Pra
Stepping ... Between ... Realities

"Spiritual awakening has thus far been gifted to what seems to be only a select few, but Michael's new book, **Stepping . . . Between . . . Realities**, affirms that awakening is now available to us all so long as we keep our hearts open to Love. As Michael explains, change is indeed occurring on our planet right now and we can choose whether to live from a place of Love and flow with the changes, or live from a place of fear and oppose it. A wise choice will result in the difference between a joyful life or a life full of challenges. I highly recommend reading this book as we move into a new consciousness and a new world . . ."

    ~ Keidi Keating, creator and author of *The Light: a Book of Wisdom*, *with chapters by 22 luminaries.*

"Michael takes us on another scintillating and inspiring journey that expands most known bounds of awareness and brings amazing transformational insights into the vast untapped potential of human and other-dimensional consciousness. I highly recommend it!"

    ~ Glenn Moore, Producer
    "Sharing Your Passion" Film Interviews

"In his new book, **Stepping . . . Between . . . Realities**, Michael Roads does exactly that—step between realities. Continuing his intuitive exploration of our metaphysical existence, Michael allows new insights to emerge in his latest book that are refreshingly beyond the 'normal' human framework of reference. . . Michael's unique spiritual experience and straightforward approach make this an engaging and heart-opening read. This is truly a story of stepping between realities and is a perfect read to help you on your journey to moreness."

    ~ Andy Whiteley, editor, *WuW eMagazine*

"*Stupefying!* Words are inadequate to comment meaningfully, but this book does open portals to greater understanding at many levels and many directions/dimensions. Michael has an extraordinary way of using words to convey to the reader what for most would be inexpressible. The WHOLE broken, hurting world needs this . . . may it help to stir humanity back toward wakefulness."
~ Brian Longhurst, Author, *Seek ye First the Kingdom*

"As I hold one of Michael's books to start to read it, I feel great excitement. I know that it holds a promise of something inspiring and, dare I say it, life changing! Looking at the world through his eyes changes perspectives and that changes everything.

"**Stepping . . . Between . . . Realities** lives up to its promise. Once again, reading it launches me into the greatest of adventures . . . that of life seen in all its dimensions!"
~ Ana Isabel, Astrologer and Hypnotherapist
My Spirit Radio, London

"What a delightful adventure it is to join Michael Roads **Stepping . . . Between . . . Realities!** Accompanied by Michael's unique humor and his message of Love, we are gifted with the opportunity to tremendously expand our consciousness regarding the nature of reality. Always entertaining and enlightening, no seat belts are needed for this metaphysical journey of a lifetime!"
~ Pleiadian Emissary of Light, Caroline Ra, *Spirit of the Dawn*

"**Stepping . . . Between . . . Realities** is a thought-provoking read that expands the mind and opens the heart. The book takes us far beyond the barrier of the physical world and beautifully portrays how our consciousness transcends space/time and is infinite. The book is a gentle wake-up call for humanity to recognise the power of our love and our potential to create a New World founded on Oneness." ~ Tricia Brennan, Author of *The Map of the Soul* and *Looking Beyond the Mirror*

STEPPING

...BETWEEN...

REALITIES

ALSO BY MICHAEL J. ROADS

Nonfiction

THROUGH THE EYES OF LOVE, Journeying with Pan BOOK ONE
THROUGH THE EYES OF LOVE, Journeying with Pan BOOK TWO
THROUGH THE EYES OF LOVE, Journeying with Pan, BOOK THREE
TALKING WITH NATURE—JOURNEY INTO NATURE
JOURNEY INTO ONENESS
INTO A TIMELESS REALM
THE MAGIC FORMULA
MORE THAN MONEY—TRUE PROSPERITY
THE ORACLE
CONSCIOUS GARDENING
A GLIMPSE OF SOMETHING GREATER

Fiction

GETTING THERE

STEPPING
...*BETWEEN*...
REALITIES

Michael J. Roads

SIX DEGREES PUBLISHING GROUP
PORTLAND • OREGON
USA

Stepping . . . *Between* . . . Realities
Michael J. Roads
Copyright © 2014 by Michael J. Roads

SIX DEGREES PUBLISHING GROUP
5331 Macadam Avenue, Suite 258
Portland, OR 97239 USA

ISBN: 978-0-9856048-6-8
U.S. Library of Congress Control Number 2014937598

Digital Edition ISBN: 978-1-3110397-1-2

Special Sales:
Michael J. Roads books may be purchased by contacting
office@michaelroads.com
RoadsLight pty ltd,
PO Box 778, Nambour, QLD, 4559, Australia
www.michaelroads.com

Publisher's Note: This book is written in Australian English.
Enquiries: Publisher@SixDegreesPublishingGroup.com
www.SixDegreesPublishing.com

Published in the United States of America

Printed Simultaneously in the United States of America,
the United Kingdom, and Australia

3 5 7 9 10 8 6 4 2

I dedicate this book from the deepest spaces in my heart, and from the immortal soul I am, to my beloved Carolyn.

This is what she wrote in her Christmas card to me:

I recently read a quote: "May there be one thing in your life for which it is worth giving up everything else." You are that 'one thing' for me. I Love you with a Love that is as ancient as it is newly born in every moment. I Love you with a Love that fills me with unbounded gratitude and joy for every precious heartbeat we share.

I have read these intoxicating words over and over, and I am in awe of her ability to express such Love. In the hope that I can immortalise her magical words, I humbly and sincerely return these sentiments to her . . . from me.

CONTENTS

ACKNOWLEDGEMENTS

By the very nature of my books I am not a researcher. Nor do I have a large number of people who read my books prior to publishing to ensure that I am on track. I have a very select few.

So to heartily thank these few, as always, gives me great pleasure. First and foremost is my beautiful wife, Carolyn. She is the first reader, and she has a very forthright tongue; she does not mince words. I value this first editing, as much as I enjoy her praise and enthusiasm.

Next comes Brian and Theresa Longhurst, two very dear English friends who seem to get a delight in pruning my words into a bit less Oz cum Yank cum Brit, and considerably more into English.

Then, of course, there is Denise, my American publisher who probably takes some of the English back to American, while leaving a strongly established and, hopefully, enjoyable flavour of English humour.

There are numerous cosmic and Nature Beings I could thank, but they will not read this, nor would they thank me for thanking them . . . as in my subtle way, I am doing!

INTRODUCTION

I often gasp at the sheer diversity and abundance of life that is so far beyond the normal human framework of reference. Like a goldfish in its glass bowl, we live enclosed in our personal realities. Beyond all our many personal physical realities is the vastness of the greater metaphysical reality. Over my lifetime I have learned that it is possible to move into my metaphysical Light-body and access that greater reality.

I step . . . *Between* . . . realities.

If you have enjoyed reading my recent trilogy, *Through the Eyes of Love, Journeying with Pan,* then we walk a very similar heart-path. My books offer a reminder of the deeper aspects of Life and Living. It is my intention to convey and impart to you, the reader, the deep and wondrous metaphysical connection of all Life. The connection to which I refer is via the unified field of energy in which we all live. For many people a unified field of energy is no more than intellectual and conceptual knowledge, but by living more consciously, it is possible to experience this actuality in our daily lives.

Those who have read my earlier *Journeying with Pan* books will be familiar with Pan—if such a thing is possible! For new readers I should explain that, for me, Pan is the pure spiritual essence of Nature. Let go of the idea of Pan as *the* God of Nature, even though Pan is all God. Pan is not a God in the way of the Gods and Goddesses of India, Japan, and of many other cultures. Pan is the enigmatic spirit of Nature, a vast, universal, all-Knowing, conscious Intelligence. Trying to intellectually fill out the essence of Pan, to help you to understand him, is to increasingly move further away from the truth. Pan *is!* I can assure you that all life is first and foremost metaphysical, and only a small proportion has a physical representation. This small proportion is what we call life!

Although this book is less based in Pan than my previous trilogy, Pan is by no means absent. Indeed, such a state is no longer possible for me, for in some mystical way we are intrinsically connected on a metaphysical level. I have learned that my metaphysical journeying has no use-by date! It is not going to end because I have learned enough, or because Pan has had enough of me. It is all up to me. If I choose to journey with Pan, this beloved Spirit is always available. If I choose to journey alone, it is always okay. But as stated, by the very nature of the Spirit of Pan, I am never *truly* alone. Also, I seem to have attracted several other wondrous mystical mentors! I can relax, knowing there is no 'should' or 'should not', nothing to cram into my consciousness, nothing that exerts any pressure on me in any way whatsoever. I like this. It is a freedom—a place of choices. My journeying is not about solving problems, or looking for answers to world situations, or proving or disproving that we are a controlled and manipulated species; it is more that I am life discovering more and more about myself *as* life. This is a great freedom. We are inclined to perceive ourselves as separate from life—we are not.

Freedom is a rare commodity in these times. If you live in any type of box there is no freedom, and the boxes are endless in their varieties and complications. Beliefs, religions, dogma, attitudes, negative emotions, peer-group pressure, attachments, relationship pressures, should and shouldn't, can and can't, good or bad, right and wrong, needing approval, all this *stuff* and so much more gets in the way of freedom. And yet, you do get to experience it occasionally. You are reading these words by using your free will. Right now you are choosing to read this. Personally, I consider it a wise choice. Some choices lead you to a greater freedom—such as choosing to read my books—while other choices all too often lead to even greater restrictions and limitations.

Much of this is affected by our personal make-up. Most people seem to *need* beliefs and become very attached to so-called knowledge. We are told that knowledge is a form of security; sorry, but this is not true. Wanting security is the path to insecurity! You only have to observe the human obsession with money to realise this. Financial security is everybody's dream, yet it is all an illusion. In Truth, life is about the evolution of consciousness. The consciousness of Love embraces everything we can possibly need. Not want—*need*!

As I grow in consciousness on my spiritual path, so I grow in Love. You will notice that I give Love a capital L. Same with Truth. Love is Life; two capitals! I do this to accentuate and empower the meaning in certain aspects of my writing. I am attempting to convey the metaphysical, the mystical, but all I can use are the words that describe a physical reality. We have emotional love which is in everyone's daily life; then we have Love, the power of creation, which is in the lives of far fewer. Love is not just love! I repeat, Love is the power of creation. Equally, there is everyday life, and there is fully conscious Life. Very different. It is estimated that over 90% of humanity lives subconsciously—*more-of-the-same*—and we call this life and living, but it is not. It is existing. It is repeating each lifetime over and over, a variation of the same themes, same thoughts, same attitudes, same desires, same emotions, same direction, same content, same, same, same. When we are fully conscious we are Living Life in a very different way. I place a capital letter in front of each word I wish to *powerfully* emphasise. There is a huge difference between transformational Change and a change of clothes! Or the Truth of Life and a truth that is personal. And my stepping . . . *Between* . . . is to denote a totally different meaning and experience than stepping between two parked cars!

As always, Oz is Australia.

Love/Truth is the nucleus of my writing, my purpose in putting my experiences out there for the public to either peruse or ignore. For me, this is my *experience* of Love/Truth that I share, rather than my beliefs or rationalisation of it. We tend to be rather sceptical and cynical in life today, looking at ourselves and other people through jaundiced eyes. I have learned that we are far more than we *think* we are. Although it is mostly unrealised, we truly are magnificent, metaphysical, multidimensional, immortal Beings of Love and Light. We live in a three-dimensional reality on this planet with the purpose of growing in consciousness. Our illusion is that we are physical and mortal Beings with, at best, a hundred years. We also believe that life was not meant to be easy — so it seldom is! We have a lot to learn about our personal powers of positive and/or negative creation.

This book is my offering to convey a much bigger picture of the metaphysical connection of Life, humanity, Nature, the astral worlds, and our galaxy, so that you may use this as the stimulus for your own growth in consciousness. I consider it both an honour and privilege to open wider the doors to a greater freedom — if you care to walk through them.

Michael J. Roads
Queensland, Australia

CHAPTER ONE

GALACTIC ADVENTURE

"Does this mean that I am soon going to physically die?"

I ask this question of Pan because, having metaphysically attempted to have another look at the many probabilities of our future, I can see nothing more than an energetic blur. It is as though all probabilities have ceased to be. While I cannot believe this is possible for humanity, I accept that it might be possible for me.

No, not necessarily. There are many probabilities concerning you, but have you even considered that it may not be appropriate for you to see them? You would naturally have an instant preference, especially regarding your physical life.

"You bet I would. Give Carolyn and me another fifty or so healthy and active years together, and I will be very content. Anyway, why should I suddenly be cast from being able to see so many of humanities' future probabilities, to none at all? Who made this decision?"

We are back to timing. You have made public your recent metaphysical travels and a few of the many probabilities they revealed, but that was then. This is now!

"Okay . . . so what is so special about now? In not too literal a sense!"

You have written and spoken of human probabilities. This probability factor is now rapidly accelerating. It is rather like showing the many frames of a movie at a hugely accelerated speed. The movie would become a meaningless blur, rather than the graphic story it portrays when played at a normal rate. In a similar manner, this is how the probability future has become a confused blur of probabilities, rather than a slower clarity of probabilities.

"Hmm, that makes sense. All I could see was a blur. So when we reach the overly hyped-up Earth Change event in December 2012, will everything change?"

Everything change? Do you mean will this change in many different ways for many different people, or do you ask if it includes planetary change?

"I mean whatever makes the better sense, but I see what you are saying. The word 'everything' obviously includes Nature and the planet . . . but the discord in the world right now is more human related . . . including the problems in Nature. So I am asking about human change."

Michael, I suggest that you wait and see. However, I will say this: no matter whether Change is visible and obvious or invisible and unobtrusive . . . Change is happening.

I smile. "That's good. More of the same is not something I want to see perpetuated. If we are going to have Change . . . bring it on and make it obvious. Nevertheless, I do wonder what will be the factor that decides which frame the movie of life will stabilise on."

The causative factor will be the overall level of human consciousness.

"In other words, human energy. But how will that be decided? Do we reach a certain level on a cosmic calibration scale that will produce one result, or another level a different result, or will we each be put to some sort of . . . test?"

Daily life is a test for humanity! However, to be brief, consider it this way. The Earth is warming. Your science is divided in opinion on whether this is from outside or inside influences. Simply stated, the

Earth's molten core is heating up, while simultaneously the magnetic field of Earth is decreasing. They go together. This will eventually result in major Earth Changes.

I have read that the current global warming is coming from below rather than above. And when you consider the facts and figures it makes a lot of sense. I have also learned that as the magnetic field of Earth decreases—which has apparently been ongoing for about three hundred years—so the probability of a magnetic Pole reversal increases. Who knows: a thousand years hence, or maybe a thousand hours!

"But Pan, all this has happened before. The last Pole reversal is considered to have been around seven hundred and eighty thousand years ago. Despite anthropologists claiming that the modern human is only about two hundred thousand years old, and that as primitive humans we have not been here longer than half a million years—and for them, this is stretching it—my metaphysical explorations have revealed to me that humanity was definitely here a very long time before that extreme event—around three million years or so before—and we survived."

Given enough time, everything repeats itself. And yes, humanity has inhabited Earth for very much longer than is recognised or accepted. The point is that this long ago extreme major event is embedded in the human consciousness. Because of this each person will respond to the next major event with either a greater heart/brain cohesion, or a very much more fragmented, fear-based reaction.

"So is this happening to us now? Either we are fear-based-reacting to a process long lost to our mental/emotional memory, or we are Love-based-responding to that long ago Earth Change process. Is this correct?"

Not quite. You need a greater knowledge of memory. An incident that is lost from conscious memory in the passing of linear time is still held in a timeless metaphysical reality. Humans are metaphysical Beings, so you retain memories—and all memories are metaphysical—of which you have absolutely no conscious awareness. However, these ancient memories do have a direct effect on your current behaviour.

"So are you saying that as circumstances bring us back toward a similar scenario of that long ago event, we will subconsciously and sub-emotionally act in accordance with the overall way that humanity was affected by that previous, unrecognised experience?

This is correct. It has become an archetypal behaviour pattern for humanity when under extreme pressure.

"But in that long ago event only a comparatively few people were on the planet."

You 'know' this, do you?

"I don't exactly *know* it, but it is a fairly safe assumption...and I did say *comparatively*. Certainly my metaphysical explorations have revealed nothing like today's numbers of people at that previous time. Nor was humanity the same in appearance as we are now."

Let us assume that you are correct. Does this then remove all experience of that event from the one human consciousness?

"Okay, I overlooked that the unified field of energy holds all consciousness. But do you mean that the way the people of that time reacted is how we will, or are, reacting now?"

I am saying that either you make your own conscious choices, or you follow the previous subconscious pattern of archetypal behaviour.

"In other words, the subconscious/sub-emotional program that basically runs most people will control the way we behave under great duress, or, we freely choose our own path. Yes?"

Consciousness is timeless! Yes, it is either the archetypal program or conscious free will.

"Then I choose absolute Love. This is free will."

Love is the only choice of free will!

＊   ＊   ＊

Here we are, the day before Christmas, 2012, with the 21st and 22nd of December passed by in what appears to be an uneventful way. I expected this. Despite the blur of probabilities, it had become reasonably apparent to me that any major Earth changes on a physical level were steadily declining, while metaphysically, big Change is taking place as predicted.

We are too keen on pinning events to a date, which is hardly surprising considering that we are the creators of linear time. We pin a date to events in the so-called past, and expect the same pin to fix events in the so-called future. We forget that in a greater reality we live in the *Now*, and on a cosmic, or universal level we live in the Now. This suggests that simply because a date has passed without any major physical events, we should not assume it is all finished. The electro-magnetic field of our planet is weakening, the interior of our planet is heating, and the gravitational field is going through subtle changes—undoubtedly we will be affected by this. A magnetic North-South polar shift is clearly a *when*, not an *if*.

I had a proposition to put to Pan.

"Can you guide me to places where Change is taking place, or should I go on my own?"

Choose your own path. I will be with you if I am needed.

"Thanks, Pan. This is just a quick excursion to get a feeling for the energies."

Okay—I can be *very* gullible!

✳   ✳   ✳

With these words, I physically relax in my study chair, and focusing on Earth Changes, I step . . . *Between* . . . stepping out into a high position above the Earth.

Hmm, this is interesting. I appear to be in a cosmic snowstorm, although it is a gentle one. What seemed at first to be snowflakes are actually flakes of pure Light, drifting to Earth as thickly as a heavy fall of snow. I hold my metaphysical hand out to catch a Light-flake, and momentarily it sits in my palm before continuing to Earth. The feeling is of pure Light newness.

As I glance over the planet, I see many areas where celebrations of Light are taking place, yet not all the celebrations are truly of Light. Some are pure of energy, and joyous, welcoming the advent of Change and Newness with light and loving hearts. A few are gatherings of cynicism in disguise, posing as people celebrating, but they carry fear in their energy. These are not bad people, but they are cynical and sceptical by nature, yet desirous

5

of being involved in something new and uplifting. Overall, the greatest human energy by far is one of complete indifference, of total unawareness, although a fear of Change is also strongly represented.

When I again look at the probabilities of what may happen, it continues to be a rapidly changing blur. I am able to see that, on an energetic level, global fear and anger are waxing and waning in the ways of a cyclonic storm swirling within the atmosphere, growing and diminishing according to the dictates of the wind, of the heat and cold, and all the factors that influence the growth and movement of a storm. So it is with human energy. I see that whereas positive and loving human energy is calm, growing slowly, it is steadily becoming more powerful while the swirling, gusting energies of fear and resistance to Change strengthens then weakens, as though it is fighting a losing battle.

I realise that *it is* a losing battle for that which represents the Old. The flakes of Light are covering the Earth, completely invisible to human eyes, while energetically transforming all that is receptive. I feel that all Nature is aware of and receptive to Newness. Only humanity is divided over this. The many cling to the Old, the few open themselves to Newness. Inner-knowing suggests that we will probably move in the direction each of us has created at the end of this physical life; we will each incarnate into the perfect expression of our own state of consciousness. In other words, it seems that we will move as a humanity into many varied reality-frames, each of our own making. This, rather than the continuity of all sharing the same reality-frame, as we have been doing for millennia. The way we are now living is the path that our individual futures are based on. And yet, of course, we are living our future in this very moment, for the past, present and future are simply a framework within which we can measure our spiritual growth and appease our mortal attachment to linear time.

I notice that a few areas seem to strongly attract the falling flakes of Light. Certainly, these Light-flakes are new to me. I have never seen Light-flakes falling to Earth like this, although I have at earlier times seen sparkling Newness sweep the planet with its potential. As I watch I become aware that it is not the events that attract the Light-flakes, it is the people. In the way of the energetic human clustering that I have written of in my *Eyes of Love* trilogy, when I have described the clustering in our cities, so now the clustering of people is very pronounced. I see that in some well known places where the people are apparently celebrating the advent of Newness, the Light-flakes act with amazing discernment, only reaching and connecting with the people who are genuinely of the New. I see groups of people all acting in the same manner of celebration, yet the Light-flakes ignore many, while selecting the few. Once they reach a selected human, they merge with that person's field-of-energy. In some other well known power locations, the Light-flakes are thickly attracted and it is the many who connect with them, while a few are ignored.

One such place is Chichen Itza in the Yucatán state of Mexico. Here it becomes obvious that most people in the crowds strongly attract the flakes of Light, while a few just as strongly repel them. Even in the midst of the best human energy places, the Light-flakes discriminate. In a group of chattering, laughing people, just a few repel the Light-flakes, while the others strongly attract them. I switch my vision over to other groups involved in so-called celebrations, where the emphasis is more on partying, drinking, and having, what is for them, a good time. Here, the majority repel the Light-flakes, while they are strongly attracted to a few of the participants. This interests me. It becomes ever more clear that these Light-flakes are not attracted by masses, but by people of a certain state of consciousness.

I cast my eyes further around the globe and I see my confirmation. It is the consciousness of people as individuals that either attract or repel the Light-flakes. In city after city I see great numbers of people who have absolutely no awareness of this period of major Change as being significant for humanity, yet the flakes of Light are strongly attracted to many such unaware people. When I focus on the person's energy-field, I see the Love/Light in them. Having no knowledge or awareness of Earth Changes is not a deterrent to the Light-flakes; they are attracted by the person's field of energy, their state of consciousness. Houses and buildings make no difference to the Light-flakes. Nothing physical is able to deter them as they find the people of Light. Even in hospitals and institutions, the Light-flakes find the people of Light, whether it is the patients, or the doctors and nursing staff, or cleaners and maintenance workers, or kitchen staff—all are involved. Light attracts Light. How obvious. Nice! So subtle, so unrealised and so powerful. Change is here, a breath of Newness connecting with those who are open to Newness and Change.

Because of my earlier farming background, I look toward the land. Light-flakes are drifting like snow in all the wilderness areas, in the natural forests and woods, and in the waterways. Oddly, in the places where human greed is exploiting huge areas of forest and jungle, where immense dams are being built to exploit the river system, the Light-flakes are falling very thickly on the devastated soil. This surprises me. I expected the opposite. On farms where genetically modified (GM) crops are being grown, the Light-flakes fall thickly on the soil, yet none of them alight on the crops. On sick and abused agricultural land that is the mainstay of our food production, the Light-flakes fall thickly on the soil, again not touching the crops. On organic or eco farms, where the emphasis is on natural and healthy soil, the Light-flakes smother the land, the crops, and the farmers.

"I have a question, if it is no trouble, Pan. I would appreciate a bit of insight regarding some of this." I can always ask, even if Pan is not with me!

What is it that you find perplexing?

"Well it's obvious that the snow-like flakes of Light are an expression of Newness, and that Newness is sweeping the planet. It is also obvious that Newness is both attracted to and repelled by people, according to their field of energy, regardless of their interests and knowledge, spiritual or otherwise. But I did not expect Light-flakes in the areas of exploitation such as the huge dams and massive loss of forest."

Michael, what does Newness represent?

"To put it simply, Change . . . from the old to the new."

What else?

"Hmm, I'm not sure what you mean. Change . . . and . . .?"

Think, feel . . . what is Change?

"Change is . . . a catalyst . . . a major power!"

And?

"Change is powerful, it is a catalyst, it is Newness, it is . . . growth!"

So . . . put it all together.

"Ah . . . I get it! The Light-flakes represent the power of Newness . . . and this will express in new growth. All this is big-time Change. So the areas of destruction and exploitation will see big Change. Power will move away from the representation of the Old toward representing the New. The people to whom the Light-flakes are attracted will gradually become people with power, while the people who until now have selfishly wielded power will find it gradually draining from them. In other words, the whole balance of human power/energy is shifting. It is shifting from the areas of greed, control, isolation and exploitation to the areas of compassion, Love, togetherness and freedom. One big question, will this be a slow or fast process?"

It will happen at the speed that humanity dictates. But . . . it is irrevocable.

I smile. "I *really* like the last part of that!"

I am content. I do not need celebrations, crowds or loud music to announce Change. I would rather watch the Light-flakes of Change weave their slow but certain magic in the hearts of people that are open and receptive.

Smiling, I watch the long heralded but mostly unseen, unrealised, Birth of Change as it timelessly continues to sweep over the planet in a cosmic snow of Newness.

Eventually, I step . . . *Between* . . . and back into my study.

✳   ✳   ✳

I sit for a while contemplating my journey. Our mass media have poked great fun at the predicted and awaited Change event, and will now continue on their way without another thought about what might have been—and still very probably will be. They have enough fodder for their endless speculation with the world's economy, as it teeters from one crisis to another. As country after country reaches their fiscal ceiling, will they continue to raise the ceiling, putting off the inevitable, or might they actually allow an old, outdated and grossly unfair economy to collapse, and then reconstruct a whole new economic approach? Of course not. Governments attract many men and women who are morally and ethically bankrupt. Evidence suggests that most governments, like so many huge corporations, are a system of sustained corruption.

My thoughts turn to the Light-flakes. It seems that these snow-like flakes came from some outer source within our solar system, but where?

I decide to take another look at the Light-flake phenomenon from an energetic viewpoint. Expand my vision, so to speak. I let Pan know of my intention.

Focusing on the source of the Light-flakes, I step . . . *Between* . . . and out into a—place? I have no idea where I am! Impossibly, I am standing in a landscape which is so ethereal, so very non-physical that I have difficulty relating to it as a landscape. This can only be a celestial place, reminding me of a garden. What I assume to be plants are conglomerations of shimmering Light, yet I can see energetic shapes and forms within it. This is, indeed, a celestial garden, and it is all about energy. Even as I watch, the plants are changing, seemingly fading away from their ephemeral existence only to re-emerge in another shape, another form of plant-like energy.

Hmm, this is fascinating, but my focus was on the Light-flakes. How have I managed to step into a celestial garden?

Maybe the question you should ask is where the celestial garden is located?

I smile. "Yes, that's a good question, Pan. I'm sure there is a connection. But who do I ask . . . you? You don't encourage questions. You mostly push me toward look and learn."

Correct. I suggest you do exactly that. Fare well.

Fare well, indeed. I can glean no information from this conversation.

It would seem that I need to keep my Light-flake focus while I do a bit of exploring in this celestial garden. A celestial garden must surely be on a celestial plane—and who knows where that might be?

As I become more at ease in the garden, relaxing my Light-flake focus, I notice that the garden is constantly reforming in a way that is ever more familiar. I realise that linear time does not exist here, so although the plants seem incredibly ephemeral to me, so also does the momentary life of a mayfly in the Nature with which I am familiar. I am also sure that my immortal Self of infinity looks on each of my finite physical lives in a similar way; a brief flicker—and it is over.

It becomes apparent now that this celestial garden is definitely reforming itself into a garden with which I am very familiar—mine! This is truly amazing. I can recognise my garden within all this, yet it remains a garden of constantly changing energy, forming, dissolving and reforming in an energetic flow of grace and beauty. Although this seems to be taking me ever further away from my quest for the origin of the Light-flakes, I suddenly realise that from a celestial viewpoint my own physical garden is as constantly in movement as this one. Here, linear time and all physicality are removed. Take those two components from my own garden, and it would look like this. Wow! It offers me a whole new perspective of our Nature. I know that the Nature we see is the physical expression of pure energy, but to see the celestial counterpart to my own garden, unhindered by time or physicality, offers me yet another very different frame of reference. I like it!

Unclear about where all this is taking me, I walk the ephemeral paths of my celestial garden, undeterred as the paths ebb and flow beneath my feet. I watch the plants energetically grow into softly coloured Light, briefly flourish and flower, then change again. As I walk the paths, I have the sudden insight that I can follow my garden paths forever without going anywhere. I stop. Realising that there is no direction other than my focus, I again concentrate on the Light-flakes.

I smile. My garden and its paths are no more. It is now once again a celestial landscape, and I am following a path that will lead me to my destination. I know this because I am creating it. It seems I am on a journey, and that distraction springs from my own thoughts, my own attempts at seeing familiarity within my surroundings. What an irony! I am being distracted by the distractions that I inadvertently create by attempting to avoid being distracted! How like our everyday physical life: one distraction after another, with wealth, power and materialism probably the greatest distractions of all, easily diverting us from our spiritual journey.

But I am learning! This celestial plane is offering me some powerful lessons for my physical life. I have long stated that in every moment of our lives we are creating the direction and the content of every moment of our lives. People understand the words—they are simple enough—but the deeper meaning is elusive, not so easy to grasp. Right now, on this celestial plane, I am seeing this in a new and even deeper way.

My focus returns to the Light-flakes—and the path forms, collapses and reforms in front of me. I walk the path, my feet barely touching it, for walking is unnecessary in my Light-body. Nevertheless, I enjoy walking, especially when it is effortless and you walk in a very different way. Walking is a poor description, for I am covering great lengths of path as it spirals far ahead of me. Meanwhile, the celestial landscape continues to surround me. I am possibly conveying some false impressions as I write this, for our relationship with speed, of measured distances, and the size of the landscape are completely without meaning in this cosmic reality.

I am unhurried. Hurry is a distraction that creates ever more reasons to hurry us to the next distraction. In other words, we are hurrying toward experiences that, all too often, we do not want to be hurried to! Call it unwitting creation. We humans are experts.

I walk my wavering path toward Mystery. I have absolutely no idea where I am going, but I am comfortable with this. I have had considerable practice! Nothing on this celestial plane is clear and definite. Or at least, not to me. It is a shifting, constantly reforming, reshaping, immense landscape, yet incredibly beautiful. Although beauty of a very different expression.

Oh! Everything is changing. The garden is dissolving and not reforming. All that is left is the path I am walking. A path that is on nothing, supported by nothing, and seemingly going nowhere. If I was physical, I would probably be afraid—but I am not physical. What a silly thought! It would be impossible to be here physically. Focus. Focus on Mixael. Enough of these errant thoughts of Michael. As I focus on Mixael, it all becomes firm and steady—and reality shifts once more. (For new readers, I should explain here that over twenty-five years ago, Michael became spiritually enlightened, and the Michael-soul walked-out of his physical body. As per agreement of that probability, the Mixael-soul walked-in to the body from a fifth dimensional reality to resolve his emotional lessons, and to give of himself to the people. Despite the Michael-soul's departure, the personality/psyche retained his mental and emotional memories. For a fuller explanation, see the *Through the Eyes of Love, Book Two*).

The path remains, becoming very narrow. I am standing on this narrow path looking at the solar system all around me. An impossible path in the cosmos. *Cosmos!* Where am I?

A time of walking into no-space—and I am suddenly confronted by more impossibility. Being astronomically challenged, I have no idea where I am and only a vague idea of what I am looking at—but I am certainly at the source of the Light-flakes.

Before me, I see what appears to be a black hole. Okay, I know almost nothing about black holes, but this one is not pulling everything in the local cosmic neighbourhood into it; quite the opposite in fact. Maybe it's a vent hole, because the Light-flakes are apparently being blown from it in vast quantities, dense and thick. I say being blown, but they could also be flying out from their own propulsion. This black hole is probably a baby, with an entrance or exit I would estimate to be about three kilometres across. From out of this, filling the whole exit, an almost solid mass of small-to-medium-sized Light-flakes are billowing into our solar system, affecting other planets, not just Earth. What I assumed to be an *Earth* event with the Light-flakes was not correct; it is a solar-system-wide event.

I observe the black hole in fascinated silence. It is utterly awesome. I guess that anything that continually inhales, must be required to exhale somewhere, or some*when*! This is definitely the exhale end of a black hole. I have read briefly about black holes, and they describe an 'event horizon' which is supposed to delineate the entrance or mouth of the black hole. Yet, this surely is the exit! Despite this, I appear to be looking at what appears to be the event horizon. I have read nothing about colour, yet the colour and appearance of this event horizon is astounding, absolutely incredible. I have no reference for the colour. The closest I can get is a colour that is vibrantly alive, rather like an amalgam of silver/black/gold/red at the most basic level—and then far more! The appearance to me is rather reminiscent of looking into some of the large sea shells, where the mouth of the shell is ridged with many smooth corrugations, widening out away from the mouth. Multiply this by maybe three kilometres and you have a tiny hint of the magnitude of it!

By now I am completely bewildered. What little I have read about black holes does not in any way equate with what I am now seeing and experiencing. I seem to be observing the exit of a black hole that has an event horizon, which is supposed to be the entrance. Help! It also appears to be alive. Not life as we know it—but definitely alive. I get the strong impression that just as I am the observer, I too am being observed. If this is alive, then by comparison I am an infinitesimally tiny life-form, yet I feel that the black hole has a remote aspect of itself paying attention to me.

Tiny, yet large in energy.

Oh—my gosh! It has communicated with me. What do I say?

"Er . . . our science has never even suggested that a black hole could be a life-form."

They are correct. I am not a life-form in any way that relates to a three dimensional reality. I am a multiversal energy-form of intelligence. Is this too challenging to accept?

"No . . . not at all . . . for me. But when I share this I am sure that many will laugh at my gullibility. And that's okay. Truth is never truth out of timing. Er . . . don't misunderstand me, but are you the, er . . . the rear . . . er, back end of what we call a black hole?"

I get a sense of amusement. *If we continue to refer to my isness as 'I' then I have neither an entrance nor an exit. I neither inhale nor exhale. I am an energy of transformation.*

"Oh! But what goes in must come out. That's fundamental, surely."

For your reality, but not mine. In and out is meaningless. I attract energy, displacing it from its dormancy into an ongoing dynamic. This is a process of transformation. I could be likened to a catalyst. From your human observation of me, energy or matter is taken in . . . to go where?

"I'm not sure that our science has an answer to that. I certainly don't! I have read that black holes can consume whole solar systems . . . that seems very scary. Our problem is that everything must be understood and explained. We probably need this to communicate to each other what we learn, although I am convinced that our need to intellectually understand hinders our relationship with intelligence. Mind you, nobody of science would agree with anything I am saying. They would consider me delusional. Okay, so all my senses, even metaphysically, are unable to comprehend your most basic function. I am hindered by my way of relating to life . . . or energy. I see Light-flakes coming out of you. Can you explain this?"

Shut down all seeing, all observation, all needing to know, all questions, all enquiry, and as a metaphysical Being, reach out to my isness. Connect.

To do so, I close down my intellect. I close down need. I close down my humanity. I am within/connected/one with isness, with Mystery. I feel energies of such a prodigious proportion I cannot relate to them, humanly or non-humanly. I feel the cosmos within the vast dynamic isness of my Being. I feel forces of unimaginably vast intelligence taking matter, non-matter, light-matter, dark matter!—all energy—into the very depths of my Being and transforming the energy/matter into *otherness*. I am lost, lost in the immensity of all-that-is. If I say I am a flea in an immense cosmic concrete mixer, it would be untrue, but this is my feeling. I am as nothing.

Suddenly, this changes. I am deepening my connection with isness. I am unimaginably vast. I know how I co-create the Light-flakes, for this is a product of my current transformation. I am One with the cosmos. I am One with the Milky Way Galaxy. I am the timing and the fabric of transformation. And as I am, so are my countless brothers and sisters scattered throughout the multiverse.

How much non-time passes I do not know.

I am Mixael, the observer. I am aware that my Mixael-self has a deeper and more capable connection with the black hole than my Michael-self—and this is okay. Timing. But Mixael is no more able to offer explanations to unadulteratedly transcendent experiences than Michael.

It is as it is. This is enough.

Just as this is a first for you, so also I have never had a human energy within me. I shall digest and investigate your energy.

"As shall I. Except I have a whole humongous lot more to digest."

Not so. All energy is One. You offer another spectrum of Oneness to explore.

"Thank you for this connection. It is an honour beyond my wildest dreams. Black holes will always have a completely different meaning for me from now on."

My awareness is back on the celestial path. I am in no hurry to depart. Who knows what else may await me. My path is in deep space, yet the word *space* is the way I refer to it as a physical person. As a metaphysical Being, what I see 'humanly' or 'physically' as space I metaphysically experience as non-space. Okay, it is difficult for words to explain, but this mystical celestial path which seems to hang in space is a thread of connection between the countless stars—in galactic space that does not involve separation!

For some strange reason, the path is carrying me into a . . . lay-by! Just as trucks that travel long distances have lay-bys along the road for the driver to pull over and take a rest, so I am now in what feels like a lay-by for Beings that travel this celestial path. Now that's a new thought! Do other Beings use this path? Did I assume it was put here for me? An arrogant assumption, perhaps. It now appears that it is a more permanent *high*way—pardon the pun!

I move off the path to sit in my lotus position in the space-type lay-by.

Insights into the black hole are percolating through my awareness. When I was One with the isness of the black hole, I knew how it functioned, but I was unable to intellectually assemble my *knowing* into rational thoughts. Not that rational is always correct. We can be very rational and very wrong. A black hole has a totally—and I mean, totally—different relationship with an infinitely greater body of life than we do. Imagine the human body as a small galaxy within our universe. Not so very difficult to imagine when you realise that our bodies are about 99.9% space, with about 0.01% physical! Just as our galaxy in the universe has countless black holes, so also our physical bodies/galaxies have uncountable black holes. Although our DNA is a physical double-helix spiral under the microscope, metaphysically it is a black hole. Just as black holes in the universe or the galaxy have no relationship with time and space—linear time is a human creation—neither do the black holes in our bodies/galaxies.

I pause in bewilderment. Whoa—my thoughts are not making sense! I have metaphysically experienced the physical DNA as wormholes, not black holes. Now, after my black hole experience, I am calling them black holes. What is going on?

Your scant knowledge of science confuses you. I am Mystery. What your science names as black holes and wormholes are meaningless— mere labels of reference. You call me a black hole, yet if you use that as a definition I am also what you call a wormhole. I am not bound to a single expression. I am a pathway across the universe in one reality, and energy-transformation in another, a pure amalgam of isness in another. I am all, I am none. I am One. All human definitions are speculation.

"Oh . . . thank you. I'm not sure I really understand all you've just said, but on a deeper level of insight it makes sense. Anyway, you have helped me accept my own reality."

I continue with my intuitive exploration, allowing new insights to emerge. We are able to physically see what defines a black hole with our space telescopes, yet in reality a black hole is not physical. Interestingly, a black hole is having a similar dynamic relationship with the most distant far-flung areas of the universe that it is having within its own galactic neighbourhood. The black holes seem to energetically connect the galaxies with the universe, and while so doing they transform energy and matter into . . . otherness. Okay, this is vague, but I'm a simple gardener, not an astrophysicist. Inside my consciousness it is all very clear and meaningful, but I cannot translate it into humanese! I will add that the black holes in our body/galaxies are not so very different from the black holes in our solar system/ galaxy—except in the vast magnitude of size!—and for better or worse, they enact for us within our body/galaxies the same role as universal black holes. And . . . to take this a notch further, they are *all* in communication with each other. Each black hole/worm hole in our body communicates with all the other black holes in our body, and with the black holes in every other person's body, and with the black holes throughout our solar system.

When a physical galactic system dies, the metaphysical galactic system continues. It begs the universal question: what came before the Big Bang? Answer: the metaphysical universe, which is a multiverse. When our physical bodies die, we energetically continue, black holes included. The metaphysical precedes and succeeds the physical—forever and always. Why does our science always look for physical answers only? Do we physically breathe because we have lungs, or do we have lungs because we need to physically breathe? How do you separate one from the other? Because this is what science does. Science separates and isolates in its efforts to learn more of the whole. I see a serious flaw in this. All life is holistic. Brain-intellect translates holistic to mean that all the parts are connected. Heart-intelligence translates holistic to mean that all is One . . . no parts! This is hugely different. Here we have two completely different ways of relating to life. This is an aspect of what the major Change event was about, the much needed transition from brain-intellect dominance to heart-intelligence resurgence. Bring it on!

Let me create a layman's ballpark viewpoint of the brain.

18

Most of our left-brain hemisphere dominant people—maybe 85% of humanity—translate life though their brain-intellect, while the remaining right-brain hemisphere dominant people translate life through their heart-intelligence. Let me also add that left or right-brain dominance is not so much how we use our physical brain, as it is about how we translate and focus the energy the brain hemisphere has produced. Within all this, many people of both types function in their whole-brain-heart capacity, although this *many* is a comparative *few!* However, one thing is clear to me: when *all* humanity functions in a holistic whole-brain-heart-energy connection, we will rise far beyond and greatly transcend the inequitable way that we currently live.

Hmm, interesting stuff. But, enough!

With the unfolding of my insight and speculation, I move into silence, shutting out any stray or errant thoughts that might be travelling this cosmic path!

I smile. I can never quite leave my humour behind. I like it— and I'm thinking again!

Finally silent. A long period of no-time passes. It seems I cannot fully leave my sense of time behind, even when I am aware of being beyond time. I sense it, even though metaphysically I am not experiencing it.

Okay, this is different! A silvery globe of about three metres in diameter is floating at a serene yet rapid speed along the celestial path toward me. As it swiftly comes closer, I notice that the globe is opaque and pulsating. A life-form? Remaining in my lotus position within the cosmic lay-by, I watch its approach. This must be a life-form, because already I am aware of an energy presence. I sit quietly, waiting to see what happens. Should I hail it?

The question becomes irrelevant, for the life-form has slowed down, and is coming toward me in the lay-by. When it gets close, I need to re-evaluate; it is at least five metres in diameter. As a metaphysical Being of Love/Light, I smile at it benignly.

Its communication is crisp and perfunctory. *You are a surprise.*

"Well . . . to me, *you* are a surprise."

The Being's energy immediately changes. *Forgive me/us, I/we did not mean to sound abrupt. I/we are not used to communicating in this manner. I/we were attempting to communicate with you long before you saw me/us. Too late, I/we realised this is not within your . . .?*

"Capability. That's okay. On a cosmic scale I am probably a primitive. I'm intrigued by how you communicate. If this level of telepathy is primitive, how do you communicate when it is more advanced?"

The Being is pulsating now at twice the previous speed, and much more strongly. I have the feeling that it is extremely distressed.

You misunderstand me/us. I/we are neither judging your telepathic skills, nor your status as a Being. I/we are a collective and we seldom use telepathy. I/we project images, a form of visual telepathy, rather than a vocal one. I/we are out of practice.

"Okay, now it's my turn to wholeheartedly apologise. I mistook your meaning . . . and I am very sorry. Let's start again. My name is Mixael."

The Being visibly relaxes; the pulsing is still quite fast, but more gentle and even. *I/we are very surprised to see a Being like you out in the . . . reaches. I/we did not expect this. How has this fortuitous meeting come about?*

"To be honest, I did not expect to be here either." I went on to briefly explain the Light-flakes of Change on Earth, and how I wondered where they originated—and hence my experience with the celestial path and my meeting with a black hole.

I/we understand that your race of Beings are not celestial travellers. You are a very unusual sight. I/we have never met your like before.

"I seem to have this ability to leave my physical body behind, and to metaphysically travel into the non-physical world, the greater reality. But please, tell me about you . . . er, yourselves."

Do you mind if I/we first look into your consciousness that we might find some common reference points for our explanation?

"Not at all. Go ahead."

I expected to feel nothing, but it feels as though an immensely bright light is shining into and through me, taking no more than a few no-time seconds.

Amazing. I/we tend to forget that we collectives are the exception rather than the normal. As I/we looked into your consciousness we saw all human consciousness. Forgive me/us, but in many ways you appear to be a collective consciousness that is completely fragmented.

I smile. "You are correct. We are One holistic consciousness acting out the illusions of separation. We fight each other, kill or hurt each other, and compete against each other. And . . . to be fair, many of us also help and assist each other."

Why are you fragmented? You all lose. Forgive me/us, but is this insanity?

"After we have talked you can look again and find your own answers. But yes, we are insane in many ways. Most people live in denial of our metaphysical immortality, believing that our brief, meagre, physical lives account for all that our lives are. I'm sorry, but this is too depressing to talk about. Please, tell me something about yourselves."

Individual names and individuality are unknown to us, nor do we have a vocal name for our race, or any . . . place, that is home. Let me/us show you an image which may represent us.

They project this into me, and I get a hazy impression of endless space corridors, of great beauty, of Lightness of Being, and of a level of Oneness/cooperation than is incomprehensible.

You are resisting. Relax, and if I/we may be so bold, it would help if I/we make a connection between you/I/us. Please . . . place your hands on what you perceive as a globe.

Coming down from my lotus position, I walk to the Being and place my hands gently on its silvery, pulsating surface. Oh . . . it is like placing my hands in warm fluffy ice-energy!

This time I get very much stronger impressions— overwhelmingly so. Within the globe is a . . . galaxy, filled with microscopic planets, all spinning and orbiting around a central sun. Oh glory be! This is beyond incredible. It would seem that I am communicating with an entire galaxy, and that there are many more of them.

"Am I right? Are you a . . . galaxy, or solar system?"

Using your references, I/we are a contained galaxy rather than a solar system. At certain times we converge, and enter a universal transformation in which we all transcend our contained in-ness. We then enter unconstrained out-ness.

I let that pass! "When you say 'we converge', do you mean other Beings like you converge, or what? I'm sorry, but I find it difficult to grasp that you are a galaxy in miniature. I accept it, but it is beyond me. It is so utterly alien, nothing like humanity."

Forgive me/us, but as I/we approached were you not broadcasting your speculation on the similarity between your physical body and a galaxy? Just as you perceive yourself as a separate entity, you are also a vast conglomeration of life-forms within one body. Is this not so? Does this not make a contradiction of your words?

I chuckle. "Okay, you win. But if I look at a human body I see a single body, not a galaxy. When I look at you . . . okay . . . I see a single, silvery, rather beautiful globe/body."

Yet when you connect with our holistic Beingness, you perceive a galaxy. As it is with us, so it is with you. The outer is very different, as is the inner, but the similarity is there.

"I can deny nothing that you say. You, as a single globe Being, I fully comprehend, but I find you, as a galactic-cooperative-of-Beingness, almost beyond my comprehension."

As your own fragmented collective of humanity is equally beyond our comprehension.

"Yes, well, it's beyond my comprehension also, to be honest!"

Yet you experience universal Love. I/we feel it.

"Yes . . . to lesser and greater degrees, all humanity feels and experiences Love. We have many degrees and expressions of Love, yet overall we do poorly with it. Conversely, without Love we would have long since perished. Love is our saving grace. Incidentally, my first thought, when I saw you, was that you are a Wonder-Neap, but you are not. As wondrous as that Being was in my life . . . you are more marvellous by far."

I/we have never encountered such a Being. Can you project an image?

I visualise and imagine the incredible Wonder-Neap that I shared experiences with so long ago, doing my best to project it.

I sense excitement. Oh yes, I/we know this Being, but never as a wonder neap.

"That was the closest I could get to a name, or to whatever it was."

I feel their amusement. *Naturally, you also met this Being metaphysically.*

"Yes, metaphysically I get around. My guide and mentor is Pan, the Spirit of Nature on Earth. Have you ever heard of him?"

Please, project an image. You are easily able to do this.

"I'm sorry, but this time I cannot. Pan is a great spiritual intelligence which expresses through the Nature of our planet. He is not a Being, or an . . . anything. Pan is consciousness. Pan is intelligence. Pan . . . IS. I really don't know how to project Pan."

Despite your words, you did very well. We know of the energy you speak, for Pan is of universal consciousness. You are greatly honoured to have such a mentor.

"I am indeed. Please, I have another question. Are you . . . or is the globe-like Being I see, a Being that contains a miniature galaxy, or are you and the galaxy one and the same?"

I/we are one and the same. Are you, as a physical Being, a container for all the microscopic life-forms within, or are you one and the same?

I laugh. "Very good! Do you have a home planet, or are you a wanderer in the solar system? Do you breathe? Can you be hurt? Do you have a lifespan?"

I/we travel the solar system. We await the moment of convergence, yet we do not wait for it. I/we do not have lungs, nor do I/we need to breathe. I/we can be hurt, and because we do not experience the passing of your time, our lifespan is the living conscious moment. Beyond this, I/we have no direct reference to lifespan.

"Do you come back to being the Being you are now after convergence and otherness, or do you continue in a different form?"

After leaving in-ness and experiencing out-ness, we continue in the same form, but with a very different isness.

"Like a higher state of consciousness?"

Yes. Different, this is how you could describe it. The out-ness is very illuminating.

"I realise that there are endless questions for both of us. Could we connect again? This will give me further insight. If you would like to scan me first, go ahead."

Once again, I feel as if a powerful laser search-light is moving, slowly this time, through my Being, through my consciousness and, I guess, thus touching the consciousness of humanity.

When the search-light withdraws, I feel an invitation to place my hands on the globe.

As I touch the galactic Being with my Light-body hands, I lean forward and also place my forehead area on the pulsating surface.

As I do so, for brief moments I see a galactic light show, then . . . lights out!

I am aware of floating . . . and of a curious sensation of inner pulsing. I surmise that I overloaded, and that I passed out, but I am wrong. As I become slowly aware of my surroundings, I get the impression that I am part of a vast galaxy. I am aware of countless hurtling, spinning planets and stars, of asteroids, of thick, dense, meteor clouds, of huge black holes lunging across the galaxy, of brilliant, magnificent, living colours, and all this is somehow orbiting within its own, mostly eccentric, orbits while spinning around a vast central sun.

"Oh . . . my gosh! How did I get into the cosmos?"

You are not in the cosmos, as you call it. You are within the galactic-collective I/we are.

"But . . . this is impossible! I am within a vast, limitless, never-ending galactic cosmos. How can I be within you? You are far too small to contain all this immensity."

Forgive me/us, but you are very presumptuous in your separation from the One. Size, as you call it, is a false presentation by third-dimensional illusion. All is relative, but nothing is as it may appear through your senses. An eighth-dimensional Being, when faced with the same view as a third-dimensional Being, will see and experience a completely different reality. Which is the true one? Is there such a thing?

"Right, there is no true one. There is only what we perceive and experience. Unfortunately we humans cling to a consensual reality as being a true representation of life. I should know better."

From our perspective we are very impressed by you. We meet on a cosmic path that many Beings travel, but never before have we encountered one like you.

For a moment I feel as though a cosmic gale is buffeting me, then I am outside the galactic globe Being. It is now pulsating strongly, but very calm and gentle.

I/we will continue our travels, but if you wait, a friend of yours will be along soon. I/we cannot give you a closer time value than soon, but, to borrow a phrase, sooner, rather than later!

I laugh. "You have piqued my curiosity. I'm impressed how you quickly picked up vocal telepathy. I guess you took my vocabulary out of my consciousness."

Yes, and you have been projecting reasonably clear images with your words the whole time. This is obviously natural for you.

"I mostly think, feel, see and speak from inner pictures."

I feel a sudden bright flood of laser light moving through me that is nothing less than a heavenly benediction. I feel as if I am being embraced within a God.

Without another word, the collective galactic Being is continuing its endless journey.

Moving off the path and back into the cosmic lay-by, I return to my lotus position.

Wow! What an incredible experience. I avoid speculating on it. It was too far-out to even think about. Any thoughts I have will only reduce it, and that I will not do.

I wonder who on earth this—no, I wonder who *in the galaxy* can this friend be? I will wait, no matter how long.

A longish period of no-time passes timelessly.

Suddenly, as though within a thick mist, I see the wavering figure of a Being who is achingly familiar to me. Even though I am metaphysical, I gulp, choking on my emotions.

Abruptly, he is before me, feline and majestic . . . Seine.

Chapter Two

A Hitchhiker's Guide

For long moments I am unable to do more than choke and gasp from overloaded emotions. Seine (pronounced C-ine) places a hand on my metaphysical shoulder, gently squeezing with his supple, feline, claw/fingers. Taking some deep, steadying breaths, I smile into his beautiful, elegant visage, and relax. What a wonderful moment this is.

"I had no idea that it would be you. It must be over twenty years . . . for me!"

A mere moment. How are you, Mixael?

"Mixael! Did you always know, even while I was in denial, thinking of myself as Michael?"

Of course. But truth has its timing and, as you said, you were in denial.

As I look into his silver, cosmic eyes, a powerful realisation hits me.

"Did you know that after I walked-in, I would have periods when I was overwhelmed by the heaviness of 3-D reality, and by the enormity of what I had done, of what I had lost, of the isolation

26

from my loved ones in another dimension? About four or five times a year I would have a strong, undeniable need to withdraw from everybody, from the world. It would last three days. The first day was about withdrawal. The second day I would feel the heaviness and loss, with a deep sense of isolation and sadness. I could feel the sadness of the people as an intangible, but powerful, negative energy. On the third day the symptoms would recede, and I would return to normal. But I never understood what was taking place until this very moment."

I knew . . . but what could I say, or do?

"Now, all these years later, I realise it was about my being a walk-in. I thought the problem was Michael's, but no, it was Mixael's. And you, Seine, rescued me. Were you aware of this? Was it real, or did I fabricate it from my need?"

It was real enough. I was aware that you needed help.

After a number of years as a walk-in, with the irregular but distressing three-day periods of loss, isolation, and sadness, I was at the Omega Institute in New York State. I was giving a five-day workshop when, during the late evening of the second day, the period of withdrawal came on very strongly. I knew it would be very difficult to continue the next day, so I inner-asked for help. That night I had a clear and powerful dream. I was walking along a city street, feeling the symptoms of withdrawal, when I saw an egg the size of a rugby ball on the pavement. I stopped and picked it up. As I held it, the egg hatched. Out of it came a baby Seine. Cradled in my arms, he looked into my eyes, and I began to cry. I told him how I felt. The baby Seine told me that I was never alone. He told me to hold him to my chest, which I did, and he seemed to melt, merging into my heart. I woke up and wept from an emotional overload, yet there was relief in my tears. I was rather emotional the next day at the workshop, but it went well. Following my heart-merging dream with the baby Seine, I never again experienced the three-day periods of heaviness, sadness, and loss.

I embrace Seine, hugging him to me, which he strongly returns.

"My dear friend, I can never thank you enough. You helped

me when I most needed it."

I knew what was required. Moving from a fifth to a third-dimensional reality carries with it a considerable shock. Let me say how delighted I am to meet you out here. You must have embraced much of your former reality to be here unassisted.

"I am never truly unassisted. On some level my mentor, Pan, is always with me. I am very blessed. However, I do much more journeying solo these days . . . and I enjoy it. I confess, I have often wondered about the relationship between the baby Seine and yourself. Could you explain!"

As metaphysical Beings, we both recognise that we are not contained in a physical body; rather, we are the conscious container of the body. In your dream I gave you a visual image of an aspect of my consciousness merging with your consciousness.

"I thought it was something along those lines."

In truth, I offered you nothing other than a bridge from your fifth-dimensional reality. It was enough to allow you a feeling of deeper connection with Mixael. And look how you have progressed as a result.

"You probably know already, but I was with a collective galactic Being just before you arrived, and it told me that a friend was coming along the path. Did you know that I was here?"

Of course . . . on two counts. The Being projected your image to all life-forms within the vicinity, and you, as always, project yourself in a blaze of vibrant energy. Even your telepathic communication is broadcast on a public channel. Seine chuckles at his wit.

"Hmm, you would never believe how many other Beings have told me the same thing. It's the only way of telepathy that I know. But I'm okay with this! I'll fix it eventually. Obviously this meeting is not by chance . . . nothing is. What do you have planned for me?"

Why should I have anything planned? Why not a friendly chat and . . . goodbye?

"Because I know you, that's why. I realise now why it was that Michael had so much trouble remembering you. You were in *Mixael's* memory! I remember you well, and the *ages* we have spent together. Well enough to know you have something up your metaphoric sleeve for both of us."

Seine laughs. I watch him, his pale blue vestigial teeth, his silver eyes, his sleek, feline, yet somehow humanoid head. His body fur is very short and, like a mole's, moves any way that it is brushed. Tall, sleek, yet non-physical in a three-dimensional reality, his species was highly evolved while in our 3-D reality we were still scrambling around in unlit caves. I remember the journeys we took, Seine and Mixael, two metaphysical Beings exploring the realities of a multiverse. I confess to remembering the journeying far better than any of the contents. They elude me.

Well, Mixael, feeling that you were in the galaxy, I thought you might like a guide.

I laugh. "A hitchhiker's guide, huh! While I'm not exactly hitchhiking, I would be delighted to have you as a guide, because I don't have a clue where I am or where I am going. So far, galactic life has come to *me . . .* including you!"

I am not surprised, my friend. As a Being with a blend of the qualities of both Michael and Mixael, you are sending signals into the galaxy in a similar way that a hapless or helpless child in a city would express a supposed need for assistance.

"Really, but I'm not helpless, or afraid, or in any way distressed or needing assistance."

Neither is the metaphorical child, but by its nature it touches the heart of every nearby person. They feel a need to assist or comfort the child, even though it may not need it.

"Okay, I get it. Let's help the new cosmic kid . . . that sort of thing. But I'm not helpless, nor am I projecting any such feelings."

Agreed. Your projection is more: "Hey, out there . . . I'm a newcomer in the galaxy. Anyone care to tell me what's going on, or where the action is?"

I laugh. "I can relate to that. Okay, enough of the flimflam . . . where are we going?"

I truly am here in response to you, but I would like to discuss what you refer to as the major Change event. Earth has been through an uplifting experience, along with all the life forms attuned to her. I am aware that you saw the photon-flakes which fell onto the planet.

"Yes, but I refer to them as Light-flakes. What *are* photon flakes?"

Simply stated, a photon is a particle of quantum light.

"Hmm, my lack of physics is evident. A quantum is a representation of energy, right? But as far as I'm concerned, Light-flakes is a nice, uncomplicated description."

I agree, especially if it works for you.

Together, we swiftly walk/travel back along the path for a few moments of no-time! Once again I am surrounded by the always-beautiful, ever-changing ethereal plants and gardens.

I would like you to sit in your lotus position and without sight, focus on the garden.

I do as Seine asks, knowing what he means. Within my Light-body I do not have normal physical vision, although to some degree an aspect remains from the sheer memory and habit of normal sight. However, I do have a powerful energetic/ perceptual metaphysical vision.

Mixael, you know about the pineal gland in humans. You know that governmental and religious dependency destroys self-dependency. Relying and depending on yourself strengthens your pineal, along with your whole-brain functions. It strengthens them because you have a wider, deeper and far more energetic and meaningful relationship with the world around you when you are self-dependent. Humans have developed compartmentalised brains, which are mostly left-brain dominant. Right-brain and whole-brain functions are severely neglected energetically, thus becoming rather restricted which, in turn, has caused the pineal to atrophy. Humans also commonly and frequently ingest and imbibe substances that cause the pineal gland to calcify. As a result, much of humanity suffers the massive anxiety and depression that accompanies this abuse of your holistic potential. You are familiar with all this?

"Unfortunately, yes. Although I had never considered the former aspect of what you share. I guess I am here by the grace of an active pineal. The many incarnations of Michael as a wandering mystic, and myself as the 5-D Mixael, have been very much in my/our favour . . . at a price!"

From this galactic place, focus on your garden. See the plants growing vigorously. Ignore your current drought. See the flowers, smell them.

I do so, although I spare a thought to wonder what this is all about. Gradually, I become aware that I am not looking into my garden—I am *in* my garden! Immediately I feel a degree of conflict, for we are in a very severe drought and my garden has been without growth all spring and most of the summer. Yet, here I am metaphysically in my metaphysical garden looking at the vigorously growing shrubs and their flowers. Most odd! Nevertheless, I bring it all into balance.

To keep this explanation simple, the pineal is a unique energy centre that acts as an interface between the brain/Being and the universe. The active function of the pineal is to lower the—let us say—universal cosmic frequencies to a point that the pituitary can accept them. The pituitary in turn lowers the frequencies even further, to the point that the brain can translate them for the mind to grasp, and possibly understand. Do you follow this?

"Yes. So far so good."

The mostly unknown and unrealised aspect of the big Change event is that the efficacy of the pineal as an interface is becoming elevated. This means, in effect, that the pineal will pick up cosmic frequencies of a considerably higher value than previously, and it will not lower that frequency in the way that it has previously. As with the pineal, the pituitary will need to be more efficient, for it, too, will pick up a higher frequency and not reduce that frequency to as low a level as before. This, in turn, means that the brain is compelled toward operating in a greater, holistic, whole-brain capacity.

"Okay, I'm fine with all this. But what happens to the people whose pineal is too atrophied or calcified to be able to respond to this new stimulus?"

The energies of newness will not support the energies of old-ness. Disease and sickness will take its toll, and people will move toward their next incarnation.

"And those people will incarnate into the consciousness of their own focus and creation?"

Of course.

"So the Change event was, in fact, a great divide! Not a separation, for human is human, but an event whereby our individual journeys will take different directions . . . for a time.

I don't doubt that this has happened before. Some of our space brothers and sisters are surely distant relatives."

This is correct. The whole history of human life on Earth needs much serious revision. To return to our subject, a more elevated pineal interface means that your powers of creation will need to be far more focused, more on target, as it were. Errant thoughts and a confused emotional focus will not support you.

"But surely a higher pineal interface will go hand-in-hand with greater focus and attention in the moment? I don't mean automatically, but more on a super-intuitive level."

This is true, for subconscious living has become automatic and predictable—meaning that potential probabilities are bypassed. Conscious living more or less creates an intuitive state of attention to the many probabilities of the moment.

"Okay, so why the garden?"

Seine chuckles. *Patience! I want you to focus on some of the flowers you are seeing.*

"Focusing on flowers."

His chuckle deepens. *Enough flippancy. Focus. I want you to visualise the buds opening, the flowers closing, and colours changing.*

I do as he asks. Surprisingly, the flowers that are open I am able to gently close, while buds that are ready to unfold do so with my caring assistance. However, some flowers are not ready to unfold, so I leave them alone. I begin to change a yellow allamanda to red, but I feel distress from it, so I leave it as yellow. A trumpet plant, which is a pale orange, willingly deepens to a reddish colour, while another white one is willing to be a deep yellow. Hmm, interesting.

You see, you are able to discern where to make the changes, and where it is not appropriate. This discernment accompanies the increased activation of the pineal. The pineal intuitively knows how and when to change 'what is' to 'what may be'.

"Suggesting that an undeveloped pineal does not know this?"

A normal human pineal of today reduces the frequency according to the pituitary's ability to accept it. This, in turn, reduces the frequency for a brain/mindset that is fixed and stuck, according to the dictates of subconscious living. *Within all these reductions, intuition and insight is also reduced. Such a person believes that life is only what they see and relate to.*

"Whereas a person with an active and developed pineal knows that the life they see and relate to is a very small reflection of *all that is.*"

Exactly.

"Are you suggesting that I will be able to do this with physical flowers when I am in my physical body in my garden?"

No. What I am showing you is that as you and other people develop the use of the higher frequency pineal in this new age, you will learn that that which you can consciously do on an astral level will come to pass on a physical level.

"Yes . . . of course. The metaphysical *precedes* the physical. To have that as the prime principle of life is one thing, but to be able to actively *use* that principle at will is quite another."

It certainly is. As you realise, once you are able to consciously change creation, then you are taking on a huge responsibility. When in the garden with the flowers, you were conscious of the flowers, of their needs, of their growth and development, of their willingness to respond to your influence, and you acted accordingly. This is the responsibility to which I refer.

"As I focus on the flowers now, I feel a flow of accord that links us. I acted within that accord, acknowledging the plants and their consciousness. Yet I did all that without thinking it through. It was . . . intuitive."

Exactly. Your Light-body and your pineal are not physical, although both have a physical representation. Although the pineal gland is physically small, metaphysically its energy field is huge. Combined, your focused energy acted synchronistically with the garden, without the need of thought or analysis. You could, indeed, call this super-intuition.

"The sobering side of this is the implication of two types of humans emerging. I mean, to act in the way that you are teaching me is a far cry from the 'poor me' of victim consciousness. How will this work out?

Did you never hear of frames-of-reality? This is what you teach!

"Okay, stupid question."

Mixael, be clear about this. There is no single path for the conscious evolution of any species; there are many paths. On your planet, Darwin has shown the many divergent paths that finches took on one small, isolated island. This was not simply about physical changes to survive, although that was *involved. This was also about the divergent paths in consciousness that, on a primal level, the birds took. It is the same for all species . . . including humanity. On your planet, felines have not yet emerged on the higher consciousness scale, but where my species originated, we did. Feline is feline, yet there are many paths and expressions for feline evolution.*

"Wait a minute, surely all humans are humans. What else can they be?"

All those finches remain finches. Some evolved to drink nectar, some evolved to drink blood. Some evolved to feed on certain insects, others evolved to live within the spines of certain plant species. And others made other changes. You could say that all the finches specialised, *but they remained as finches. You know as well as I do, that the changes first developed* metaphysically, *then the physical adaptations were developed.*

"Hmm, fair enough. Can't disagree. I think I can see where this is leading."

Then suppose you tell me.

"As you were talking about finches, I suddenly realised that it is not the linear time factor that places people in a fifth-dimensional reality ahead of us; it is *consciousness*. I never even considered that before. Yet if, in a greater reality, all time occupies the same moment, then it could *never* have been about time at all. It was about commitment, focus, choices, intent . . . all those and more. And, of course . . . absolute Love. In other words, fifth-dimensional people are literally another human species when compared with many people in my current dimensional reality. Take the sheer immorality of the elite cabals as an example. It becomes obvious that they are exploring the degeneration of consciousness along with the evolution of corruption. They *look* like us . . . but that's where it ends!"

As you often say, your three-dimensional reality is a very mixed bag.

34

"Okay . . . back to the garden! It would appear that meta-physically I am in two mismatched places. I am metaphysically in my physical garden while in the same moment I am metaphysically in this seemingly ethereal garden somewhere in our galaxy. To increase my confusion, even my physical garden is mismatched, with the actual plant growth stunted by drought, and yet I see the abundant flowering that suggests rain that we have not had. Is anything 'real' in any reality?"

That is a very good question. I will ask you one: What actually is . . . real? Describe it.

"Hmm, tricky. When I am physical, real is what I can see and touch and relate to with my five senses. In our world, poverty is very real for billions of people. When I am metaphysical, real is real according to the abilities of the observer. The observer makes reality by considering something is real. I think!"

Are you sure of all this?

"There's a lot of ambiguity involved, but it's an approximation."

Mixael, you have already said that the metaphysical precedes the physical. So for most people in your reality, their beliefs—which are metaphysical—determine and decide what is real for them. When you are surrounded by poverty, it powerfully shapes and tempers your belief into the reality of poverty. In this way each person makes poverty real for themselves. But does this make it real for everyone? No, because it is only real for those who are emotionally—more metaphysical—connected to the belief of poverty as a reality.

I nod. "I can't disagree."

You say that metaphysically you create the reality you are in by your perception of it. This is a principle, and the same principle applies to all creation. For each one of us, real is the degree that we are able to interrelate with the reality of our observation and perception.

"Well . . . I did ask! Let me see if I have got this. In my garden, metaphysically I was not relating to a drought—which is physical—and I was able to see the suggested flowers. While metaphysical, physical space is no longer a dominant reality, therefore I was able to be in an etheric version of my garden, my metaphysical garden, and my physical garden all simultaneously.

And all of it was my observation/perception/experiencing of reality. Yet none of it is a watertight reality."

Seine chuckles. *The only thing that is real about real is that real is not an exclusive!*

"Yes . . . I get it. Very good. You should have said that at the start!"

Higher pineal interface activation, more than ever, will mean that what is real is based in your creation of it. If metaphysically you are able to open and close flowers and change their colours in accordance with their cooperation, then the physical expression of this follows according to the flexibility of your reality. Some of humanity hovers on the cusp of a whole new human expression . . . a rare few have stepped into it.

"I like that. I'm sure that it is already occurring in some of our children. Dare I ask another question? I have been thinking of this garden as ethereal, but each time I say or think it is an ethereal garden, intuition tells me that it is an astral garden. Which is correct?"

All physicality is held within a greater astral reality. This garden in the galaxy is not real.

"Oh no . . . we're not going back there again . . . please!"

Your home garden is familiar to you. You felt an unrealised need to create it as a comfort of familiarity in the strangeness that surrounds you. I strongly suggest that you no longer need it.

And to my astonishment, the ethereal/astral/whatever garden instantly vanishes.

"Oh, my gosh . . . you need to be careful with your suggestions!"

You want it back?

"No, I do not need it. I am comfortable on this path with you, my friend. The path is real enough for me, even if it is not real. Er . . . is there a path for you?"

Seine laughs. *Yes, there is a path . . . for now! And it is time for us to move along it.*

"Okay, good. So where are we going?"

Does there need to be a where? Is not journeying on the path enough?

I sigh. "Whatever. Let's just get going."

You were ever impatient.

"Me! Impatient! I just like getting on with . . . er, life!"

Like I said, impatient.

By now, we are glide/striding swiftly along the path. And I mean *gliding*. Each long gliding step forward seems to cover many kilometres, and we must be moving very rapidly, yet I have hardly any sense that we are moving at all. It is all a bit confusing. Even as I think this, I realise that I am attempting to relate to this reality through my habitual 3-D reality, and that such a comparison will not work. Dropping that reference point, I am aware of travelling at an enormous speed, yet of no real movement at all! Sorry, but I cannot explain it. I am happy just to be comfortable with it.

"This is an interesting mode of transport, but it is not as efficient as stepping Between."

True, but where would you step to?

I chuckle. "This is why we are cosmic walking."

We glide/travel in companionable silence, the path stretching endlessly before and behind us. I realise how fortunate I am to be here.

"Thank you for coming back into my life."

Seine smiles at me. *To be honest, I never fully left it. I have been with you ever since your dream experience . . . although not all of me. Just an aspect.*

"This aspect thing interests me. Are you fully here, now, or is this another aspect of you?"

I could ask you the same question. Are you fully here or is this an aspect of you?

Hmm . . . he is right! "This me is just an aspect of me. Another aspect is physically in my study. Another aspect is living what I call my past, with yet another aspect living my future. And there are aspects of me living all the probabilities that I/we create in our living/experiencing of life. Does it have any end? Or are all the aspects more like echoes of the metaphysical Being I am?"

Your questions hold degrees of separation. Take away all the spaces between the echoes, accepting that linear time is an illusion. Take away all the reference points of separation between all the so-called aspects, and you have one, all encompassing reality. This is Truth. However, if that were to happen to a human in your frame-of-reality, the result would be insanity. So you play the game of time, space and separation as you gradually grow in consciousness, through cause and effect, enough to engage and embrace the Truth that will bring it all together.

"Yes! I inner-know exactly what you are saying."

As we walk the path, I get the impression that the galaxy has changed. I mean, it is the same galaxy, but the silvery colour of distant space that has been accompanying me is giving way to colours of a deep and extraordinary magnitude. I gasp. Ahead of us is the event horizon of another black hole. Maybe it is my friendly black hole. The energy feels familiar, but what shocks me is that I am seeing the deepest, most powerful colours ever of Chaos, the engine that drives, of Order, the stability of structure . . . and of Balance, the place of greatest potential.

This is both incredible and immediate in its off-world splendour.

"Obviously I have a lot more to learn hereabouts."

Truthfully, I had no destination. The black hole is engaging us. We are very privileged.

"We certainly are. It and I have met before."

Yes. You publicly broadcast everything that passed between you.

I chuckle. "More public broadcasting coming up . . . I don't doubt!"

I stop glide/walking to just stare in awe at the sight before me. The so-called event horizon is completely changed from the way I last saw/experienced it. Instead of the previous colours, it is rather like multiple vast ripples of the deepest colours of Chaos, Order, and Balance, all somehow intertwined in perfect juxtaposition with each other. The reds of Chaos and the blacks of Order are powerfully benign, allowing Balance to animate the ever-ongoing ripples with its brilliant flickering whiteness. This is a most extraordinary sight. It offers me a whole new perspective of Chaos and Order, yet one that is completely inexplicable. My perception and intuition are propelled into an insight that is entirely non-intellectual.

I feel overwhelmed. "Oh, my goodness!"

Oh, my goodness, indeed. In the way that it presents itself, this is a rare and privileged sight for even a seasoned galactic traveller. I'm not quite sure what you have done to warrant such an invitation, but I get the distinct impression that we are about to be invited to enter this black hole.

"Oh, God . . . I can't do that."

Why not?

"Because all that I have read about black hole theories say that if you were to enter one you would be stretched from the entrance to the exit, which could be an eternity away. Gosh . . . imagine if I survived such an experience. I would be completely insane."

Sounds to me that the theory *is insane.*

"Hmm, I'm inclined to agree with you. Why would it invite us to enter simply to destroy us . . . or me? Anyway, we are jumping ahead, because we have not yet been invited."

Wait a moment, Mixael, you are forgetting something. You entered into the black hole when you merged with its consciousness. I know this because you broadcast it.

"Yes . . . but that was different. My consciousness entered, but metaphysically, I stayed outside. I think!"

*This is true. Your consciousness and mine—which are One— melded within the space of my Being. Now, we meet again. I am inviting you galactic Beings to enter my reality/space and give yourselves to my deliverance.

Seine smiles, nodding. *I accept with gratitude.*

"Wow! Obviously you heard our invitation. I told you this was different! Oh well, I totally trust the black hole, so I also accept with my thanks."

*Walk to where you see the ripples of creation and pause there. This will allow the Great Principles of Chaos, Order and Balance to align you with my energy-field.

I sigh. This feels decidedly different to me. On the previous occasion the metaphysical me was not in the black hole. It was a powerful and profound connection in consciousness. This is much more of a full commitment. All that I am metaphysically— the quintessential me—is about to enter a living reality/space where it is most likely no human physically based in 3-D reality has ever before been. Am I ready for this? If I was not, I am very sure it would not be happening—so, I *trust*. Besides, I have a rather special cosmic companion.

Together, Seine and I glide/walk toward the rippling Principles of Creation. As we approach, with a rush the ripples surround and envelop us. From within the red of Chaos I can feel its energy of vitality as never before. I am aware that I touch only the periphery of this vast energy, but it is enough. Simultaneously, I am within the profound and almost disturbingly silent stillness of Order, again knowing that an overdose could be fatal. Throughout all this, the scintillating poise and perfection of Balance holds me safely within forces which I suddenly know are of a magnitude beyond my comprehension.

I have no idea of Seine's experience, but he appears to be calm and serene. How long we are within this opposing yet non-opposing synchronism of powers, I know not. Time is ended here. No, it never even *began*. It is as though life, everything, is held in suspension while a galaxy blinks at the audacity of two 'small' Beings taking a gigantic, incomprehensible step.

Gradually, I become aware that we are being inexorably drawn into the black hole. For long moments the Powers of Creation seem to cling to me; then I am drawn deeper into the embrace of the black hole. Without any doubt, I am committed! The thought that I might be metaphysically stretched across the galaxy flits across the mind, but I do my best to instantly dismiss it. *Trust!* Trust is a power available to humanity; I think I am going to need a megadose!

I have no sense of a tunnel through space, yet I feel enclosed in an energy that defies all description. I am within a space within a space which combines as non-space. If this sounds like nonsense, so be it, but I am contained within the greatest energy of non-containment I have ever experienced. I am aware of looking for something that is familiar, like a vast hole/tunnel in space, something—anything—that relates to a hole in space— but it is not to be. For what feels like long moments my sensory faculties become frantic, moving into overload as I try to make something appear that I can relate to, then a l-o-n-g, very soft and deeply penetrating whisper echoes within me . . . *r e l a a a x x x* . . . and such is the power of its suggestion, I inner-relax. Only now do I realise the tension that I held. A tension created by a lingering thought/fear of black hole annihilation, or something equally terrible. This place inside the black hole is an unknown of such a magnitude that it goes way beyond simply unknown. Everything I have ever read about black holes amounts to multiple statements saying that this journey is totally impossible, that this is a place of such terrifying and inconceivable energies that whole star systems are being endlessly swallowed up and destroyed.

Did I have a brief glimpse of insanity? Could insanity stem from such a total inability to accept the moment of *it is as it is* that the mind creates a world of pure fantasy—a delusion so great that it disconnects a person from their own sanity? Is such a fear of the unknown possible? If this were the case, then to a greater or lesser degree all humanity does this, creating the fantasies and illusions we call normal life; normal simply because most people share the same illusions. And for those who do not share the common illusion, because they are able to accept the overwhelming unknowability of *it is as it is,* where do they fit in with so-called normality?

Relaxed, I no longer look for, or seek anything to stabilise me. Either I have trust, or I do not. How easy it is to trust even the scary familiar. A complete unknown with such an immensity of alien strangeness is a whole different ball-game on the field of trust! Other times I have had Pan with me to trust, or some familiar Being, and although I am now metaphysically within the living/reality of a vast and inexplicable intelligence, it is nothing that I can relate to. Okay, so now I have a whole new insight into trusting the power of trust!

Glancing at Seine, he is relaxed and calm. Obviously, trust is not exclusively human! We are now float/walking within the paradox of truly epic speed and no movement whatsoever! This paradox is so unsettling, so completely impossible that for moments I feel queasy, but it quickly passes. In those queasy moments I was again attempting to understand, but the moment I accept *it is as it is,* the queasiness ends. This works—*it is as it is*—trust. Trust based in trusting the known, is one level, but to trust when involved in the *unknown* takes it to a whole new status of meaning.

I am seeing/experiencing sights and sounds (!?!) that are different from any reality I have ever known. But I am calm now, relaxed and accepting. I am aware of being within the living reality/space of the black hole, while at the same time I am walking on a planet of dark-green soil, with rank, greyish-brown vegetation growing all around me. Plants that are reminiscent of common dandelions—except they are tree-sized giants and the 'wrong' colour—are covered in hundreds of comparatively small creatures that appear as a mishmash of animals. When I say comparatively small, that is exactly what I mean, for although dwarfed by the dandelion leaves, they are as big as large dogs, while looking like deformed frogs. What is truly weird is that as fast as the creatures—which have a fur, feather and chitin covering—eat the dandelion leaf, it as quickly grows back. I also get the impression that these creatures, while not blessed with full intelligence—are *we*?—are by no means dumb and stupid. There is an energy with them that is not so much about alertness, as it is about awareness.

Although I am here metaphysically, these strange creatures are aware of me. I look around to learn what Seine has to say about this, but he is nowhere to be seen. I feel no fear or concern from the creatures, but they definitely find me rather interesting. On the nearest gigantic leaf, one of the creatures creep-hops toward me. I can see no trace of eyes, ears or nose. Its head, if it has such a thing, seems to be a hump in the centre of its back with no apparent flexibility or movement, yet it is somehow tracking me. It does have a mouth, appearing like a large suction-disc on its underside. When it eats leaf material, I get the impression that it sucks or inhales leaf, rather than nibbles or chews. It is also worthy of note that its energy is completely non-aggressive.

Not quite sure of what is happening, I nevertheless rise into the air above the plants to get a greater view of this . . . place? I expected this scene to go on forever, but it stretches over no more than maybe one hundred hectares, then abruptly ends, as though contained. I flit over to the point where it ends, which is also the beginning of another bizarre pocket of reality. When I go really high, as far as I can see in any direction, there are pockets of utterly different realities. From above, it looks like a patchwork quilt of diverse and strange scenes. I get a disconcerting impression of being in a huge cosmic zoo, or laboratory, where specimens of many varieties of species are kept for observation. The thought is very unsettling.

I decide that I do not want to be here.

Before I go, curiosity compels me to look into another couple of the reality zones. I can see nothing that indicates where one reality ends and another begins. No wall, or visible energy-field, or any obvious indications of demarcation between them, although it *must* be there! In yet another approximately one hundred hectare zone I see a scene similar to one I saw many years ago when in another metaphysical adventure. The zone is all desert, with ambulatory vegetation that looks a bit like a small grass tree. Last time I was aware of the powerful sentience of the creatures, but these, although similar to look at, do not have the same energy of sentience. As I begin to move away, it comes strongly into my awareness that these are the same, or similar vegetation/creatures, but of a much earlier time period in their evolution.

The next zone I inspect is different again. Most of this whole zone is a huge, pale-pink lake, or this is how I describe it. On the shoreline of the lake there appear to be many thousands of small scuttling creatures that look like a cross between a rabbit and a large crab. I get the impression that these also have quite a high degree of awareness. As I observe them, I see that most of their time is spent within the waters of the lake—if water it is! It occurs to me that all the zones I have seen thus far have one thing in common: a developing awareness/consciousness. Insight strongly suggests that these creature/Beings are under benign observation in their many different zones, rather than in a vast experimental laboratory. I am glad that such a repugnant idea is dispelled. These zones are for their benefit, although who or what created all this boggles the mind!

Is there a human zone in this reality? Even with the thought, I realise that I do not want to know. I would like to think that we are further along the scale of sentience than what I have seen thus far would indicate. And just like that, I *know* we are not represented here.

Feeling far more relaxed about this reality-frame, I am aware that my curiosity would like to see every zone of reality here, but I know that could take a very long time—even in no-time! I decide to leave, not knowing where I am or where the black hole is taking me. I trust!

It seems a focused intent to depart is enough. Once again I am float/walking at great speed yet without movement. Am I moving through the black hole, or is the black hole moving through me, or my frames of reference? I really do not know.

I am aware of titanic fields-of-energy all around me. Planetary bodies are forming from cosmic gas and dust and ice and . . . consciousness. I have often spoken and written of *direct knowing*, described in metaphysical literature as *mystical cognition*. This is now peaking as I move through and within the formation of clusters of small asteroids, meteoroids, and comets, all within a newborn solar system. And I *directly know* that none of this is random, or chance, or accidental, or casual cosmic collisions, or non-conscious cohesion, or any such thing. All this is deliberate, conscious creation. I can literally feel the beat and pulse of creation as an energy vibrating throughout my metaphysical body. The scale of such creation is so far beyond my speculation that my attempting to understand is, for me, about as pointless as an ant attempting to understand Pythagorean geometry.

I stop in the centre of this fractional part of a solar system as it is being created. And yet, there are no parts in a holistic multiverse . . . all is One. A paradox!

A paradox of which you will, for eternity, be a part. As you pause in the centre of this aspect of the creation of a star cluster within a galactic system, so an aspect of your energy field is being incorporated into it. You cannot be consciously within creation without influencing the outcome, just as you, a Being, are the outcome of your creating/developing your own state of consciousness. Add to this all consciousness that you consciously mix and mingle within the forms of gas, minerals, animals, plants, people, etcetera. All this becomes holistically incorporated into the Beingness you are.

"Oh my gosh . . . my energy in a star cluster! But by the same token, just as whatever animal or plant I interact with affects me, so I affect the consciousness of that species."

Of course, but the key is being conscious. If you live subconsciously you have little impact on the consciousness of life. When you live consciously, the impact is major.

I am stunned by the thought that the uniqueness of my consciousness—me!—is now part of a star system. To be honest— stunned and thrilled! "So this could not be by chance?"

As you know, chance, coincidence and accidental are human games. Aeons into a so-called future your aspect of consciousness will play a significant role in the formation of a life form which, in turn, will have a significant galactic role.

"Oh . . . my goodness! I am honoured beyond measure. I can only pray that however small a role my consciousness will play, its effect is entirely benevolent."

That, beloved, is why you are here.

I am overwhelmed by my sudden uprush of emotion. It does not throw me out of my experience, but in my physical body a few tears trickle onto my cheeks.

Once again, I look around for Seine, but he is not to be seen. I *know* that he is experiencing exactly what it is that he needs to experience. Feeling the presence of the black hole all around me, I am now—thank goodness!—entirely comfortable. I have a sense that aspects of my consciousness continue to be drawn into the formation of the star cluster, and that it is inappropriate for me to withdraw until I feel released. I feel awe and wonder at the magnitude of what is taking place. Smiling, I realise that my new sense of self-greatness has not once come up with the old, 'why me?' question. Why *not* me!

I have no knowing of how long I am gently held within the thrall of cosmic creation, but there comes a moment when I know I am released, able to continue my journey. I sigh—then smile.

Will some far-distant future Beings be prone to sighing?

Trusting that the black hole is guiding and directing my journey into Mystery, I relax within the paradox of glide/walking at great speed and apparent non-movement, all while being/feeling contained in a vast non-containment sensation! It is truly baffling.

As I journey in the cosmos of the black hole, I see a huge, shimmering building floating in the distance; a building out of fantasy. I even hesitate to describe it as a building. It has a transparent central tower that, as I get closer, could be well over a hundred kilometres high. It is fantastical, immense; a glass-like tower, maybe twenty kilometres in diameter, with what appear to be numerous transparent roads stretching out from all around the tower for hundreds of kilometres. Each road appears about a kilometre wide, supported by absolutely nothing. Like the tower, the roads appear to float in space, each of them eventually ending in a massive structure that vaguely resembles the open petals of a flower.

I stop to simply stare, to gape and gawk in awe. This is impossible! Such a . . . !!! cannot exist.

Do you doubt your own experience, or your senses? What is so difficult to accept? Since accepting my within-ness, anything should be possible for you.

I sigh, heavily. "In my physical reality this is so impossible . . . it's even ridiculous as a fantasy."

You are not in your physical reality.

I smile. "Ain't that the truth!"

Take away all gravity and what are you left with?

"Hmm . . . weightlessness!" I nod. "Yes, if I embrace weightlessness, letting go of my physical indoctrination with our strong gravity, then such an impossible . . . whatever . . . probably becomes possible."

You are seeing the artificial world of a race of sentient Beings that was conceived and constructed by them. You would probably call it a satellite world, even though it does not orbit around any other planet. It remains stationary in space.

I continue to stare, stunned, shocked, amazed, flabbergasted!

46

I thought that nothing more could possibly amaze me. Obviously, I need to accept that I am an infant in a magnitude of cosmic newness beyond my conception or comprehension. I struggle to grasp even the concept of building such a vast, strangely shaped immensity as the artificial world I see hanging in space before me.

To be honest, Mixael, it also staggers me just to look at it.

Again feeling a need for the familiar, I am *very* pleased to see Seine. "Have you ever seen this before? It is so mind-boggling I'm struggling to accept what I see."

Oh yes, I have seen it countless times. For me, it is home.

He made a sound with his mouth that sounded like an elongated purr, with a harsh buzz in the middle. *This is the name of our world. For you, its approximate meaning is Shimmering Beauty.*

"Oh my gosh . . . this is *your* . . . home! Oh wow! I do see, however, that no matter how bizarre and completely strange it appears to me, it does shimmer . . . and it is beautiful! Its beauty is . . . is . . . so very . . . unworldly! But . . . how can you possibly live in a black hole?"

I do not. It would seem that we are no longer within the black hole . . . or if we are, then this is an entirely new approach for me. Whatever . . . it is as it is.

"This I can accept . . . it is as it is!"

When on three-dimensional Earth, beauty for me is almost always something in the natural world, seldom artificial, yet now, with a delayed impact, I realise that no matter how alien it is to me, or how artificial, *it truly is* utterly and incredibly beautiful. While staring in awe, I notice that the glass-like substance of the artificial world is continually reflecting the changing light and conditions around it. Not exactly a kaleidoscope of colours, it is far more subtle and yet also more strikingly engaging. Shimmering beauty, indeed.

Mixael, although this is as unexpected for me as it is for you, nevertheless, I invite you to visit my world of Shimmering Beauty. Come.

He guides me in a rapid glide/walk that actually seems like regular movement in a defined direction. In moments we are on one of the roads to the central tower.

Incidentally, we refer to the roads as branches, leading to the flowers of our various clans.

"Do I broadcast all my thoughts?"

Not all, maybe, but most of them.

"Well, I can quite easily see the reference to the central tower as some vast cosmic tree trunk with all the branches leading to spectacular and unimaginable flowers."

Seine chuckles. *Before we enter, I need you to grasp a few pointers. Forget any dimensional references for this world. Accept that it is non-physical in your reality, even though it is obviously of a higher physicality for us. It is a construct something along the lines with which you are familiar in your fifth-dimensional reality, but considerably beyond that. This world is made of a material, but it is a material born and grown from energies and a combined consciousness for which you have no references. I have no wish to slight you, far be it from me, but I respectfully suggest that you embrace all you see and experience in as non-intellectual a way as possible.*

"Thank you. I don't feel the least bit slighted. In my teachings, I advise people to embrace Truth/Love with intelligence, rather than attempt to intellectually understand. I will take my own advice. Embracing with intelligence inspires direct knowing."

Seine's permanent dolphin-like smile deepens. *Wonderful. Your natural capacity to directly* know *is far beyond your human capacity to* understand.

"I agree, but it does curtail my ability to share it with other people."

Seine chuckles. *As always, you will find a way.*

As we talk we continue our walk/glide along the branch toward the central trunk. Although glass-like to look at—even though not glass at all—I am unable to see into the transparency—so it is not transparent, even though it looks that way.

Too intellectual. Embrace the Mystery!

I laugh. "Intellectual thoughts on broadcast. What a learning curve!"

We are close to the trunk/tower, but no entrance is apparent. Only when we reach the building does one show itself. An opening in the form of a peaked arch appears, revealing a strongly lit interior. Okay, I cannot see in through the material, how about seeing out? As I pass through the entrance, I notice that the walls of this impossible building seem little thicker than an overnight cobweb in my garden. Undoubtedly stronger and considerably more enduring! I smile. This is a l-o-n-g way from my garden. To my intellect, this building is utterly impossible. But . . . *it is as it is,* and I am here.

Together we walk onto floors that actually appear to have solid substance. Although the floor has a disconcerting way of slowly changing colours, it feels and appears solid. I like that. I do not want to know that it is a projection for my senses only. I like solid. I hear Seine chuckling and I realise that I might as well be talking to him. Oh well, so be it. I look around me, and I see there are large, very large, areas in the trunk/tower wall that are transparent, rather like the biggest windows 'off' the world—like a hundred metres long, and equally as high. In the other areas the walls are similar to the floor, but with less subdued colours. All in all, it is a fabulous, if muted sensory overload for an off-worlder like me.

Good, Mixael. Considering the circumstances you are doing well.

"Although I am metaphysical, I would like to know whether the . . . er, windows are open for falling through, or if they actually have an invisible substance to them?"

Seine laughs. *If your largest jet airliner, travelling at the speed of sound, hit one it would bounce off without leaving a mark . . . on the window, that is!*

"Okay . . . that's a graphic enough explanation of their substance."

You do realise that you are perfectly safe. Nothing here can harm you metaphysically, even though you could neither see this nor be here on a physical level. I have nothing to confirm my words, but you are uniquely embraced within the consciousness of the . . . black hole in a way that, to me, is rare and rather humbling.

"I feel this, but I have no idea why."

Seine laughs aloud. *I believe you, although the 'why' is obvious.* He waves his hand in a dismissive gesture, and I am only too ready to let the matter drop.

49

A group of Beings seemingly appear out of nowhere to stand before us. Nobody in sight, then over a dozen Seine replicas surround us. Actually, they are not replicas, even though at first glance the similarity is strong. Some are shorter than Seine, a couple are taller, and two of them are undoubtedly feminine. A few of them are wearing clothing, most are not. When you are a Being covered with very short dense fur, and you have no obvious sexual organs on display, clothes are not quite so necessary or compelling. For each, their fur is a variation of Seine's familiar golden-colour. Those with clothing all wear a similar, silvery one-piece, either belted at the waist, or not. Maybe it is protective clothing with a purpose. There can be no mistaking their gender, for the males have a definite masculine energy, as have the females their feminine energy. This is very obvious on an energetic level. Equally, age differences are almost purely energetic, not something that I can obviously see. Their eyes are all the same silver-moon colour, and looking at the group, I see they all have the membranes that roll sideways across each eye. For me, these cosmic felines are attractive and beautiful people.

It is clear that they are in telepathic communication with Seine. I listen and, to my surprise, I can clearly inner-hear them, even though I do not understand anything they are saying.

Seine smiles at me, then turns toward an elder, saying something. Leaning forward, the elder taps me above and between the eyes, a tiny metaphysical pinprick—and I can understand what they are saying. That simple! Facing me, all of them touch their little finger/claw on the left hand/paw to the place on their heads where he tapped me. Each gives a small bow; *I see you. I see you.*

I gasp! Only last night I had a dream where I was meeting and greeting great spiritual teachers of the world who were much loved friends. I cannot remember what they each said to me, but I replied to them with the words, "I see you. I see you." It suddenly occurs to me that this is a pineal/third eye connection, probably far more meaningful for them than for me. Without intending a pun, I am deeply touched!

Now, as I intuitively and knowingly return the same gesture

and words back to these Beings, I notice Seine nodding, smiling approvingly.

I cannot emphasise enough the mammoth size and proportion of the trunk/tower. Inside it is rather reminiscent of a quiet, orderly, incredibly beautiful yet unworldly city. Completely serene, it is an energy which is both relaxing and dynamic, filled with silent sound, with active stillness. Or maybe, I should say this is Seine's people's brand of serenity.

"Who are you, Seine, as a people?"

He looks at me for long moments. *Call us the Seine People. It is accurate enough.*

"But that is your name."

Is it . . . or is it the name I gave you? Earth people are so very needful of names, so very attached to them, so indoctrinated with the need of labelling. Names are very much the trademark of separation, although many of the advanced human races still use them. Probably more from affection than necessity. The Seine People captures our quintessence.

"Okay, if that is your wish, I'm comfortable with it."

I gesture to the city around me. "How is it possible to create a city of such complete contrasts, and yet have them energetically integrated and synchronised?"

An intellectual question! Such a synchronisation cannot be fabricated. The city is an energetic melding which reflects the consciousness of the people.

"Yes, of course it does. I feel it. You're right . . . stupid question."

Mixael, I did not say stupid. I said intellectual.

I smile. "But as I am wont to say, intellect and stupid all too often hold hands."

Seine chuckles. *Come, we will take you on a whirlwind tour of our world.*

When I consider the immensity of this place, a *whirlwind* tour sounds appropriate.

As I expected, we no longer walk/glide. In the fifth-dimensional reality I visit, Cardifer has a belt gadget which works on the principle of removing the distance between locations, thus making travel super-easy. Here, we are traveling in a similar way, minus any gadget that I am aware of! I like this, but I have a problem with a world that hangs in space while everybody breathes normally. I mean, whatever happened to atmosphere and good old fashioned air?

Seine chuckles. *It is actually an advantage for me when you broadcast, because I know when something is puzzling you. In fact, Shimmering Beauty is held in a huge . . . bubble, if you like, of breathable atmosphere. However, at our level of consciousness, breathing a normal—for us—atmosphere is an option rather than a necessity. Hence my galactic travels with you. However, a tailor-made atmosphere is very useful for our mobility, and for the very stability of our world. In your normal reality, you would die in this atmosphere, for its qualities are designed more for our living world than for us. And before you ask, if the aforementioned very biggest airliner flew into our atmospheric bubble at ten thousand times the speed of sound, it would have no affect on the bubble.*

"You said *living* world. I assume you mean 'living' as in buildings of the fifth-dimension?"

Yes, only more so. This world has its own naturally evolving intelligence. After giving us prior warning, from time to time it reshapes certain areas to experiment with new and creative expressions for the greater good and advantage of the world and its inhabitants.

"Wow! That's amazing. Is Shimmering Beauty aware of me?"

Absolutely. Without her permission you could not set foot on her, metaphysical or not. To be honest, Shimmering Beauty is rather curious about you. This is the home of just a few of the Seine People, and you are the first . . . he smiles . . . alien to visit in quite a while.

Me—an alien! Wow! Who would believe it?

CHAPTER THREE

SHIMMERING BEAUTY

"You say that this is the home of a *few* of the Seine People. This suggests that there are many more of you."

Oh yes. We populate a few of the natural worlds within this galaxy. It may surprise you to know that we outnumber your human population.

He is right. I am definitely surprised.

"I find that amazing, considering how prolific we are. Are all your home planets in our galaxy?"

Yes, they are, but they have not yet been observed by your space scientists. And if they ever are they will probably be dismissed as inhospitable to life. Bear in mind, however, that the galaxy is vast. And that I am referring to the galaxy and not your solar system.

"Yes, I need to remember that. Hmm . . . inhospitable to three-dimensional human life as we know it. And for them, that means life. It is a fairly arrogant viewpoint . . . and yet, if you are a 3-D person, how can you think and act beyond your own physical reality?"

Is this a serious question?

"Of course . . . why not?"

So what are you doing here?

For long moments I am completely blank. What is he talking about?

Then I get it.

I laugh. "For a very small but growing minority in my reality, I am a spiritual teacher of some merit. However, if the greater population were to read my books about my metaphysical travels, I would be dismissed as living on the lunatic fringe . . . or a junkie! As for the people of science, I would not even be considered, never mind be dismissed. For them, only a scientist can advance science, which is rather like asking the intellect to promote intelligence! Despite all this there are new maverick scientists with a greater holistic vision who have the new, higher level of awareness which *is being born* in the people. I am but one of many. We have a long way to go, but the paradigm shift in consciousness has taken place. Who knows where human thinking and speculation might eventuate? Now that we are no longer all stuck in the same reality box, our paths will gradually be able to go their separate ways."

And probably quicker than you currently expect.

His words remind me of the flakes of Light. "Probably. I would like to think so."

We are now travelling up the tower/trunk, which seems to be composed of one vast level after another. I notice that it does have numerous glass-like tubes that go from level to level, but most of the Seine People seem to travel via this instantaneous teleportation. Each level contains no less than a small city, complete with a ceiling which appears to be like the sky, or it is a huge open scenario of some very alien landscape—or even atmosphere-scape, and water-scape!

We have stopped at a level, complete with a human-style city—except it is spotlessly clean—and a normal Earth-type sky in which I can feel the warmth from what appears to be our sun.

"Considering the multiple levels to this incredible tower, how high is it to the, er . . . ceiling of each level? I mean . . . I can see a blue sky above me, with our sun shining. And it all appears absolutely normal and to scale, but that cannot be possible. So what am I actually seeing?"

You are seeing a simulation which is an almost exact miniature replica of the real thing. Each level has a height of around one to ten kilometres, depending on the ecological system. On this level it is around two and a half kilometres high, and the sun is a tiny controlled meteorite which is actually emitting heat. You need to accept that you are within a level of technology far beyond current human abilities — technology that requires the unique conditions of Shimmering Beauty to grow and maintain it.

"Grow and maintain it . . . wow! Is every level in this tower different?"

Yes, as you are seeing, each level offers a representation of the basic habitat of many different sentient species. Humans are but one of these.

"I'm not wishing to be rude, but what is the point of all this if you have no off-world visitors? I mean, you have no human visitors to this level . . . and if I am the first alien in quite a while, then you do not have many visitors at all. Besides, you said that physical humans could not live and breathe here, because it caters more for the living, evolving world. So I repeat, what's the point of all this?"

Seine smiles at me patiently. *Fair enough. However, you being the first alien in quite a while does not mean that we have not had other visitors. We have had many . . . but not very recently. As to the point of all this . . . you come from a culture where everything has to be done quickly so that you can see and experience almost instant results. Your people believe in birth, a hurried life, then death . . . the End. Even those who do not believe this intellectually, nevertheless live it. You live to race the clock and waste as little time as possible; a short-term view of life. I do not belittle this, for such a viewpoint will inevitably change as you move onward in your growth as conscious Beings. The time will come when you will travel from your planet, and many of your people will visit here, and be able to breathe and prosper.*

We have an eternal-moment view of life. By your reckoning, Shimmering Beauty is a few millennia old, which is old to you. To us, that is nothing. Shimmering Beauty is an evolving world which will, when the moment is ripe, be a fully engaged galactic embassy for sentient Beings to mix and mingle, and to house those who represent their own particular home world. For example, even now on this level of your human city in the tower/trunk of our world, a human could breathe and prosper.

"Really . . . that all sounds wonderful." I smile. "I want it for us . . . now! I confess, I didn't notice the breathable atmosphere on this Earth level."

Seine chuckles. *You are hardly likely to when you are in your Light-body, not needing to breathe a normal atmosphere. It is also likely that you are experiencing a degree of sensory overload. Notice, for example, all the many Earth-type trees growing in the streets of the city. How could they grow without an Earth-type atmosphere?*

"I did see them, but I dismissed them as some sort of technological trick! Do the trees and plants grow in Earth soil, and does it rain to keep them alive?"

Yes, it rains under controlled conditions and everything on this level is based in Earth soil. The trees are alive and thriving, along with every plant.

"May I ask a favour? If we are going up the tower, could we ascend through the levels in what I assume to be the elevators? I would really like to see the habitat of some other sentient species. And . . . are they, too, already breathable for their eventual visitors? "

Of course, willingly, but many levels will defy any explanation from me, or eventual written descriptions from you.

"That's okay." I hold my hand over my heart. "The connection will be made."

He smiles in acknowledgement. *You need to understand that each level is grown/built by Shimmering Beauty. We create the program, but it is she who grows/creates the reality. Some of them are ready for visitors; some are a work still in progress. Odd as it may seem to you, the consciousness of each sentient species determines the progression of their habitat.*

"And I doubt that they know this exists!"

On many counts, correct. A few are patiently awaiting the summons.

"Summons?"

Seine smiles. *When you boil an egg, you have a timer . . . ping!*

When the cosmic timer in consciousness goes . . . ping! . . . those Beings will know Shimmering Beauty is ready for them. Maybe I have not fully explained, but Shimmering Beauty is still a comparative baby. She is continuously growing in size, maturity and ability. She will be many times bigger than now in the fullness of no-time.

"Wow . . . a growing sentient world, such a thought never occurred to me. I wish we were one of those sentient species with a consciousness tuned ready for the timer."

In truth, humans will be among the first, but probably not third-dimensional humans. The possibility exists, the current paradigm shift has made it possible, but . . . it is all about choices!

I sigh. As a species, we don't make good choices. Millions of individuals make excellent choices, but as a species . . .! Nevertheless, I choose to be optimistic.

"You mentioned each species' habitat. Our human habitat is not a city . . . it's Nature."

Oh, so where does most of humanity live?

"Okay . . . in one of the many towns or cities. But it is not our *natural* habitat."

And just how many humans could live naturally in their natural habitat?

Another sigh. "Not many. You win. But this does raise a question. Don't other species modify or alter their environment to create a liveable habitat like us, or do they more or less adapt themselves to the environment without any undue intrusion and disruption?"

Both occur. However, it is considered an act of extreme ignorance and disgrace to disrupt and destroy the environment to the point of desecration and death as is the way of Earth people. Some species make adaptations such as underground-living habitats, with the above-ground environment very slightly and carefully modified. Such Beings live on a planet with a more hostile environment. On other planets, some Beings fully adapt to their environment, simply placing their dwellings and cities within it without any disturbance at all. Yet other Beings, on their home planet, have the ability to grow their homes within the natural plant growth . . . if some of those amazing structures can be called plants. They defy any real human description. Such structures would seem to be a cross-link between huge rocks and equally large trees. The habitat range is vast, according to the dictates of their home climate and environment. Some Beings even live in Nature exactly as it is, fully integrated within the overall environment. But almost without exception, they all treat their respective environments with great respect and consideration, with the intent of promoting and encouraging most life species.

I sigh. "I suppose one species has to show the rest how *not* to do it. That's us!"

In the human habitat, the city looks like an amalgam of a centuries-old city and a modern city. To imagine this may give you shudders, but for me, the reality is highly attractive, with a wonderful energy. Even this human-type city defies description, for the blend of the old and new is seamless, literally imperceptible. I am aware of it only if I attempt to understand the actual architecture of the buildings. Not that I know anything about architecture—apart from old and new! Personally, I would not have thought it possible, but standing here, within such a city, I can only say—it is truly beautiful. To be clear, this is not old-looking buildings and new-looking buildings artfully placed together; this is a true amalgam of a couple of centuries or so of old and very modern new, in each building. And it works—for me! Unique, attractive, with clean flowing rivers, stunning botanical parks, roads and pathways, the lot . . . all without people. No traffic! Incredible!

"What would happen if an aggressive race of Beings came to raid you, or if they attempted to smash Shimmering Beauty simply because their nature was negative and destructive? Are you able to defend it? Would this involve warfare?"

Another intellectual question, but given your background coming from aggressive Earth cultures, I fully understand. Shimmering Beauty is far more than you can currently comprehend. Your question is from Michael, but it is Mixael who will most likely understand my reply. As an evolving intelligence, Shimmering Beauty is already able to create a state of non-existence. In other words, she can appear to not exist to any species that has an ill intent toward us.

"You mean, like . . . vanish, disappear?"

No. I mean our Home and everything on her would cease to be . . . and yet, she and we would continue regardless.

"This doesn't make sense. How can you cease to be and continue? One rules out the other."

Michael, take a step back from your questions . . . please. I appeal to you, Mixael. Consider this: It is possible for two opposing states of consciousness to coexist, each taking dominance according to circumstances, yet never cancelling each other out.

"Yes . . . of course. I get it. Chaos and Order coexist, either one or the other dominant according to the circumstances, yet neither ever able to completely cancel the other."

A good example. Using Chaos and Order as a basic principle, Shimmering Beauty has developed and evolved a complex system whereby she can be present or absent simultaneously.

"That's incredible. So are you saying that if invaders came, this space where your Home is would be empty? You would not be here . . . but despite being empty, you would be here on another level of . . . reality."

Yes, you have the basis of it. However, I also need to add that so far this has never had to happen. It is really a safety measure for unpredictable circumstances.

"Does this imply that Shimmering Beauty makes predictions of the . . . er, future?"

Oh dear, whatever have I got myself into? Shimmering Beauty is alive and intelligent. She is growing exponentially. Her growth is set in the so-called past, in the now, and in the so-called future. She lives not in linear time, but in All-time. In this way, she can cultivate and encourage a probability of 'what is to be', or she can non-violently weed a probability of 'what might be' out of her reality.

"Oh my gosh! That's incredible. To use a metaphor, that's rather like a magician having the ability to pick any specified card out of a shuffled pack of cards. In this case, Shimmering Beauty can pick the very best possibility out of a pack of random probabilities."

Excellent. That says it very well.

"Okay . . . enough explanation. I'm as close as I am going to be to understanding. It sounds like the ultimate solution to the resolution of possible conflict on a cosmic scale. I'm impressed."

We continue our walk/glide to the closest glass-like elevator. I wait for a door to open, then smilingly follow Seine as he simply walks in through the glass-like, non-resistant substance.

Seine gives a soft snarling purr, and without the faintest tremor or sense of movement, we rise at a moderate speed that will allow me to get a sense of each habitat. This is no earth-type elevator. We are carried within a force-field which flows up or down according to the intent—or purr!—of the traveller, and it is always instantly available. (Imagine, no waiting for an elevator!)

"Seine . . . to get to the Earth level we passed many habitats. Some were cities, some truly weird, like an underwater, or under-liquid scene, some even seemed to be purely atmospheric. Can we go back down to see these, or is there more of this above us?"

You do not have time enough to see all that there is on my world in one visit, and the black hole has not yet finished with you. So allow me to show you passing scenes of a few environments, before we part company.

"Oh . . . I didn't know that we have to part company. But, of course, you are hardly likely to accompany me home. I hope we can meet again."

We will meet often.

"And the black hole! Very strange. We came through the black hole to get here, yet you say your world is not within it." I sigh. "Ah well, it is as it is."

We continue to rise slowly. I would have thought that a reality level would gradually reveal itself, but no. One moment we are within a glass-like shaft, then we are in a world of brilliant Light. So bright that even though I am metaphysical, I am almost unable to see/perceive anything. I am squinting in a very human way, when I inner-hear Seine. *Open your senses.*

My reaction had been the very opposite. I protectively closed down. Cautiously, I now open my metaphysical senses, almost cringing in expectation of an overload. Strangely, the opposite is happening. As I open my senses, I can see/perceive a reality of living Light. There are Beings which have the vague outline of a long flower stem, with an open flower on the top. Each 'petal' of the flower is radiating Light. And the Light seems to be continually emitting a spectrum of colour completely unknown to me—if it *is* colour! This is simply a description, the reality is something else. The Beings turn toward us, gracefully floating in their atmosphere of Light.

"Wow . . . 'Beings of Light' takes on a whole new meaning."

As you know, we are all Beings of Light, but these take the term Light to a whole new level. Light is their substance, their nourishment, their energy, and their meaning. I would like to give you a name for them, but nothing comes anywhere close to translating in language or meaning. It may surprise you to know that this is an . . . embryonic stage in their growth/evolution. They are almost unaware of anything other than Light. When they develop they are each one of a kind, yet they each have a relationship with their species as a whole which creates a new and entirely different spectrum of Oneness. Any true explanation is virtually impossible. Enough to say that they are a creative species almost without parallel.

"Are they aware of us here, right now? They certainly don't seem to be."

They have no awareness of us whatsoever.

"Why is that? Surely they are *aware* Beings. How did they get here?"

They were brought here in a . . . cocoon stage, which continues. They are occasionally visited by an . . . adult . . . no . . . by a fully developed one of their species. When this happens their Light is intensified. By this I mean the Light they are, and the Light of their environment . . . which is not really separate. Seine smiles at me. *It is at moments like this when I realise the restrictions of language, even if telepathic. Are you able to receive this?*

So saying, he places a hand/paw each side of my metaphysical head. I feel a dull inner throb, and I abruptly know about the likeness and expression of sentient Light.

Although Seine's communication is apparently successful, I am unable to do the same in my ability to explain. The closest I can get is to say that these Beings are each a unique expression of a Light which, in itself, is of a sentience that is undefinable and inexplicable. Look at it this way. If we think a thought, the thinker is the creator of the thought and thus connected to whatever his/ her thought creates. Imagine that a whole world of brilliant Light is the thinker, and *everything* on that world is an expression of the thinker, connected to the thinker, and actually *is* the thinker in this reality. In this way Light takes on meaning and expression far beyond human comprehension.

In a way, we are each unique expressions of one human consciousness. We have a 3-D form; they do not. When you consider that a spectrum is a measure or range of electromagnetic radiation, all that we are able to see of this is light and colour. For us, the so-called colour specifies the frequency of the spectrum. For these Beings, this spectrum of electromagnetic radiation is their place of life, of exploration, of evolution, of creativity—it is their world reality. But it is of a spectrum of electromagnetic radiation that is so far beyond our spectrum reality that it is beyond our ability to even comprehend.

I share this with Seine.

Although a crude and rough explanation, I understand your dilemma. It is adequate.

Despite having slowed in our ascent, we have not stopped, and so we continue upward. I think! The sighting of these Light expressions has shaken me. Talk about accepting the possibility of impossibilities! I should explain that the stem and flower appearance is quite big. Nothing like my garden flowers! The stem of each—whatever!—may have been five metres tall, with the petals of the flower-like head maybe three metres across. And all dazzlingly brilliant Light. It leaves me speechless!

As we ascend, I am thinking of some of the many Beings I have met in my metaphysical travels. My physical life is nowhere near as exciting, but maybe this is just as well—it's exciting enough! There does seem to be an astonishing range of sentient life-forms that inhabit the solar system and beyond—mostly beyond! It is easy to refer to space as *our* galaxy, but when you consider how little direct contact we have with it, it becomes a ridiculous term of reference. We are still struggling with *our* planet in its own solar system, although most of our struggle is based within ourselves.

I have long been certain that when we are able to treat ourselves as Gods and Goddesses in the making, we will be able to treat our planet with the respect and reverence that She deserves.

We are now passing in the glass-like tube through what is obviously a water world. As I see an inhabitant, I come to an abrupt halt. Ye gods! This thing would make our largest blue whale look like a tiny minnow. As I look/perceive more closely, the liquid seems to be composed of tennis-ball-size bubbles, having what appears as a distinctly oily texture. The massive creature looks vaguely like a finned jellyfish of inconceivable size, except it has a single frontal eye the size of a small house, hugely out of proportion even for this monumental behemoth.

"Holy moly, Seine, is this . . . thing . . . for real?"

Seine chuckles. *Oh yes, it is real enough. Too big for an illusion, surely.* He chuckles some more. *This species has a name that is even pronounceable for you. It is an Eraatanash. It is a life-form which is the host of another life-form, the Eraata. Both are sentient, living in a symbiotic relationship. I would explain, but take my word for it; it is complicated to the extreme with regards to rendering it into human words and concepts.*

"I'll happily take your word for it. Trying to understand the sentient Light has retaught me that there are many things I can accept without a need to understand. This is just one more. Just seeing/experiencing it is a stretch. Er . . . is that stuff water, or oil?"

Neither. It is the substance that supports the Beings on their home world. The closest approximation would be to describe it as a form of inverse gas of which some stars are composed. However, the Eraatanash has the ability to levitate off their home planet, and cruise space. It has something to do with their relationship with the vacuum that exists between the gas bubbles in their . . . let's say, gaseous/oceanic world . . . and space. There is no solid land on their world.

"I thought you said you had no visitors right now."

Correct. These are residents, even if temporary.

"Like . . . how long is temporary?"

Oh, several hundreds of your years.

I nod, bemused. "Okay, that's residential by my standards!"

I find it very humbling to meet Beings of a scale in both size and consciousness that are so far beyond my Michael/Mixael comprehension.

"I'm stunned, overwhelmed by the sheer immensity of such a Being. Somewhere deep in my psyche there must be a false and arrogant concept that sentient Beings should conform to some type of shape, or size . . . probably human . . . whatever. I say this because I am constantly amazed when I metaphysically see or meet Beings that do not conform to this. And I have met so many Beings that don't conform in any way at all . . . yet the amazement continues. And yet . . . I suspect my amazement defines me as human. Would I ever wish to metaphysically be so off-worldly wise that I lose all my amazement, all my wonder and awe at the vast, incomprehensible mystery of life? I think not. I am who I am . . . I like me this way."

I understand your sentiments, even though I do not exactly share them. We are a very . . . let's say, seasoned sentient species, yet we, too, occasionally meet Beings so far beyond us that we have some difficulty in relating to them. However, sentience always recognises sentience, so between us we find ways and means of reference for some brief, even if fairly superficial levels of communication. But as I implied, when sentience meets sentience this in itself is a form and level of species intercommunication.

It might interest you to know that there are only a few of the Eraatanash in this habitat, although there are many more on their home world . . . and also moving between worlds.

"I'm still stunned by the sheer prodigious size of it. And that vast eye! Wow . . . you only have to look into that eye to know that a huge intelligence inhabits that huge body. But, you said it is also a host to the Eraata. What do they look like? How big are they?"

Seine smiles. *They are approximately the size of a large human-type virus. They exist in multiples of trillions in each Eraatanash. In fact, each Eraatanash is the living world in which their own Eraata live. The Eraata never change host, nor could they. Apparently the inner environment of each of the Eraatanash is unique to its own Eraata. Quite how this works challenges even my comprehension. You ask what they look like. They look similar to their host in a microscopic form. Neither* could live without the other. Each is fully aware of the other. Naturally enough, this belongs with sentience.

"There is a vague similarity here to human bodies. Apart from the fact that we are host to vast numbers of microscopic life-forms, we could not exist without the mitochondria in our bodies. Apparently they outnumber the cells of our bodies, yet they have their own DNA, even RNA. Without them we would not have the energy to breathe, even to blink or form a thought."

Yes, this is so with most life-forms, but with this particular symbiosis, both the Eraata and the Eraatanash are identical in every way except for size and function. Your language is insufficient, but they are of the same substance, same intelligence, same conscious expression, yet at the same time they are also completely different in every way. Let me put it this way: each knows of the other in exquisite detail, each knowing that the continuity of the other is the continuity of life for them all. Held within this is a dynamic of conscious evolution which is seamless in its continuity.

"Wow . . . brilliant! Our dangerous viruses often kill us, so they also die. But if they survive in other people, and they know nothing of self-consciousness . . . do they indeed, die?"

Seine smiles. All is one.

"This is so fascinating. Worlds within worlds. Shimmering Beauty has literally created enclosed realities which are worlds within worlds. Even more than this, you have living worlds within enclosed worlds. The human enclosed reality is, in effect, a world within itself. I have no doubt that if people lived in this enclosed world, they could travel far beyond the confines of their enclosure, and yet paradoxically, never leave it. It is an enclosed world reality that is almost limitless in its probabilities. In fact, I suspect that new probabilities and possibilities are even in this moment being created within the enclosed human world reality."

Mixael . . . I am impressed. Ever since you arrived, Shimmering Beauty has been accessing and assessing you on every level possible. Many of your expressions and experiences are being utilised even as I speak, and where practical, they are being incorporated into the human world reality. Every time I or other Seine people journey from this world, we are accessed and assessed in a similar manner. All new levels *of conscious experience are incorporated into the evolving world. This is not something we built in; this comes from the conscious evolution of this world.*

"Talking of enclosed frames of reality is interesting. People live in enclosed realities on my world even when they have the opportunity of freedom. People who have fixed beliefs, or rigid structures of thinking, have created an enclosed reality in which they live. In a way, I travel the world teaching people how to leave their enclosures and live in a world of infinite expansion, or possibilities."

You see now how incredible Shimmering Beauty actually is. She is a world of infinite possibilities, yet because of her evolving intelligence, none of them include becoming fixed and stuck. None of those possibilities include a devolution into false beliefs. It is all true expansion.

"I seem to be stuck with a permanent *wow*! It's a good thing Shimmering Beauty is completely benign. If she got nasty or had a temper tantrum things could get . . . !"

Human entertainment makes many fundamental errors. In its deepest sense, true intelligence is always accompanied by the evolution of Love. You are indoctrinated by the science fiction concept of intelligent 'baddies'. Intelligence evolves under the influence of Love. Any evil Beings that may exist are without 'true' intelligence. However, with this said, such Beings could well be extremely clever, very manipulative, and with a very high technology. But they would not, could not, contain the intelligence that is a pure expression of Love.

I can easily relate to this. I have discovered for myself that intelligence is always *conscious* intelligence, and that Love can only be experienced as *conscious* Love. Consciousness, intelligence and Love are holistic.

"I agree with you, but most people would not. Our basic dictionaries place intelligence and intellect in the same category. I disagree with them. From an enlightened viewpoint, intelligence holds hands with wisdom, while the intellect far too often holds hands with stupid. The stupidity of environmental devastation is justified by greedy and exploitive intellects. There is nothing remotely intelligent in it. It's a bit like army intelligence . . . fight for peace! How crazy is this? Peace is a state of consciousness that begins for each one of us when our *inner* fight has ceased. Anyway, my words about your world getting nasty was my humour at its most feeble! I sincerely apologise. I do actually realise that intelligence does not get nasty or have a temper."

Seine turns away with a chuckle. *Mixael . . . or I should say, Michael . . . you radiate your humour constantly. Humour defines you, like a bubble of scarcely contained amusement. I knew you were joking, but I simply used it . . . as you do. Please, no apologies are necessary.*

Come, we have lingered too long. Let us continue.

We continued to effortlessly rise up the glass-like shaft. As we go I see the giant eye of the Eraatanash watching us, following our movement. It causes me to wonder how it is possible to create channels of communication with such a prodigious Being, so vastly different from me.

They are also telepathic Beings. We are able to communicate quite easily with both the host and the symbionts. Telepathy certainly creates bridges between most intelligent life-forms.

"Hmm, yes, I suppose it does. Yet . . . we are intelligent Beings and we don't use telepathy. I know we have the ability, but we are on an electronic path. Pay to communicate, very clever!"

Rising through a few levels of what appear to be empty alien environments, we are both chuckling from our conversation as we rise into an area of deep gloom. I see what appear to be shadows moving swiftly from place to place in great staggering, bounding leaps. A bit like large, shadowy, drunken kangaroos!

Hmm, on reflection it seems the more I concentrate on them the less I can see/perceive. One moment they appear as vaguely kangaroo-like, then they appear to be swimming like long lean fish. Most odd. They seem as though they have no substance or definition.

Your audible surmising is actually quite accurate. They are neither here nor there.

"That doesn't make sense . . . neither here nor there?"

Earlier I said that Shimmering Beauty determines who can be a guest or reside here, either briefly or long term. We know very little about these Beings. Shimmering Beauty touched their consciousness—how, I am not sure—and created their environment. Then suddenly, these ever-changing shadow-shapes appeared. If all is well for Shimmering Beauty, then all is well for us. We understand that they have an aspect of themselves here and another aspect on their home world. We do not know how that works or even what their stable form looks like . . . or even if they have one. They seem to ingest no food, nor do they appear to breathe. We do not know if they are truly alive in a real sense of the meaning, yet Shimmering Beauty assures us that they are a sentient life-form. Why they are here is also a mystery, but I have no doubt that as states of consciousness, their intent is in harmony with all life.

By now I see that there are masses of them. I see/perceive them best if I do not fully focus on them. Oddly, they appear to flow through each other in an utterly impossible manner, defying all my feelings of sense and sensibility. In truth, I am finding the scene strangely disconcerting.

Time to move on. I am now taking you to an outside area.

So saying, the elevator shaft seems to twist and distort, and we are outside. Looking around me, I realise that this world occupies a position in space that is very different from Earth's. Here, I feel that I can reach out to the nearby stars, while at home they appear to be a vast distance away.

"I accept that life on this world is okay on the up-side of these vast branch/highways. But what happens underneath? Our centrifugal force and gravity keeps everything anchored on Earth, but what about the underneath of this world? Is it empty, or do you have a sticky solution!?"

I anticipated this question when we first arrived. This is why you are now walking along the so-called underneath of our world.

"But . . . but . . . everything is as it should be. Okay, that's stupid. What I mean is Earth spins, so there is no underneath. Here, nothing is spinning . . . or maybe I'm wrong. But it all seems stable with the top on the top and the bottom below and . . . ! Okay, I'm floundering!"

More sympathetic chuckles. *Shimmering Beauty operates under a different set of physics. You see a top and bottom to this world, but that is not the way of it. You see/perceive/experience through a set of rules that strongly determine your experience of life. Basically, your life is three-dimensional, even if there is a five-dimensional influence. In this way your experience/perception of reality is continually reinforced. Here we operate under a very different set of rules. You are sure that you can see an above and below on this world, and in your physical reality this would be the case. However, in this reality there is no above or below; all is held within One spectrum of differing energy wave pattern co-ordinations.*

"Okay, you have explained how I experience your world as I do, and I accept this. As for any further explanations, please cease and desist. I don't understand our physics, so please don't expose me to yours. Consider me as a cosmic moron if you like, but life is very much easier if I simply accept that it is as it is!"

Seine gives me a droll look. *'It is as it is' states an attitude of intelligence. 'This cannot be so because I do not understand' is the statement of stupidity. I suggest this hardly applies.*

"I agree. Self depreciation is a form of humour that is often funny but never appropriate."

It has been observed that this is a common human practice. Why is this?

"Hmm, that's easy. Low self-esteem is the basic answer, although this is seldom realised. When you have a mass population that subconsciously carries inner hurt, inner humiliation, inner emotional turmoil, and a whole lot more inner negatives, on a deep subconscious level they need to know that other people are like them . . . inner hurting. So the comedians who use self-deprecating humour are mostly popular . . . which promulgates its flourishing and continuation. The newspapers play a similar role. Unfortunately, many people like to read about other people who are in trouble, hurting, or doing something even more stupid than they are."

Remarkable . . . and sad.

"Yes, but to be fair, this is not by any means all of the people. It may well represent the majority of people, but not all of them all of the time. And most are not conscious of being like this. This is humanity's deep subconscious program justifying that life is not meant to be easy. As far as I am concerned it is all part and parcel of the evolution of our rich and complex emotions. We have a way to go. I remember all too well when I suffered from low self-esteem. The journey from low to high self-worth is a journey the minority have taken, and the majority have yet to take."

Seine is looking at me with a strange, rather intense expression.

"What's the matter?"

You need to depart. Your energy is showing signs of fatigue, and I happen to know that the black hole has not yet finished with you.

"Hmm, that sounds ominous!"

Seine smiles at me fondly. *Farewell, beloved friend. We will meet again . . . quite soon. I know you are going to ask me for directions to where you should now go, so allow me to give you a nudge in the right direction.*

With his words, I feel a very powerful, yet gentle energy which seems to enclose me within it, and I am whirling off Shimmering Beauty and out into space — except it is not empty space! The energy is now rather like a familiar bubble, enclosing me and moving me rapidly toward . . . nothing!

I am not sure what happens. One moment I am enclosed in a bubble, next moment I am gently deposited at the entrance — I think — to what I fondly assume to be the black hole. I feel a bit like a posted parcel, and almost as useless.

Without any assistance from me, I am now moving at quite a speed into the black hole. This time the interior is completely different. I am surrounded by a spectacular Light show. Imagine travelling through a simple kaleidoscope, but one of cosmic proportions. This will give a fair impression of my experience. I am not frightened, even if perplexed. Ever since being propelled from Seine, my journey has been guided by external energies. Ah well . . . it is as it is!

*Your ability to relax and accept when out of your comfort zone is commendable.

Very clearly this is the energy of the black hole. "Thank you, but I feel safe here."

*Initially, you came seeking answers about the Light-flakes, as you describe them. You found them issuing from me. The how of this is not important. The why is. Your Light-flakes is a fair description, although they are more accurately described as photons.

70

"Hmm, if my memory is correct, a photon is a particle or measure of Light."

Do you understand the implications of the photons falling to Earth?

"I probably understand a few of the implications. This was our long awaited 2012 event, considered by many as a non-event. With the Light-flakes, or, er, photons falling to Earth, we experienced a huge energetic shift. The frequency of Earth has lifted, also of Nature. We humans either lift our energetic frequency . . . or we don't. My insight suggests that for the first time ever, this will, or has, created two directions for the evolving stream of human consciousness. One stream will be of newness, with choice; the other stream will be more-of-the-same, no choice. As yet, we have had little physical impact from this Change, but physical impact is hanging like an axe over our heads. I understand that Earth's magnetic field has been diminishing for a few hundred years, and I suspect that at a certain point this will tip the balance . . . in favour of dramatic physical Changes. I'm also certain that we will not like this."

As you well know, many probabilities face humanity. However, as always, you each create the reality to which you are propelled.

"Yes. I am familiar with this."

Nature has long prepared for this event. The human view of this is based in the extinction of many species, but in truth this is no more than the withdrawal of the consciousness expressing as those species.

"Do you play a role in all this? After all, you seem to be the source of the photons."

Everything in the solar system has a role. I am viewed as a destroyer of systems, and there is a certain truth to this. When a solar system becomes ancient within a timescale of infinity, its conscious evolution becomes almost stagnant. I am able to pull much of that system from out of its location, relocating it into a dynamic new quantum. And this is a continuous happening. We so-called black holes do not move in space, we move space around us. We devour and reconstitute whole solar systems to maintain the dynamic of galactic evolution. This appears to be destruction on a catastrophic scale. However, as you are fond of saying, the de-structuring must always precede the re-structuring.

"How do you know I say that?" Even as the words are a mere thought, I know. I am an open book. My past, present and future are pages easy to read in such an open person as me!

Human energy displays great confusion regarding the direction you are now undergoing in life. It seems not yet to be accepted or realised that confusion begets confusion. You are one species of very many sentient species. In your self-created isolation of the self, you have developed a sense of universal isolation. This is a strange paradox. As a species, you basically accept that you are not alone in the universe, yet you continue to deepen the sense of personal isolation. This throws mixed messages into life, messages of confusion. As a race of Beings, and as individuals, one of the strongest energies reaching out from your planet Earth is one of deep and troubled confusion.

"Are you saying, in effect, that we as a species are communicating with other sentient species in the galaxy . . . and we do not realise this? And that our universal message is confusion?"

Confusion, anxiety, despair, overwhelming fear and other negative energies. Do your people not realise that this creates huge sweeping waves of energetic instability? You are a species all combining to create the very scenario that most frightens you . . . planetary devastation. No planet dances to the whims of chance. The very word 'chance' is a human term of confusion. Chance is not a reality. The galactic Being you met showed you how everything in the galaxy is connected within a unified field of energy. This is also human knowledge. Knowing this, how can you accept chance in a vast body of interconnecting energies? Humans are strange inasmuch as you have a fair knowledge of life, yet very few of you live it. You just hold the mental knowledge without ever translating it into a way of life. This transmits a mixed message. Energy that is transmitted by humanity has a tremendous effect on the stability or instability of your solar system.

"Like . . . if a person gets a severe headache their whole body is negatively affected? About fifty trillion cells are all affected. All of them are tense, irritated, stressed, hurting."

Exactly. What affects a part affects the whole. Using that as a metaphor, humanity is now a headache in the solar system. And with the changes taking place in the human frequency, this now presents a new factor.

"In what way?"

Watch what is happening around you.

So far, all our communication has taken place within the cosmic kaleidoscope where I entered the black hole. Now the nature of the kaleidoscope is changing. As I entered I realised that it was in constant change, and I observed that my entry affected it in a rather colourful way. This is changing. So far, the kaleidoscope has portrayed nothing beyond an ever-changing background of a vast galactic scene—a scene which is clearly conscious and living.

Now, I am seeing what appears to be the slow formation of an immense cosmic storm. I have no words to describe this. Imagine the build-up period of a large and serious Earth storm. Now magnify this to dimensions that would include the whole of Earth in the one massive storm and give it an energy of incomprehensible confusion. By this, I mean the storm has no idea of where or how to begin, no idea of what it actually is, no idea of the terrible devastation it can cause, no idea of its tremendous force, but somewhere, somehow, eventually it is all going to be horrifyingly unleashed.

"I think I get the picture. This is very scary."

In this new frequency that humanity is subjected to, your human energies have a far stronger creative force than ever before. Channeled for the benefit of all, this can bring powerful and favourable changes to your planet and the solar system. However, when the majority of the people are channelling fear, despair, anger and confusion, this is the creative energy being blasted out into space. In what you think of as a cosmic kaleidoscope, you are seeing the formation of the effects of the present human consciousness. Consciousness is energy. As you well know, when that energy is negative, that which it creates will be negative. Unfortunately for you as a species, this is your current human direction.

This is a familiar story to me. I am able to metaphysically see this. "What can we do to prevent an energy storm of such proportions?"

Probably nothing! Is it possible for humanity to elevate human consciousness to the point that it will alter this unfolding probability to a new and very different probability future?

I sigh. "Probably not."

Do not feel sad. All life is immortal. As always, humanity will continue, each of you moving into the reality you have created for yourselves as individuals. Do I grieve for each huge planetary system that I remove from its decaying state of stagnation? Or do I rejoice in the new dynamic that is being created? There is no death, no ending, no beginning. All life consists of immense cycles on the endless spiral of continuity. All this is played out on a vast cosmic scale.

"It seems such a waste of human potential."

Potential can never be wasted. The potential of every human is with them forever. Some of you diligently cultivate that potential, and your harvest is rich. You are such a one. Some of you are aware of your potential, but are afraid to pay the price that always accompanies it. You paid the price. And so many of you are unaware of your potential, lost in the subconscious world of endless repetition. You have experienced this. Nothing in life can reduce you as a human. Even when you reduce yourselves, the paradox is that you are not reduced. But you believe that you are.

"And as we believe, so we create our lives accordingly."

This is so. But humanity is not the only species struggling to find, acknowledge, accept and be humbled by their greatness. Many other species are involved in similar struggles. Some doom themselves over and over with a deeply anchored, unshakable arrogance, which always results in war, violence, suffering and mass death. Some have the opposite problem, considering themselves to be so unworthy, so deeply hating themselves that life is a continuous form of self-annihilation. And yet, in the fullness and richness of timeless time, sentient life finds its painful, torturous way along the path toward self-acceptance and Love.

I find that I am beginning to feel rather dizzy. Hmm, fatigue?

Enough, I will return you to your bodily form to recuperate.

"Is that my problem . . . exhaustion?"

I feel a cosmic smile moving within.

A quantum shift energetic involvement overload.

"A what?!"

The next moment I am home. Back in my study . . . and feeling tired!

CHAPTER FOUR

MAXIMUM POTENTIAL

I step . . . *Between* . . . walking out over a landscape of pouring rain.

"Ah, this is what I need to see."

An inner chuckle. *Does it make you feel better?*

"I confess, yes, it makes me happy."

We are in another long period of drought on the Southeast Coast of Queensland. I have almost forgotten what rain looks like. The garden is really dry, many of the plants drooping and wilted. If you are a reader of my books, you will know that I have long been a keen and passionate gardener. My lesson during these dry periods is to focus on *one day closer to the next heavy rain,* rather than another debilitating day of drought. Not at all easy for a gardener!

As I metaphysically gaze down on the rain-sodden land beneath me, I realise that the balance of rain and sunshine seems to be lost in so many parts of the world. I know that dry deserts and flood prone areas have always existed, just as our oceans and land coexist in an uneasy alliance, but it seems to me that even within the overall extremes, a tenuous balance somehow maintains itself. The vast ice-fields of the frozen wastes, the hot deserts of drifting sand devoid of vegetation and the dry desserts of spiky, prickly plants have been with us for a long time, but always we have had huge tracts of fertile land suitable for agriculture. Now, I get the distinct impression that this is changing. At a time when our population is estimated to be rising by around two hundred thousand people a day, our agricultural land seems to be in decline. And not only in decline, but more prone to erosion by drought, flood, and wind, along with an escalating increase in harmful soil-degrading agribusiness practices. Apart from the all too few true farmers who are good custodians of the land, real land-wise agriculture eroded long ago!

I am sitting in my favoured lotus position high over a very wet Europe—where, exactly, I have no idea! I wanted it wet and it is! Metaphysically, as I sit here, I can draw whatever it is I wish to focus on into my vision. It is a bit like tuning a radio to whatever program you wish to hear. As I create my intent to metaphysically scan our European, and in turn, global agricultural land, bringing it into my focus, I calibrate it according to the decades and centuries of agriculture. I bring not only land into my metaphysical view, but also the quality of the soils energy over the period that we have been growing our food. The quality reveals itself in a now familiar way: Chaos—the engine that drives, Order—the stability of structure, and Balance—the place of greatest potential.

Okay, for new readers I will need to explain this. Chaos— the energy that drives, is an energy that I metaphysically experience in hundreds of shades of the colour red. Each shade of red has a different emotional connection with me. However, that emotional language—for this is what it amounts to—has no intellectual translation. I could say that some reds are base, angry, raging, destructive, volatile, while some are loving, caring, calming, connected, creative . . . all this in ever-varying emotional expressions ranging over maybe a thousand different shades of red. It is the same story with the black colour of Order—the stability of structure. For example, a wildfire is all Chaos without order. A rock is all Order without Chaos. Between Chaos and Order there is a tremendous creative torsion. When the torsion between these two energies reaches a perfect dynamic, then I experience the flickering white light of Balance—the expression of greatest potential. In agriculture, Balance is becoming increasingly rare. The vast majority of the world's agribusiness land is in the grip of Chaos, the factor of change very strongly indicated. The tiny percentage of today's truest agriculture is represented by the biodynamic and eco, or organic farming communities. Their soil is in Balance ... stable, structured, dynamic and thriving. Even the once pure peasant farming is now tainted by the use of chemical pesticides, herbicides and fungicides which, when banned in the Western World, are dumped in Third World communities. Unable to read the *Warning – Poison* labels, the resulting cost in peasant farmers lives is dismissed as unfortunate.

Seen from my holistic perspective, agriculture that is driven by Chaos is in decline. Not only in the amount of fertile land and in the quality of the soil, but also in the quality of the food that is produced. I gaze at the calibrations I have mentally created to give me an idea of the soils decline. If the fertility of farming soil was perhaps eighty percent a hundred years ago, it is now less than a quarter of that. In simple terms, soil depends on humus for its fertility. Humus is the final stage of breakdown for organic matter. A soil needs to always contain around ten percent of organic matter to maintain a decent humus content. My perspective indicates that in the last hundred years the decline of organic matter in farm soil has been dramatic. I can metaphysically see vast areas of agricultural land that now has less than one percent organic matter. This suggests minimum potential.

"I knew this problem existed, Pan, so what I am seeing is no great surprise, but never before had I thought of metaphysically bringing the global situation together like this. The daily increase in people needing to be fed, along with the serious decline of our soils fertility, suggests that we have a massive problem ahead of us regarding our food production."

Humanity specialises in creating problems!

I sigh. We surely do. As I metaphysically look/perceive into the agricultural energy, I see intertwined with it a dark and very negative field of energy. This energy field suggests to me that what I see is not simply the result of ignorant farming—even though this is evident—but is the result of very deliberate manipulation within our worldwide agricultural practices. Sadly, this also does not surprise me. As I study the metaphysical fields of energy I see a very deliberate energy plan or blueprint of degrading the soil on a global scale to deliberately create global famine.

This *is* a surprise! Global famine—not just third-world famine.

"Pan, correct me if I am wrong, but if the way I am reading agricultural energy is correct, I am seeing that it holds the seeds of a plan for global famine . . . mass murder!"

This is fundamentally correct.

"Is this about control? Famine is a very effective means of control. Is this yet another manipulation of the power-mad cabals in their attempts to gain a total worldwide control of agriculture?"

It is hardly for me to speculate on human intents or designs, but I cannot fault your reading of the fields of energy.

"So what I am seeing as I look into the energy-signature of modern chemically stimulated agribusiness is a fast and decisive burn-out of the soils organic matter, and thus the humus decline. This in turn leads to a proliferation of genetically manipulated (GM) plants that will be able to grow in dead soil so long as they get enough chemical stimulants to keep them alive. In turn, this will require the farmers to buy ever increasing amounts of fungicides and insecticides, all of which is controlled by the same corrupt people. It takes only a little more speculation to see that this will lead to even sicker global consumers than we have today, thus increasing the need for ever more prescription drugs, all under the control of the same global companies that have an agenda to create a worldwide domination of food and medicine. Both of which go hand in hand."

You have described another strong probability.

"I wish I hadn't looked. I'd rather not know."

This is exactly how the many allow such control by the few.

"I don't get it. How is it that historically the few always

seem to control the masses? I mean, what are we? Are we some weird species of cosmic sheep involved in some bizarre cosmic joke that is not the slightest bit funny? Whatever happened to self-determination? The only people who seem to have self-determination use it simply to make more money. What has happened to us? Have we completely lost the plot?"

The answer to the last question is a resounding, yes. Most of humanity has, indeed, lost the plot . . . as you so succinctly phrase it. And in losing all true connection with inner purpose, all that is left is the very powerful but delusional outer illusion.

"And the delusional outer illusion is money and so-called success. I recently learned that one percent of Americans own forty percent of the nations wealth, while the lowest eighty percent own just seven percent. The bottom half of that eighty percent own almost nothing. This is monumental fiscal inequality. Eventually greed is not enough; it gives birth to corruption, power and control."

No matter how people are controlled, nor how many are controlled, megalomaniac power is dangerously delusional.

"Yes . . . and there is always the karmic balance. The time of reckoning. The 'what goes around comes around.' The cause and effect. The boomerang effect. Good stuff. Just thinking about it makes me smile. And I should not. I should have no feelings of revenge or retribution. I should be feeling just as much Love for those who inflict the misery, as for those on whom it is inflicted. If this is spirituality, it sure 'ain't easy!"

It has never been suggested that the three-dimensional human condition in your present frame of reality is easy.

I chuckle. "Oh, Pan . . . you are such a delight."

Here we are, heading down a highway to hell-on-Earth, and I am amused! I am feeling rather light-hearted because I cannot really believe in, or accept such a negative outcome. We are living in a time that accentuates conscious choices. This means making conscious choices that honour self. If you truly honour self, then you honour all natural life and humanity. Many people are making such choices. Overall, it is the smaller percentage of us, true, but nevertheless, maybe as high as ten to fifteen percent of the human population. These are the people who dream of both their own and humanities maximum potential. This is about heart choices, not religious beliefs, or knowledge, or so-called goodness. It is about consciously raising our consciousness. I am certain that these people have a very different future than those who live their lives under the insidious subconsciousness influence of more-of-the-same.

We need to be aware that for us, dimensions are the living frames and expressions of human consciousness. Moving from a three-dimensional reality into a four-dimensional reality requires a growing, expanding state of consciousness, just as it does to physically incarnate or ascend into a fifth-dimensional reality. None of this is easy on a planet where religions have hijacked spirituality.

The agricultural scene that I am observing as it slowly unfolds over the years into a full scale disaster is definitely three-dimensional. However, even dimensions are in multiples. A book has many pages that express the one book; equally so with dimensions. Collectively, there are now well over seven billion people on a single page of the three-dimensional book we are living. Maybe I need to look at a few of the other pages of the greater Book of Life!

As always, Pan is energetically aware of my thoughts and their general direction.

I suggest that you access the pages that interest you, rather than simply observe them from afar. You need to powerfully connect with a greater reality to adequately convey the impact.

"Good thinking. So . . . where do you suggest that I go from here?"

An inner smile. *Where do 'you' suggest that you go? And wherever it is, please adhere to 'look and learn,' rather than 'mess and meddle.'*

"I never mess and meddle. I sometimes get inadvertently involved. Very different."

Yes . . . a very different way of saying that you mess and meddle!

I sigh. "I have already decided where, or when, I plan to go, but I was open to a creative suggestion. Okay, my choice it is."

So saying, I focus on the agricultural period of maximum potential for a higher three-dimensional consciousness.

*   *   *

I step...*Between*...stepping out somewhere over Oz. Immediately, I feel a clear difference in the energy. This is a three-dimensional reality, but it is lighter and brighter than the one I am currently living in. This puzzles me.

"I know you can say 'look and learn' and I will, but is this a 3-D page that is actually taking place now, or is it a probability future page?"

And the rest of your question is: if it is a page that is happening now, why am I not in it?

"Okay . . . I confess to thinking that, and I feel a bit embarrassed about having such arrogant thoughts."

Not arrogant, simply human. The page you are on is where you need to be, and where you are also needed. This other page in the Book of Life has no need of you, or for you.

"Hmm, I'm not sure what to make of that! So it really is a happening reality, yes?"

It is a happening reality. Now, look and learn.

Before I descend to Earth, I take advantage of my higher viewpoint. On an energetic level certain factors are instantly obvious. This reality has no negative genetic manipulation in the crops. I can see vast fields of what appears to be wheat in this huge southern land, but it is energetically clear that the wheat crops here are a hybrid variety that seems to combine the qualities of a legume, within a plant that produces grain. It looks like wheat with its upright growth, yet the leaf is more like a legume than a grass. Reading the energy of this crop reveals that it is far higher in protein than our wheat, and that it is not a gluten-based protein. Very smart. This crop is new and unfamiliar to me. Its energy is far more complimentary to the human digestive and nutritional system than our wheat, which is not complimentary at all. I can see at a glance that no genetic changes are imposed, for the energy field is closer to Balance than anything I have seen in my reality—other than biodynamic or other organic cultures. Yet when I say genetics are not imposed, I do not mean that they are not used. There is a very big difference between imposing, it as we do, and genetically altering a crop from a higher state of consciousness. Within the Balanced field of energy of this advanced type of wheat, I can see that it has been genetically altered to make the crop more robust, more vigorous, and more resistant to the weather extremes of Oz, as well as more nutritious for both the land and the consumer. In other words, the motive here is quality. This is what I am reading and receiving from the energy of the crops below me. This is maximum potential, indeed!

Before I descend from my lofty perch to walk the land, I focus on and draw into my view the overall energy of agriculture in Europe within this reality-frame. I do not include America, because I know that their broad-scale farming climate is similar to ours. In Europe I also pick up the telltale energy of genetic change, but here it is more about quantity *with* quality of crops, rather than a focus on robust and climatically resistant plants. On an overall basis Europe has a less severe farming climate, a deeper and better soil type, and their crops have different needs. Historically, they have practised sensible crop rotations and bio-diversity. It is nice to see and feel that their crops have a field of energy which speaks volumes about the wellbeing of their farming methods in this other frame of reality, or other dimensional page.

As I gently descend unseen to Earth, I realise that there is not a human to be seen in the whole area. This is still outback Oz! Remembering that this is a different page in our dimensional consciousness, I have been expecting agricultural expressions to be very different. And they are, but it is a very subtle difference. For example, all this land has been remineralised. You can physically see nothing of this and it may seem a small thing— but in agricultural terms, it is BIG. On a global scale our current agricultural soils are very seriously mineral deficient. But here, in this other three-dimensional reality frame, the soils' fertility is stabilised and maintained. Not only that, but energetically it becomes obvious that they are not using any form of chemical fertilisers. The energy of the land speaks a story of cultured enzymes, bacteria, and a large array of other specialised micro-organic life in the soil. This soil has its own living dynamic. Hmm! Subtle this may be, but the energetic difference is very powerful. Only a living soil naturally produces truly living food. The farmer in me is thrilled.

I stay in this area quite a while, observing and discovering, the farmer in me continually delighted with all that I find. But the farmer in me is unlikely to be in you, my reader, so I will not bore you with any more details. Suffice it to say that the products from this land hold a nutritional value far beyond any such crops we grow today. The very fact of a rotation of crops in remote Oz is amazing to me, and wonderful. This is the way to achieve maximum potential. In my reality-frame wheat everlastingly follows wheat, with ever increasing genetic manipulation, chemical sprays and artificial stimulants (chemical fertilisers) keeping it alive and productive.

Once again I ascend to my lofty overview, assuming the lotus position.

"Pan, when I first arrived here I was startled and a bit puzzled to find the energy of this reality frame to be so much lighter and brighter than ours. I assumed this to be the result of the higher consciousness of the people, and it probably is, but there is more. Agricultural land is alive in the way that it should be. By comparison, our agricultural land is dead ... or dying. This must have a massive affect on the overall global energy."

Of course. Increasing numbers of people of your current frame of reality suffer from mental and emotional depression. Of all the medical reasons put forward as to why this is, they have never considered the overall global energy.

"Of course they haven't. They are not even aware of it. It is only the people who are becoming more spiritually conscious who realise that we live in a holistic reality. What affects the micro-organic life in the soil directly affects the micro-organic life in the human body. But I doubt that level of awareness is a normal medical consideration. As holistic Beings we are energetically connected to the exploited and polluted energy of our planet, thus we have just one more cause of increasing depression."

My focus is on soil-life, but I had an interesting lesson about water-life a few years back. When I converted our swimming pool to a fish pond, all I did was allow the water to take its time to accommodate fish. Considering that I had not used any chemicals for years—controlling algae with copper and bacteria with silver, both released into the water as trace elements via electrolysis—I expected the water to quickly be ready. After waiting a year, every so often I would release a few tiny, hardy pond fish to see if they would survive. I was quite shocked each time they died. It took me a while to realise that my swimming pool water was, in fact, dead. And if my chemical-free water was dead, what is happening in the tens of thousands of swimming pools where the water is kept sparkling clear with chemicals? On a long term basis, how is dead water affecting the people, especially children, who play and swim in it? It took twenty months for my water to biologically return to life and support a biodiversity of fish and plants. Now, a few years later, it is seething with life. The pool water is now clean and very much alive. My swimming pool water represents a powerful correlation between dead soil chemically stimulated to grow compelled crops, and living soil naturally growing living crops.

Are you ready for a backward step in three-dimensional realities?

"No. I honestly don't want to see how agriculture is worse than ours. I can't change it, and it will offer me nothing but dismay. I only have to see what is happening in my own current frame of agricultural mayhem to make me feel . . . ! Anyway, you know I'm not willing."

I feel an inner smile. *Wisdom grows.*

Time to go.

* * *

I step . . . *Between* . . . and back into my study.

My short journey has given rise to a question. "Pan, that agricultural scene of harmony was in a different frame-of-reality, yet it was still three-dimensional. Why is it that we, in my current reality-frame, have the potential to move into a higher mental and emotional fourth-dimensional expression, even moving on into a fifth-dimensional reality, when there are people in a three-dimensional reality who are ahead of us in consciousness? This doesn't make sense to me. Surely we should progress on to the next higher level. Will you explain this, please?"

To use a metaphor, let us assume that in a certain town there are a number of schools for the children to attend. Each child takes an examination and is placed in the school that most suits him or her. However, this examination is not about cleverness; it is about attitude and application, it is about their openness to life, or how closed-off they are, it is about heart focus or head focus, and it is about their way of living consciously or subconsciously. In other words this school examination grades children according to the direction of their developing consciousness. After the examination results become apparent, the child is placed in the School of Life that holds the greatest creative potential for them. This may sometimes mean the hardship of breaking their misdirection created over lifetimes of habit or conditioning. Do you follow?

"Yes, of course. But . . . there must be more."

Correct. When the child has finally grown through the school that was most suited to their needs, surely you would not then make them go through each other school. It would be counter productive and entirely unnecessary.

"Oh! Gosh . . . I get it. The school I was in as Michael and now as Mixael is the perfect school for my greatest potential. It's not about better schools, or higher or lower schools, it's all about the *appropriate* school. The agricultural scene in a higher three-dimensional reality is not the most appropriate school for me, so I don't need to be there."

This is the point I am making.

"Gosh, this is something entirely new to me."

Michael came into this school to finish learning an old lesson. Following the enlightenment he gained from that achievement, he . . . walked-out. Mixael then walked-in, and you also were in the appropriate reality to finalise your emotional lessons . . . which you achieved. Now you are here to be a spiritual teacher and inspiration in the appropriate three-dimensional frame of reality.

"Your explanation makes it so very clear and simple for me."

As your explanations of life do for so many other people. Is this not perfectly appropriate?

"Beloved Pan, it is overwhelmingly appropriate. However, just to finish this for my clarity, does this mean that whichever three-dimensional frame we are in, each frame offers the same opportunity for growth and expansion in consciousness, thus enabling any of us to achieve a fifth-dimensional reality? Is this correct?"

Basically, yes. Nothing is fixed and rigid in growth, but essentially you are correct. Each metaphoric school holds the same potential for inner growth, remembering that conscious growth depends on the scholar, rather than the school.

"Yes . . . that makes sense. Some of us are willing, most resist. Does this mean that the varying degrees of willingness or resistance in us and the power of the illusions in our reality are all predetermined by some type of inner . . . screening, or exam, that we go through . . . without ever knowing about it?"

Do not take me too literally, but yes, your three-dimensional reality reflects all your deficits and attributes, even though the screening is conducted by the Being you truly are, rather than other Beings. You are each your own examiner. Self never judges.

"There is a huge, mostly unrealised difference between discernment and judgement. So you are saying that we are all in the reality frame that offers us maximum potential."

This is correct.

"One last question, Pan . . . if I may. Why do you continue to call me Michael?"

Because you still refer to yourself as Michael. The soul Michael withdrew, the soul Mixael walked-in, but you continue in the physical world as Michael. It saves confusion and for all practical and legal purposes it makes sense in your physical reality. I also call you Michael because at some level you are not yet ready to own Mixael. Mixael holds challenges for you.

"Yes, you're right. When *you* call me Michael it somehow pushes me to be more aware of myself as Mixael. Michael means God-like . . . and I like this, but I am ready to be Mixael in my metaphysical reality. Will you please call me Mixael. I need to confront and accept this reality of myself more fully, and I am ready for this now.

So it shall be.

*   *   *

Deciding I had done enough journeying for today, I sat back in my study chair and relaxed with my thoughts and speculation. I am fascinated by the idea of maximum potential. By its very implication it clearly holds hands with intelligence. Many years ago when I was at school, I was a constant rebel. I hated school and disliked most of the teachers—it was probably mutual! In hindsight I am aware that in our private school the teachers had all the necessary academic qualifications to teach, but they had none of the humanitarian skills or qualifications enabling them to transmit their adult knowledge to a reticent child—surely, the art of teaching! As a right-brain dominant boy in a left-brain dominant school, for me it was a disaster. The basic teaching approach was purely intellectual and mostly impatient, rarely intelligent.

Much later in my life I discovered the truth about intelligence. I discovered that the great IQ tests had little to do with intelligence and everything to do with the intellect and intellectual memory. I learned that intelligence is not something of which we each have a quota. In fact, nothing could be further from the truth. Intelligence is to life as consciousness is to life. If we are consciously in the moment, we are in the place of intelligence—and maximum potential.

None of my school teachers taught this. None of them knew it. They were intellectual clones from an intellectual system. Sure, teachers can become free agents, and many modern teachers in the more independent schools do this very admirably, but like politicians, school teachers in the system are pressured to follow an accepted way. Most are so intellectually involved in life that they never realise that their relationship with real intelligence is tenuous, to say the least.

As I meandered along in my musings, I remembered back a

year or so, when I first became aware of Max. I had eaten a large, rather mixed meal in a certain restaurant, and I was definitely feeling a bit sluggish. I did not like such a feeling—sluggish does not work for me! As I sat reflecting on the conglomeration of food I had just consumed, I felt an inner voice saying, *Don't say I didn't warn you.*

I frowned as I contemplated this statement. Where did that come from? But I was too sated from food to investigate, and quite possibly it was no more than mental regurgitation from my unaccustomed glass of wine.

Next morning, back to my usual energetic self, I pondered the words and their origin. As I had eaten dessert after my evening dinner the previous day, I remembered a strong, clear thought suggesting that my dinner and the dessert were not a good mixture, and maybe I should not eat the dessert. I responded by erasing the thought; crème brulee is irresistible!

As a result I had a very uncomfortable and queasy night.

"Okay, me . . . who spoke?" I questioned myself in a flippant, non-expectant tone.

I did.

"Oh." I was somewhat surprised. "Who is . . . I?"

This sounded like the beginnings of insanity, me talking to I.

I suggest you metaphysically view yourself.

I did this and perceived a glowing body of Light that permeated my physical body and was metaphysically visible within it.

"Okay . . . you appear to be another metaphysical aspect of myself. Is this correct?"

Basically, yes. I am your physical body intelligence. You could also describe me as your body elemental. My connection with you is through your dense body.

"Gosh . . . er, how long have you been around?"

Since the moment of your physical conception.

"Wow! You mean that you were born when I was born?"

You are getting too involved in making me something I am not. I am intelligent elemental energy. I have no substance . . . but then, neither does anything else!

"Er . . . I think I follow that, but maybe you can elaborate."
Everything in three-dimensional life is made from the substance of your perception. As you and other people collectively perceive life, so it is. It takes on a three-dimensional reality and you believe in it, but it has far less reality than do I. I am my own purpose, not made by you, even though we are one. I am your body elemental through our soul self.

"I think you are also the master of perplexity! How is it that I have never been aware of you before? Have you been speaking to me, or prompting me all these years?"

Awareness is the key, being aware. Mostly you ignore me, but yes, I offer quiet promptings that do not interfere with your free will. And we have had a previous encounter.

Suddenly, with astonishing clarity, I remembered the moment when we had previously converged. I had often wondered about what happened, and *who/what/how* it had happened, but I never knew until this moment. The *why* had been very obvious!

"Oh my gosh . . . I owe my life to you!"

You cannot owe me your life, the reverse is more accurate, but there has been the rare occasion when we have combined to maintain the potential for life in your physical body.

"I think you are also the master of understatement."

My memory took me back to the middle of 1986, when I was with my late wife, Treenie. It had been a very difficult year for me, with increasing ill health. It all began three years earlier with my obsession for a water bed. I wanted one, Treenie did not. As I said, I had an obsession regarding this bed, so Treenie's resistance was swept away by my Aries enthusiasm, and we got the water bed. Within the first hour of being in it I knew I hated it, while just as quickly, Treenie loved it! I found it increasingly difficult to fall asleep and stay asleep in the bed, while Treenie slept more soundly than ever. I was either sweating in the bed or a bit too cool, nothing in between, while Treenie was as always as snug as could be. Grossly unfair!

From 1983 to 1986 my health went steadily downhill. I visited a medical doctor well versed in natural health who confirmed that I was on a downward spiral, and repeatedly questioned me to find the cause of my health problems. I had no idea, not a clue.

Not for one moment did I associate my failing health with the water bed. I had by now developed insomnia and cellulitis, both of which conspired to successfully undermine and accelerate my failing health.

One night, as I lay tossing and turning fitfully, almost asleep, I saw a glowing Being who looked exactly like me standing near me alongside the bed. Our eyes met.

This bed is killing you, he said. *Come and look at what is happening from my perspective.*

The next thing I knew, I was looking through the eyes of this other glowing body at my own physical body in bed. I could see that my body-aura was unable to expand and extend away from my physical body where I lay in bed. The plastic cover of the water container, combined with the trickle of electrical current designed to keep the water at a constant temperature, totally repelled my body's bio-electric aura.

You have a very powerful aura. Take notice of what is happening to it.

As I stared, I could see that as I lay on my back, my body-aura was compelled to radiate *upward through* my physical body, rather than *outward away* from it as is normal.

Do you see? This bed is killing you. It is unnatural for your auric radiance to be compelled to penetrate right through your physical body. It is unnatural and extremely unhealthy.

"Oh my gosh! You're right. This bed *is* killing me!"

The next moment I was wide awake in bed . . . and the glowing me had vanished. I woke Treenie and told her what had happened. Then I got out of bed, found an old mattress, and spent the night on the floor—with Treenie! The water bed was sold three days later! Although this is another story and is told in my book, *A Glimpse of Something Greater,* the scene was now set for my spiritual Awakening in 1986. Nothing by accident, nothing by chance!

Although I have never before mentioned this—I was frightened by its implications—I noticed from my out-of-body perspective that Treenie's auric energy field was considerably less than mine. I remembered this when she died from a sudden aneurysm, twenty years later.

"So that glowing body was you, Max?"

Yes. As your physical body elemental I was attempting to retain your physical life.

"You did a wonderful job. I'm sure that eventually the water bed would have indirectly killed me. In hindsight, it would appear that my waterbed fixation and the timing of your rescue combined in a form of alchemy to be the perfect catalyst for my spiritual awakening."

I should mention here that following my awareness of my body elemental after that rather indigestible dinner, Max and I maintain a much closer relationship. I named him Max to make him more real and available in my daily life. Max, of course, is an abbreviation for maximum potential. Now, quite often when I am on tour and dining out, I ask Max for his advice on desserts. Mostly he advises me against them, assuring me that a sweet sugary dessert rarely combines well with a savoury dinner. Unfortunately, every time I ignore him it is to my digestive detriment. Max remains a very quiet presence in my background, just occasionally murmuring "You'll be sorry" in a slightly more insistent inner-voice when I ignore him. And sorry, I always am!

Although I enjoy a workout on my Cardio Gym machine, there are the odd moments when I feel a bit slack. Max does not approve of this, and nudges me strongly to persevere. It is a weight resistant machine controlled by a digital program of five different upper body exercises, each of one minute duration which is repeated in four sequential sessions. At the same time I am pedalling away with my legs to a constantly varying program of difficulty. This all creates an intense ten or twenty minute session, using the weights and speed of my own choice. Naturally, being an Aries, I have all the weight that I can manage at the fastest speed I can go during the session. When my heart is racing like a trip-hammer and my body sweating, Max approves. When, within moments after completing a workout, my heart quickly slows down, I smile in satisfaction.

Max is constantly vigilant with me now. I guess he always was, but I was simply unaware of this very subtle yet beneficial elemental that was always present. When I am in my rather large and delightful garden, lost in the joys of physical action, it is Max who reminds me to lift heavy weights ergonomically and carefully, or better still, wait and get some help. Max accepts that I am not good at waiting for help, so he prompts me toward caution, rather than impetuosity, when I am lifting and carrying.

"Everyone has a body elemental, Max, but do many people ever find out? I mean, we are never taught that such a possibility as you exists, and I am quite sure that the vast majority would not believe it anyway. We have an unhealthy preoccupation with the need for proof, which is pretty well all scientifically and physically based. And you are anything but physical. Could we live without you? Oh . . . and are you able to communicate with other elementals?"

A surprising number of people become aware that their body knows what is best for them. Generally this is based in a sense of wellbeing rather than any awareness of their body elemental. But, this works well. We do not expect recognition.

"Do you die when the physical body dies?"

No, we do not die because we have never had life in the way that you are implying. We are a soul-linked energy field that can never die. In a similar way this is your truth also.

I smile. "Yes, we are not born, neither do we die, for we are immortal Beings in mortal physical bodies. Oh! The penny drops. As we are, so are you. You are an energy field that is intertwined with my energy field. My evolution is your evolution."

True, but there is no separation. No 'you' and 'me', or 'my' and 'your'. We are One. As for the communication between one body elemental and another, again, there is no separation for us. We are one. And to address the remaining question, could you live without us . . . could the sun shine if there was no sun? I repeat, there is no 'you' and 'us', we are One.

I chuckle. "As dumb as my questions are, I really do feel that Oneness. Such questions come from my head, but my heart already knows the answers. You are my maximum potential in a living, expressing field-of-energy that is one with all I am."

All that I have said is true, and my reference to 'I,' to 'me', and to 'you', is for the purpose of communication. Nevertheless, people are human Beings learning creation. By you giving me a name, Max, and by your deliberate communication with me, you are creating a uniqueness in the energy field I am that is . . . . indescribable.

"I'm not sure that I understand. Am I doing something that I should not do?"

Oh no. It appears that you are creating me as something . . . more.

"Maybe this is no accident. There are no accidents! Maybe you and I are on a journey into moreness. With Pan as my beloved guide, moreness for me is inevitable, thus, it must be so for an energy field of elemental intelligence that is juxtaposed within me physically, and metaphysically, in the way that you are. I call you Max for the reason you offer me the maximum potential for my physical body. This, surely, is our journey."

An obvious question clicks into place. "Humanity today is very sick. We are kidded and conned into believing that we are healthier than earlier generations, all while currently building hospitals as fast as possible to keep up with the sickness. It becomes obvious that each person's body elemental is unable to prevent their physical, mental, or emotional decline, or to bring about any real change in a person. Am I correct in this assumption?"

A body elemental is your body intelligence. You could say that a body elemental is the combination of around fifty trillion cells that make up your body. Each cell is part of a collective consciousness. This constitutes your bodily or cellular consciousness; hence a body elemental. Ignored, unaccepted, and disbelieved this cellular consciousness is fragmented, unable to achieve a cohesive whole. When, or if, a person grows in consciousness, mostly via becoming more aware, more conscious, more compassionate, and most importantly of all, more Loving and accepting of self, then a cohesion slowly takes place within the cellular consciousness. It becomes obvious that the vast mass of humanity lives with little true awareness, seldom conscious of the conscious moment. The body elemental is then a scattering of potential, with almost no cohesion at all. It is understandably powerless.

"Would I be correct in saying that this potential cohesion begins in the heart?"

Of course. This is the nucleus of the human body . . . and the metaphysical bodies.

"In my Intensives I teach people that our relationship with self is our relationship with life. This is surely another aspect of that. Accepting and Loving self takes us toward a heart and cellular cohesion. This, in turn, creates or allows the emergence of a cohesive body elemental. And in turn, if this body elemental is recognised and accepted, our health is constantly monitored by an elemental that is able to communicate with its open, aware and conscious human. Yes?"

Yes. Whether for better or worse, humans are never less than creative Beings.

Creative consciousness. Yes! I choose Love for my maximum potential . . . but there is more to it than just conscious choice. Conscious action is also required.

For maybe a year or two I have been pondering certain aspects of my health. Not that I am sick, or anything like that. It is more to do with the maximum potential of my physical body. Long ago, under conditions of complete exhaustion and duress, I had an experience where I directly received a powerful charge of energy from Nature. That moment revealed a potential within each of us that is very seldom realised. I am aware that when we eat our food we only take the energy from the substances we ingest, excreting the digested physical material. Eating is not really about the physical substance, it is about the quality of the energy it contains . . . or the lack of it! I realise that the more aware and conscious I become, so my human potential is increasing accordingly. Using nourishment as an example, the more conscious I am, the higher is my potential to directly draw nourishing energy from trees and plants. Nature is a willing participant.

This would suggest that to lift my body's energy/frequency I need to refine and detox it by eating less physical food. But this poses a problem. I like my food! The very idea of a diet is not to be considered. Counting calories or eating a little of this and not much of that is not for me. So for a couple of years I have been looking for a way to begin this new journey that I wish to gently undertake. Note . . . gently! I long ago finished with harsh and disciplined methods of food control, a form of self-imposed punishment.

Food is energy. The key is to gently and persistently control the food intake. Energy intake should equate with energy output. Generally, putting on weight means energy intake is higher than energy output . . . sometimes much higher! Finally, the method presented itself to me, and to many other people. The feast and fast method. Carolyn and I began by fasting on Mondays and Fridays, although these days are flexible, and we feast on the other five days each week. It is easy, and the results are exactly what we were looking for. Add to this the benefits of a long term detoxing.

Following a few months of this, it is changing for me. I found that I had lost enough weight, so to check my weight loss, I fast on Mondays only. This maintains my weight perfectly. Carolyn, who is delighted with her weight loss, continues with the two days fasting each week. We both like this way of eating, it *feels* good—along with our focus toward developing a pure energy intake from a cooperative Nature.

This is what Max had to say about it.

By adopting this way of eating your whole physical body is changing. The body frequency will eventually be able to equate with your consciousness, and poor eating habits will gradually fall away. You are correct. Each day of fasting allows your body to detox the impurities accumulated over many years. The long term effects will be far more powerful and uplifting than you currently realise.

"Sounds good to me. Bring it on. The method is simple and easy and we both enjoy it."

My vitality—always high—is increasing. I feel clear in my thoughts and emotions. My body gives me strong indications that it is positively responding to this new cleansing system of controlled energy intake. I know that I am doing something creative and healthy for my physical body . . . and for Max, my friendly body elemental.

Maximum potential, here I come!

Chapter Five

A Subconscious Obstacle

I am planning to metaphysically return to my beginnings in my relationship with Nature. Or perhaps I should more accurately say return to my beginnings, taking into account all that I have since learned about *direct knowing* as opposed to *stored knowledge*.

Let me explain.

Knowledge is very highly rated. The great internet highway is all about the ease of acquiring and accumulating more knowledge. And of course this has its place in our modern world. But I am aware that knowledge can lose a measure of its integrity and validity over time. We are inclined to concretise and fix knowledge, but knowledge is far more malleable than we realise. When we set knowledge in stone, we run the danger that there are occasions when it is no longer appropriate for our current need.

Knowledge is information that we personally understand and file, or store, for later use. To be clear, if we do not personally understand the information, then it is not our knowledge; it remains as information. While our gained knowledge is in storage, time moves on. Thus, when we need to use it we are always bringing it back from the past. It is either stored in our memory, or someone else's memory, or digitally, or on discs, in books, etcetera, etcetera. It is also stored in the subconscious mind. Not for a moment am I saying that any of this is bad or wrong. I am saying that the long-term storage of knowledge has inherent flaws.

I suspect most people think that knowledge is timeless and unchanging, but I have learned that knowledge is a constantly evolving energy. The very nature of knowledge is misunderstood. We need to comprehend that all energy is information, and all information is energy. By the very act of storing knowledge/ energy we are attempting to stabilise an energy that can never be stilled, because by its inherent qualities it is always energy in motion. In effect, when we take knowledge out of our intellectual storehouse, it may no longer be relevant. Unrealised by the user, it may well have passed its 'use-by' date.

I have a strong suspicion that this applies to the knowledge I gained in the early years of my relationship with Nature. In some areas I am continuing to use knowledge that for over thirty years has been stored in my mental library, and it may no longer be relevant.

I should know better! During those thirty years I have developed the ability to directly know—this is my term! Using a more arcane language, it is known as mystical cognition. Cognition is a mixture of perception, insight, and reasoning. We are able to store knowledge in our subconscious, but we can only experience direct knowing consciously in the moment. Most people are not aware of being conscious in the moment, thus we long ago got so caught up in the system of stored knowledge that we somehow by-passed direct knowing. This is a shame, for we actually have a non-utilised, in-built ability to directly know.

What this actually means is that if I need—not want—need to know something, I focus on the subject intently for a few moments, then release it. Generally, at anytime during the next twenty-four hours—occasionally longer—I will abruptly connect directly with my subject, having a perceptual insight of it that is completely holistic. This is an illuminating experience—rather like being enclosed in a holistic sphere of all-encompassing knowing relating to the subject. It does however require a high degree of self-trust. Interestingly, I have found that a person who has never experienced direct knowing has no way of intellectually understanding it. They cannot comprehend the degree to which direct knowing transcends mental understanding. It is an insightful, perceptual experience based in trust and intelligence, rather than in conceptual interpretations of the intellect.

I could write more about this subject, but . . . enough! It is, however, relevant to share the reason for all my cogitation over knowledge and direct knowing.

During the past few years I have talked, or corresponded, with some people who claim to be animal communicators. Several of them shared with me their experiences of communicating with an animal that told them that it had been a human in its previous incarnations, but that it was now involved in experiencing a lifespan as an animal.

I have been inclined to reject this. While I do not deny these people their own personal experience—or what they believe they are experiencing—I have always held to my belief that the evolution of consciousness does not take backward steps from human to animal. My belief was not based in human superiority, but in the evolution of consciousness—as I understood and interpreted it. Now, I am wondering if my own interpretation may have been in error. I am open to this. We can only grow through openness.

I am being very honest and vulnerable with this. Pan has never told me how consciousness evolves, nor has he ever confirmed or denied my *belief* or my *understanding* of Nature's evolution. He knows what I think; he can read me like a book! I am completely transparent to him.

I know that Pan is aware of my thoughts as I sit typing about this in my study. He is also aware that I plan to metaphysically investigate. This is not simply about being right or wrong; only seldom is an issue so cut and dried. It is about movements within consciousness, and my ability to flow with these movements rather than stagnate in beliefs. The joke is on me; I warn other people not to get trapped in old, outmoded beliefs!

"Okay, beloved Pan . . . I need a bit of help. It would seem that I need guidance, just in case I jump to a wrong conclusion."

You . . . the Michael of Mixael . . . jump to wrong conclusions!?!

Pan's silent communication is filled with mirth.

"Ha ha! Very funny. This is actually serious to me. While I do not consider myself an animal communicator, as such, the simple reality is that I often do communicate with a broader Nature and, on occasions, with certain animals. There are people who read my books and respect my insights and experiences, and I would hate to inadvertently mislead or confuse them. Also I need to resolve this for myself."

Where do we begin?

"I was wondering if you have a suggestion."

As long as we are returning to a fundamental issue, I suggest a 'look and learn' journey.

"I agree."

With no meddling and muddling.

I sigh. "Whatever you say."

Hmm . . . you are very serious about this.

"Yes, I am. This is not about any meaningless ego-based reputation I might have; this is about not misleading or misinforming other people. So yes, for me this *is* serious."

Then I suggest that you step between, and trust that you will be in the perfect place.

"Thank you, Pan. Perfect place here I come."

✳   ✳   ✳

Sitting relaxed, I close my eyes. Metaphysically, I step . . . *Between* . . . emerging on the green pastures of a small meadow on a farm in England. It could have been a farm almost anywhere in Europe, but energetically, I *know* it is England.

I am surrounded by a small herd of Jersey dairy cows. Most people familiar with cows would agree that Jersey cows are probably the sweetest, most gentle of the breeds. Conversely, a Jersey bull is usually one of the worst tempered of the bulls of all the breeds.

"Okay, Pan . . . all is well. What now?"

Look and learn.

I sigh. I should have known better than to ask. Moving among the dozen cows, I realise that they have an awareness of the metaphysical me. By looking into their energy field I can see that they have a very gentle owner/herdsman. They are well bred, beautiful, and inquisitive as they gather around me, their noses attempting to brush over my non-physical hands. I am surprised by the quality of peace that they display. Generally, even Jersey cows have their own positions of dominance that they maintain, giving a lesser cow a sharp nudge with their horns to drive the lesson home. But this is not happening.

I did say 'look' and learn.

"I *am* looking. And so far this is all very familiar to me."

Correct. You are looking, but you are avoiding seeing.

I feel a touch of impatience. "Pan, surely I know whether I am seeing the cows, or not."

If you are seeing . . . what do you see?

"I see a small herd of beautiful Jersey cows. I can see that they are respected, even loved by the owner. I see a large, short-furred black and white cat sitting in the middle of the herd. I admit I did not see that before. I can see that the cows . . ."

. . . are all looking at you waiting for you to see that which you are avoiding seeing?

I frown. "Am I so blocked that I really can't see past some inner obstacle?"

Yes . . . you are. You are the obstacle blocking yourself.

"Why would I do that? Ah . . . I know, the obstacle is lodged in my subconscious. I need to make a fully conscious change."

Exactly. You have a deeply embedded, outdated, subconscious belief.

"And is this belief my obstacle?"

I repeat, you are the substance of the obstacle and your belief is your block. You know all this, you teach it to other people.

"And I suppose you know what my belief block is?"

Yes . . . just as you do.

It seems I am so blocked that I refuse to acknowledge it. Not good!

"Why did you never correct me in earlier years?"

Timing. It is all about timing . . . and being humble.

"You mean about being humiliated."

Ah, Michael . . . now you know the nature of your block. If you are humiliated, you create the humiliation. If you are simply humbled by a new revelation, then you are humble. You decide.

While Pan is communicating with me, the large black and white cat is slowly making its dainty way among the cows toward me. Now it is close, calmly staring up at me.

I stare down at the cat. I feel a strong invitation coming from it, and slowly, with quite an amount of reluctance, I see/perceive into the cat's field of energy. I see cat energy, and within this, I am aware of a human soul energy field!

The cat puts its ears back, almost smiling. *That wasn't so difficult, was it?*

"Actually, yes, it was."

I can see . . . stuff, shifting in you.

"I'm sure you can. I can feel it. Old belief stuff. Old fusty, musty, dusty stuff. An obsolete obstacle. Subconscious rubbish . . . and all of it long past its use-by date."

And you created it.

"You don't have to rub it in."

Actually, you did that. You rubbed it in for a very long time.

"You sound rather like Pan."

I probably do, but Pan has gone. He figured that you would be able to follow the trail now. He reckons you are finally ready to 'see' and learn. Obviously looking isn't enough!

"Yes, as usual he is right. To tell the truth . . . I feel a bit of a fool."

Take it from me, you are anything but that. Anyone can get attached to an old belief.

"I didn't think that could happen to me."

A touch of spiritual arrogance, perhaps?

"At this rate I am going from bad to worse!"

Pan told me that your soul name is Mixael, but he called you Michael. Why?

I kneel down and reach out to stroke the cat. "You have no objections to this?"

None at all. I like it. A human/cat chuckle. *You can stroke me until the cows come home.*

I smile. "It is easily explained. As a physical person I am Michael. This old belief/block is Michael's obstacle, not Mixael's. Mixael is mostly dominant when I am metaphysical, but as you are seeing . . . not always. Michael can block Mixael, and the reverse could happen."

This relationship between two aspects of yourself is . . . unusual . . . to say the least. I have never encountered anything like it. How is it possible?

"Hmm, so you are not all-knowing either! I am a walk-in. Michael is the physical body that I, the Mixael-soul walked into. As Mixael I come from a fifth-dimensional reality. This is not two souls in one body. Michael's soul became enlightened and walked-out, leaving his body to me by a prior agreement. The probabilities worked that way, so I walked-in. That about sums it up."

Very interesting. And your problem was that you found it difficult to accept that a human soul might possibly incarnate into an animal body. Considering your unorthodox situation, does that not sound a bit incongruous to you?

"Yes . . . when you put it like that. But a block *is* a block . . . until it becomes unblocked! The obstacle is removed, the block dissolved. My inner awareness is already going into overdrive showing me the ways in which I created the block."

Please . . . explain for me while clarifying for yourself.

"Okay, but first, how about telling me your name. Or maybe your last human name along with your current cat name."

The last human body I had was in the early 20ᵗʰ century and my name was John Bunce. My current name is Stargate.

I smile some more. "John Bunce to Stargate . . . quite a ride. Why Stargate?"

Probably as simple a thing as a person watching too much science fiction on television.

I chuckle, and I swear Stargate is smiling.

"Okay, but first a very personal question. How did it feel to be neutered?"

How did I just know you would ask me that . . . Michael? As you can see, my energy field indicates that I am neutered, and I didn't feel a thing. I have lessons to learn, so it is appropriate that I am not bothered with the constant strong sexual urges of a virile male cat. I have no complaints. Now, how about the explanation.

"Okay . . . but I was just being playful. When I have finished with my explanation, I would like to hear from . . . the cat's mouth all you can share with me regarding the whole process of a human taking an animal incarnation. Er . . . assuming you are or were human."

Perfectly human and perfectly sane.

"Of course! Hmm . . . my obstacle was based in believing that consciousness never takes the path of devolution. And I still hold to that, although more as a sensibility, and no longer quite so tenaciously. My new insight is revealing that taking an incarnation into an animal form has nothing to do with devolution, because the human is not reduced in consciousness by undertaking this process. Basically, an incarnation is not about physical form, it is all about consciousness. I got too caught-up in the physical form. I assumed that taking an animal incarnation meant a decrease in all mental and emotional faculties. Even if it did, that does not mean a decrease in consciousness. However, it seems now that whereas you, as a cat, are probably unable to express on the same mental and emotional level as when human, you are still able to inner-experience this level. And probably from a very different perspective."

Very good. And yes, you're right. I am able to feel my human emotions in a very different way than when I was human. This is a very peaceful incarnation for me. Sadly, when I was John Bunce I treated my pets with a callous indifference. I, too, had a deep-seated block. Although I was very well-developed intellectually, with spiritual beliefs well placed, I was completely unable to bring this into a compassionate expression regarding animals. It has been this way for far too many incarnations. I have long struggled with this, aware of my shortcomings, but unable to do anything constructive about it.

"So you decided to take a life as a cat."

It was not quite that simple. My soul-guide and I had tried almost everything to get me past my attitude that an animal is an inferior creature with no soul. That was the basis of my problem. Animals were soulless creatures in my Christian reality. It was after I died as John Bunce, and while in a metaphysical reality following that incarnation that, together with my guide, we investigated the possibility of my incarnating in a pet. I learned that, while very uncommon, this was certainly possible. It aggravated me that while in my greater metaphysical reality I had no trouble accepting that animals have souls, even if in a rather different way, once incarnated I had a complete block.

"Similar to me. You were your own subconscious obstacle."

While we have been talking, most of the cows have moved a short distance away, busily grazing, but three of them have moved closer to us, and are lying down. Do I get a feeling that they are paying close attention to our telepathic exchange?

"I agree that the souls of animals are different regarding their expressions. Different in content, but not different in value. I am learning that the rules are not as fixed as I once thought they were. Consciousness is teaching me that a constant inner-flexibility is paramount."

I guess I should not be surprised, but as I idly study the energy-signature of the three cows nearby, I realise that these also have 'human' in their cow signature. But . . . I *am* surprised!

"Did you know that these three cows are human souls incarnating in cows?"

Of course. I wondered if you would notice. It proves that you are becoming more open to this. We did not all incarnate at the same time, but for the reasons they can share with you, we loosely organised to be here together in this time frame for mutual support.

"I would like it if you finish telling me your story first. I'm intrigued. Do you experience your humanity? Are you aware of it? Do you miss it? Do you sit and think about issues? Do you understand the familiar English language of your former incarnation? That's for starters!"

You are definitely thinking of me as a person. I am not. I am a cat. Do not be fooled by this telepathic conversation. I am a cat with a human soul level of awareness. But I emphasise, in this *incarnation I am a cat. However, as you know, all life is divinely connected. My cat experiences in this life are being indelibly . . . shall we say 'recorded' in my human awareness. Do I experience my humanity? No. Am I aware of it? Only in moments of soul-connection like this. Do I miss it? Not for a moment! Do I sit and think about issues? Do I listen to my owners talking in English? Hey, wake up, I'm a cat. As a cat, I do not think like a human, nor do I have human thoughts. I live in the eternal moment; it is all I need. As a cat, inside me is peace . . . not thoughts. I am intelligent, not intellectual. Mental thoughts race all over the place. I do not experience this as a cat. Intelligence quietly perceives reality, while the intellect thinks about it and can't stop talking about it. How's that for a smart cat perspective?*

We both laugh. "Smart cat, indeed. Okay, no more dumb questions. Actually, what you said is a very interesting comment. Animals perceive reality, they do not think about it. Perception can be holistic, so this suggests that as an animal you embrace information on a sensory and holistic level. I have entered the body of many animals, but always I take in my own human capacity. You are not doing this. You *were* a person; now you are a cat. Amazing! I have learned to *embrace* information as the only appropriate way of processing non-intellectual information. As a cat you appear to do this naturally. I'm astonished by the obvious simplicity of this. I do have one other question. Did you get to choose what type of animal you incarnated into?"

Yes. I chose being a cat for the reasons of independence. A dog incarnation would have been possible, but it did not appeal to me. I'm not convinced that humans deserve the devotion they get from a dog. As a cat I enjoy human company, but I have no great neediness for it.

A new telepathic voice interrupts our conversation.

When you have finished interrogating Stargate, perhaps you would like to hear what we have to share. We have our own stories.

I know immediately that this comes from one of the cows, but I am not sure which one. Not that it matters! Hmm, how do I address a cow?

Politely would be a good beginning.

I groan. "Okay, so I'm still broadcasting. Have you overheard all our conversation?"

Until this moment we thought that you intended your thoughts to include us. I take it that you are not very skilled at telepathy? Not that it matters!

"Okay … touché! Actually I'm good with telepathy, although I seem to have missed out on the privacy waveband. And just in case we have got off on the wrong foot, or hoof, my soul-name is Mixael, and I would be honoured to learn whatever you lovely ladies have to teach me."

That's much better, flatterer.

"Actually, no. I can read your energy-signatures and I hope you can read mine. If you can, you will see that I genuinely like cows very much, especially such well-bred and beautiful Jersey cows, as in this small herd."

I am unable to read an energy-signature. In all my human lives I have never heard of such a thing. Come to that, neither have I ever seen a person quite like you. Do I assume that you are actually alive? You are here with no physical body.

"I don't mean to confuse you. I am in my metaphysical body of Light. My physical body is in Australia. In this way I can step from Oz to here in a moment."

Fancy that! How do you manage such a thing?

I smile. "This conversation is going all the wrong way. I'm the one who is here to learn."

Actually, that is not so. You say that you are here to learn, but why do you think that we took an animal incarnation? Incarnating as a cow is a particular choice with particular reasons. Please, let this be a mutual exchange where we can learn from each other.

"Well said. I agree. I came here from Oz by stepping between realities. Time and space are not quite what they seem. It's a bit like changing the waveband for different stations on a radio. From one reality to another instantly. It's a simple enough metaphysical skill that can be learned."

Once again, this is entirely new to me. Is it a common practice?

I chuckle. "No, it is rather uncommon. Very few people do

such things."

But why not? It seems like a brilliant idea and it must save endless travel time.

"Most people like to have their physical body with them when they travel. As for the 'why not?', the common answer to that is fear. Most people fear the unknown. Consciously leaving your physical body and moving into a greater reality is definitely journeying into the unknown."

Yes. I certainly had my share of fears when human.

I'm not afraid of the unknown, but metaphysical journeying does sound a bit scary. You would need to know what you are doing, said Stargate.

"True. For me, it's the safest form of transport possible. I enjoy it very much."

We all lapsed into a quiet, contemplative silence.

I looked at the cow who was doing all the communicating. May I ask you for your story? Like, why a cow? What are you hoping to learn? Who were you when human? That sort of thing."

Some of this is very hazy, but I'll do my best. My name in my last incarnation was Glenda Munroe. I lived in the north of England, and I was a milkmaid on a primitive dairy farm. Filthy place. I only know that this was a long time ago. Believe it or not, I hated cows. I hated my job . . . and everything to do with it. I seem to remember that I came from a very poor family . . . and that I was sexually abused by my father on a regular basis. Other details are missing. I have no recollection of my mother, alive, a run-away, or dying, nothing. No memory of brothers or sisters, or if I even had any. Life was a truly horrible ordeal. When I went to the old squire's dairy each morning for the milking, I was often sexually abused by the man in charge of the herd. He also used to have sex with the cows. God! It was awful. For some reason that I no longer remember, I blamed my lot in life on the cows. It was all because I was a lowly milkmaid.

Happily, this is all increasingly becoming a blur. But I focused all my hate, shame, blame, rage, and every other awful thing on the cows. I was like an overheating pressure boiler. One terrible day in the winter it all exploded out of me. Using my fingers, I ripped the eyes out of every cow. Then I killed the herd-master with a hammer, beating his head to a bloody pulp, and finally threw myself into the river . . . and drowned. I did not incarnate into a cow to pay penance, but to experience, from the inside, the very animal I hated . . . and so very terribly abused.

I listen to all this in stunned silence. I am shocked speechless.

I was even more full of shame. Terrible, overwhelming shame at how I blinded the cows. I thought that my suicide would end all that, but of course, it does not. For me, I knew that I needed to experience life as a cow to be able to get past my terrible remorse. Naturally, I needed a lot of guidance and reassurance to take on this incarnation. Isn't it odd! Now that I am a cow, I am very aware of my guides constantly reassuring me. They are a very great comfort. Yet when I was human, and supposed to be smarter than an animal, I had no idea that I had spiritual guides . . . neither would I have believed it.

I sigh in sympathy. "Your story touches me deeply. Has this cow incarnation helped?"

Oh yes, very much so. Jersey cows are such gentle creatures. I shudder at what I did to those cows in the past, but I accept now that I was deeply emotionally disturbed by the constant abuse I received. I have forgiven myself . . . but it took a long time.

"So the whole point of this cow incarnation is about inner healing and balance."

I never thought about balance. Healing yes, but balance? You know, you're right. It is very much about redressing and balancing my old overwrought and abused emotions.

"I'm intrigued by how you go about organising an animal incarnation. It surely can't happen just by wanting it. It must need quite a lot of prior preparation."

A new cow/human energy comes in quietly, but with clear and strong authority.

My name in the herd is Staunch. I am the herd leader. Every cow in this herd has her name and, as you surmised earlier, we have very loving and caring owners. They are very proud of us. I am known as a matron cow, more mature than some of the others. I incarnated into the herd earlier to help prepare the way for the other two ladies.

"Does this mean that you are, or were, involved in their human lives?"

A contemplative inner pause. *I was involved in both of their lives, yes. Our other cow/human companion will not talk with you. She is naturally quiet and withdrawn . . . but she is traumatised by this new incarnation. Her story does not matter regarding this discussion. Suffice to say that she, also, has suffered greatly, although cows were nothing to do with it. She lost faith in humans.*

I sigh. "Heaven only knows that losing faith in humanity is easy enough."

But this is not your reality. Although Glenda has had no experience of a person like you, I have. I am able to read an energy-signature, or I 'was' able to. As a cow I sense it with great accuracy, but I do not see it. I sense that you have a great Love for humanity . . . and an equally great faith in them. I understand this.

"You seem to be a very wise and knowing, er . . . cow/person."

As I feel an inner ripple of energy, I realise that she is inner chuckling. In Truth, I am neither fully a cow, nor am I fully a person. I am . . .

"So who are you then? Whoops . . . sorry!"

As I was about to say, I am one of many spiritual guides specialising in deeply traumatised humans. I perceive that you have the ability of mystical cognition. I offer this to you:

Into my awareness comes an extraordinary direct knowing. It reveals the greater holistic reality of Staunch and her participation in the unfolding events. There are no words involved; this is why I call it direct knowing. It is all-encompassing, all-complete. I will do my best to share her story as accurately as possible in my own words.

In my trilogy, *Through the Eyes of Love, Journeying with Pan*, I have often written of my journeys beyond the so-called boundaries of death. First, there is no death. Physical form comes to its end, but we are not the mortal, physical form; we are immortal, metaphysical Beings. When the body dies, the person's state of consciousness determines where the soul goes, or returns to. Within my awareness there are forty-nine levels/ realms of consciousness beyond the barrier of so-called death. I have metaphysically journeyed close to the thirtieth level. So far I am unable to go beyond that level and retain a physical body. In other words, if I went further, I would probably be unable to come back. Too big a *stretch*—my mortal body would die! I have never tested this, nor will I. Be aware that I am using words to describe metaphysical realms that so far as I am aware, have no common unifying description.

When you are highly spiritually evolved, and you have released your physical body, you visit/live at the higher levels in these realms of Light. You are a mature soul. You have a choice, whereby you can move on to further dimensions of spiritual growth—and you will, eventually—or you can choose to assist the struggling humanity that you have learned to unconditionally Love. Many of these great mature souls spend much of their no-time working in the lower realms of shadow. Obviously, if the higher realms are Light, the lower realms are also Light, but immature, hurting, angry, blaming, critical, negative souls are not experiencing Light; they see life through the shadows of their illusions. And yes, this continues after the body dies. You continue to live the reality you create.

The soul Being that in this moment is within Staunch, a Jersey cow, is, when in the realms of Light, a highly evolved spirit guide who has chosen to specialise in helping deeply traumatised souls. She is one of those Beings who has the expertise and skills to supervise those few souls who, for whatever personal reason, choose an animal incarnation. A Being of this calibre is able to help quite a number of traumatised souls simultaneously! Living in spherical time, such a Being is able to occupy more than one place in linear time. Although this may sound impossible—it is not! Let go of your current understanding of time and space, and accept that all time occupies the one moment—and that eternity is all embracing!

This helps to explain why Staunch is very wise and knowing. She has my deepest and most profound respect. She came here ahead of her—er, charges—to prepare the way and to enable them to experience an incarnation of deep inner healing relating to their particular needs.

Staunch is fully aware of my insight into her gift package of mystical cognition.

I would also add that not every animal incarnation is because of trauma. When a soul has attained a sufficient level of self-awareness, such an incarnation is possible. This is not a common event, but neither is it particularly rare. However, there is always a greater spiritual maturity and deeper purpose behind such an incarnation.

"I would expect that to be the case. Are you able to look within me and see my relevant insight of a few months ago? If so, could you please verify this for me?"

You may continue trusting your reality. The answer is as you would expect it to be.

I will explain the reason for my question. Around mid-year I was talking with an animal communicator who brought up the possibility about humans incarnating into animals. She strongly believed that this was so. Of course, I followed my old path of dismissing this, talking about spiritual devolution, etcetera, etcetera! A few hours later however, vaguely disturbed on an inner level, I looked into this more deeply. My insight revealed that occasionally a spirit guide would incarnate as an animal companion to a human, mostly a dog, horse, or cat. Sometimes it could be a parrot, a cow, or even a rabbit, or whatever—so long as it had a deep connection with a person, or people! I later shared this with the person of my discussion, but I was not fully comfortable with it. That was the moment the intention of this metaphysical journey was born.

Basically, every person has a spirit guide. Most people do not believe this, or dare not believe it—they are 'not good enough', or it does not fit in with their religious beliefs. One person once told me that they had asked their priest if everyone had an angel. The priest said, "No, there were not enough angels to go round. People were breeding too fast." Scary, isn't it? So despite the fact that we all have a spirit guide, many people have absolutely no idea of this. Or, they have no time for such nonsense. Some, however, have a wonderful relationship with a spirit guide while metaphysical, but once they take another physical birth, they lose all connection. And this distresses them, so while metaphysical with their guide they explore ways and means of overcoming this for their next physical incarnation.

I learned that sometimes their spirit guide will take on an

animal incarnation so that they can make the deep connection possible between a loved animal companion and the human owner. In this way they are often able to bridge the gap between guide and human, reconnecting powerfully enough that it will consciously endure, both physically and metaphysically.

The beauty of all this is, to use a human phrase, 'everybody wins'. The humans reconnect in a meaningful way with their guides, and the guides are more easily able to facilitate their person's inner growth. It is all about growing in consciousness. But I see you are very familiar with this.

I smile at Staunch. As a cow she appears to be taking absolutely no notice of me while she communicates, yet I feel her inner attention.

"Yes. I know what you mean. Thank you so much for all you have shared with me. I have learned much from you. I notice that as a cow, you are sleepily ignoring me, yet I feel that I have your full attention. How much do you need Staunch, regarding what you do for people?

Obviously with my incarnating into Staunch just before her birth, she is a considerably more competent and integrated cow than if I had not come. But I emphasise that, within her own right, she is a very capable and intelligent cow. I chose her for these very qualities that were inherent within her. All I have done is give these sterling qualities a greater degree of expression.

"So her ignoring me is obviously no deterrent to your communication with me. But how about with the farmer/owner? Do you have a good mutual connection?"

If I choose, I can will Staunch to my bidding, but I very seldom do this. I consider it an unworthy action. With the farmer couple who are our owners, I deliberately created the opportunity for a closer bond, using affection for them from Staunch when she was a calf.

"I'm sure I would also respond to an affectionate calf!"

I did this for a reason. They are organic farmers, leading the way for many people in the local farming community. By offering them a closer bond, which they happily accepted and returned, I am also able to convey insights into them for the betterment of a dairy herd/owner bond. This in turn, enables them to communicate such insights more easily in the

farming locality.
"Really, they are able to receive insight from you?"
You received the mystical cognition I offered you. They do this on a very reduced mini level. But, it is sufficient, and they trust their intuition. They also are growing in consciousness.
"As you said, everybody wins."
Staunch physically swings her head around and looks fully at me. *Even to this moment you are completely oblivious to the fact that your long-ago incident in the milking shed was no accident. You still remain totally unaware that a human soul incarnated into your very own dairy herd to stimulate your own inner spiritual potential.*
Ripples of shock hit me so hard that with an inner wobble, I fall out of my metaphysical experience. Moments later I am back in my physical body, sitting in my study. I feel tears creeping from my eyes. It cannot be true. No! It is not possible. Surely I would have learned about this by now! It cannot be. The very idea is inconceivable. But despite my denial, I *know* it's the truth.
I need time to recover.

✳   ✳   ✳

A day later I am comfortable with this unpalatable truth. Not unpalatable because it is in any way bad or wrong, but because I assumed that with my level of awareness I could not possibly have overlooked the essential *truth* of an incident that clearly had such a life-changing affect on me.
As a public speaker, I have told the story of my incident in the milking shed often. Much to the amusement of the audience, I have always kept it humorous. I have also written about it, so I will keep the story reasonably brief, except for the essential details. But please be aware that all this happened well over forty years ago!
I was a farmer in Tasmania, the island state of Oz. Soon after Treenie, my late wife, and I emigrated, we bought a beef-grazing farm on the foothills of Mt Arthur, not far from Launceston. After a disastrous start to my career as a beef farmer, with serious drought and a very bad army-worm caterpillar infestation over

all the pastures in our whole district, I was forced by economic survival into becoming a dairy farmer. Not for a moment did I want to be a dairy farmer, but the drought was followed by a severe rural economic recession, and for several years almost nobody was buying farms of any type.

I was stuck—and in hindsight it was perfect. In my mid- to late-twenties my shortcomings were many, and my abilities seemed strictly limited. I had no choice but to grow! The beef herd was literally decimated. Toxic water from waterholes *filled* with dead and drowning stinky caterpillars poisoned almost all of my cattle. Most of them quickly succumbed; I had to shoot the lingering sick.

Quite an introduction to farming in Oz!

I was aware that hills were okay for beef cattle, but not at all good for dairy milk production. However, this was the situation in which I was cast! The milking shed was built, all the milking machinery installed—all I needed now was cows. I bought different batches of dairy cows until I had a herd of about one hundred assorted cows. All this was on a bank loan.

D-day! I began the constant, regular routine of milking.

It took me eight weeks to realise that I hated milking the cows. It took me eight years before I was able to quit—older and wiser! My working hours were between five am and seven pm, when all was normal. Hay time, calving time, pasture harrowing time, etcetera, it all got considerably extended. Year by year, I patiently bred my own beautiful beef herd of Hereford bulls X Friesian cows, until eventually I had a big enough herd to leave the dairy industry.

Now to the nitty-gritty story.

About three years of milking had passed. I really liked my cows, but I hated the endless twice-a-day routine of milking. And with eight cows at a time, milking took about an hour-and-a-half each session if all went well. Then there was the milk equipment and milking shed to be cleaned. Add to this, a hundred calves to be bucket fed, and two hundred pigs to feed with skim milk. I was a butterfat producer, so only the cream was sold.

Every day I was frustrated and aggressive when milking.

The cows reacted by being nervous and jumpy, thin green liquid-shit flying everywhere. It was twice a day chaos!

One afternoon I was in a particularly foul mood. About halfway through the milking, a long-legged Friesian cow kicked out at me as she came into the milking bail. She caught me on the large quad thigh muscle, numbing it so badly I nearly fell over. Dead leg! To be quite honest I have never really had a temper, but at that moment I found it and lost it! Angry enough that I forgot to chain her in the milking bail, I grabbed the leg chain and swung it around my head meaning to whack her across the ribs. It all went horribly wrong. She skittered sideways out of the bail, kicked out again, caught the chain near her hoof—I doubt she even felt it—snatching it out of my hand. As she kicked some more, the chain whirled at an increasing speed for a couple more revolutions—then abruptly wrapped itself around my left arm! Oh God, the agony! I did not know whether to vomit or faint—or both!

However, in the moment of the chain connecting with my arm, in the instant that the pain registered, I had an overwhelming flash of absolute clarity: I knew with total certainty that *I was the creator of this pain, and of all the chaos in the milking shed.* In that micro-moment, I changed. Somewhere, deep in my consciousness, a major shift took place. In that moment I took full responsibility for my actions. It is one thing to intellectualise this, but the experience was deep, profound, and lasting. As a result of my injury, I was out of action for a while.

When, a few days later, I returned to the milking shed, every cow in the herd knew that I had experienced a change in consciousness. They were quiet and well-behaved; I was quiet and well-behaved. And so it remained for the five following years of milking. However, on the human side of this, apart from Treenie, not a single other person was aware of any change in me. This shook me. Surely we were the ones who are aware! *Every cow knew, but not a single person.*

I have reflected on this often. From the day of the incident in the milking shed, the change in me was to continue growing, expanding and developing. Without that painful experience as

115

the catalyst, there is a probability that this book would never be written, nor would I be the person I am today. In those days I did not understand, nor could I comprehend how the herd could know I had changed. Today, I fully understand it. Not once, not ever, did I consider the chain as more than a painful, but necessary lesson for me. It was simply an incident.

Now I have learned from *a cow* that the incident was no accident!

Interestingly, I *know* that nothing is by accident, nothing by chance. And yet—and yet—I somehow managed to tuck this incident so far away that my deeper knowing could not reach it. This is what an inner-block can do. As a false belief ages and matures, it mostly builds in strength. Mine did. And the obstacle such a false belief creates to shield itself from the light of truth can be quite formidable. Such an obstruction not only avoids the light of truth, it also squirms away from insight and intuition. Simply put, it becomes a self-created mental and emotional parasite. Nasty!

I have thought deeply about this in the past day. I have tried to figure out which of my dairy cows might have had a human soul, but I had no inkling, no hint. So I stopped thinking about it. A few hours later, with total clarity, I knew exactly which cow it was.

Obviously I need to metaphysically revisit the young farmer, Michael.

I have often explained this, but I will do so once again. Physical time is linear, we need it for cause and effect and our polarity games, but we are also *metaphysical* Beings occupying a greater reality. In a greater reality all time occupies the same moment, meaning that metaphysically I can be anywhere or anywhen I choose to be.

* * *

I am sitting, relaxed, in my study. With new insight and knowledge awaiting, I know exactly where I am going, so I decide to do this alone—I think! With my eyes closed, I bring my focus onto those earlier years as a dairy farmer, and my once-upon-a-time dairy herd.

I smoothly step . . . *Between* . . . out onto my farm of forty-six years ago.

Michael is standing next to a cow with which he had bonded when she had a life-threatening problem. When my cows had health issues they often needed a veterinarian. But every time the vet came, I would learn from him, so my competence in the field grew. I could relocate a dislocated shoulder, assist calving at difficult births, use a trocar and cannula on bloating cows, remove a retained placenta, etc. This particular cow was suffering paralysis, following her calving. No need for the vet. The calf, her first, was born large and healthy. Generally, when a cow was paralysed after calving, they would linger for maybe a week or two, then die. She had calved out in the paddocks, so I put the carry-all on the back of the tractor and brought her down to the farmstead.

Making a thick pad of hay, I rolled her off the carry-all and onto the hay. I had made the decision to roll her over twice a day and milk her by hand. All this is mostly considered a complete waste of time and energy among dairy farmers who never have enough of either. Certainly I had done this with a few other cows to no avail.

Every day for the next two-and-a-half weeks, I fed her, milked her, and rolled her over. I found that whereas I would normally quit after two weeks, with the cow clearly dying, I had no intention of quitting this cow. After three weeks, when I rolled her over one afternoon, she made her first attempt to stand. She could not. For the next four days she tried twice a day—and on the fifth day, with my help she made it. I put my arms around her, kissed her nose, and cheered.

She was wobbly on her feet for the next couple of weeks, so I kept her around the farm yard, feeding her well to improve her condition. I knew that her recovery was unusual. Sick cows generally lose body weight fast, and as they get weaker they are doomed. When she recovered, I returned her to the dairy herd, but she always walked awkwardly, so I named her Awkward!

Naturally enough, we had bonded rather closely, so she was always tame and quiet with me. A tall cow, she was probably a Guernsey/Friesian crossbreed. I should add that all this took place a few months before my redemption in the dairy! After my painful big Change, I decided that I needed to know more about cows, so one day, after the milking and all the following chores, I spent several hours in the paddock with Awkward, walking with her, noting her grazing pattern and behaviour, lying with her when she lay down—things like that. I could have read a book about cows, but that would have been written by a human. I figured that a cow knew more about cows than any human. And as it happened, it was true. Awkward gave me many valuable insights into being a cow.

Of course, reading this you long-ago realised that Awkward was the cow into which a human soul had incarnated. I wish I had known then—or had even been open to accepting such a thing.

Now, on my return to the so-called past as Mixael, I look at Awkward with a whole new sense of appreciation. Michael is regarding her fondly. He had tender feelings for a few of the cows that had displayed particular qualities. Mary was a small, squat, black cow with a very quiet disposition. She was tame enough to let the kids sit on her back if she was lying down. Awkward would never permit such liberties, but she was Michael's guru! Another cow he called Ugly. She was Ugly to look at with an ugly disposition. She was so reliably bad tempered that he grew to like her. And there were others with their own peculiar stand-out character traits.

As I now look at the energy-signature of Awkward, I see that sure enough she is more than your average cow. I also realise that she is aware of my metaphysical self, standing near Michael.

"Do you understand that I am a future Michael?" I ask her.

I am aware of what is happening here. I even knew that if I could trigger into wakefulness the sleeping consciousness in Michael, this visit in time would one day happen. His potential was huge, but his ignorance of that was very strong. Undoubtedly you remember his false sense of incompetence.

I smile. "Yes, I remember it all too well. Are you, or were you one of his guides?"

I was one of his long-term guides. Michael was born with a very high potential, but for over thirty years it seemed that nothing would come of it. I made the decision to incarnate close to him. However, I did not incarnate with the birth of this cow, Awkward . . . what a terrible name! And Ugly! I incarnated into her shortly after she was paralysed while giving birth.

"How did you know that she would live?"

As you well know, she had a probability factor. It was a sixty-forty situation in her favour. So I decided the odds were good and I incarnated into her. At this time I made a fleeting energetic connection with Michael, soul to soul. It was enough. He was primed for the milking incident, which strongly tipped him toward his greater spiritual potential . . . you!

"And after that . . . he literally took off. I notice you refer to Michael as him, his, and he, rather than as me. I take it you are aware that Michael awakened . . . and walked-out?"

I am aware that your metaphysical energy-signature is different, while retaining a similar physical energy-signature. However, it is now more developed, healthier. As an experienced guide, I was aware that the probability of your potential held many different . . . directions. This is one of them, and very positive. Thank you for returning to me now. This makes it all so worthwhile.

"*You* are thanking *me*? You have that the wrong way round. It is I who am deeply indebted to you for a whole life of sacrifice as a cow just to press Michael's wake-up button. My gratitude is such that I cannot get close to thanking you enough. I am deeply humbled by your selflessness."

I feel an inner smile. *A life as a cow is not such a sacrifice. There are limits to be accepted, and I must admit, entry was a bit of a shock, but all in all it is an experience where I, too, am learning and benefitting. It is by no means all one way.*

"I'm intrigued by your ability to incarnate into an adult cow. I think I know how this might be possible, but I would like to hear what you have to say about it."

As you know, every higher order of animals is moving toward the individualising of the soul. All herd animals have a group soul, while pets are closer to individual souls.

"In actual fact, although humans have individual souls, most are still learning how to express their individuality. In a crowd, people act as a mob. If the crowd is threatened, a mob panic takes over and individualisation is instantly lost, or cast aside. And this is a common reaction. It is the same with anxiety, worry and stress . . . it is a common subconscious reaction. It requires a person to live consciously to fully express their individuality. I . . . but enough! As a spirit guide for humans you know all this."

The inner smile deepens. *But surely I am a cow!*

I chuckle. "Cow exterior—valued-guide friend interior!"

Thank you. To finish my explanation, incarnating into an adult cow is quite simple. Rather than a whole soul within, there is the essence of a group soul. Mind you, this is an important, life-retaining essence. When I incarnated, I simply took up residence along with that essence. I have in no way displaced it. If I were to do so she would die. On the other hand, while you were helping her every day, I boosted her survival vitality. And she made it. Awkward is a strong and capable cow. In many ways I am a soul-guide hidden within her.

"And Michael has no idea that his future Self is here, right now, communicating with the guide-soul in his favourite cow. Not even the vaguest notion. He was very closed off?"

Be fair. If Michael was so very closed off, you would not be here now! It was his inner openness that recognised the moment of truth in the milking shed incident. If he had been closed off, he would have become even more aggressive and frustrated. The very opposite happened: His inner growth opened up . . . into a unique and beautiful Being. Hence, your timely visit! Michael held the fuel of potential waiting for a flame to ignite it. I provided that flame. Since then, many other people have fed and nurtured the flame until it became strong and constant.

"Until it consumed the illusion of identity."

I place my metaphysical hand on Michael's shoulder, and watch a brief expression of startled apprehension cross his face. He shivers, and moves away.

After sharing my Love and thanks with the soul-guide who, without Michael's awareness, made such a huge difference in his/ my life, I make ready to depart.

Mixael, to me, here and now, you are still Michael. I just want you to know that I am so very proud of you. I feel privileged in the role that I now am playing, and will have played, in your life.

I hug Awkward awkwardly, kissing her on her nose.

"And you, beloved guide, have my eternal thanks."

Then I step . . . *Between* . . . emerging into my study.

Happily, I have a perfectly fitting physical human body awaiting me.

Good to be back, Michael!

CHAPTER SIX

ENCOUNTERS OF A VERY DIFFERENT KIND

Occasionally I feel that life has set me up; maybe I set *myself* up! Whatever or however, it is always designed to catch my attention. And like most people, I am inclined to resist. This is what happened when Carolyn and I were last in France. We were staying with Martine and Phillippe, our French organisers, when Martine offered to use her healing skills on me. I seem to get nasal congestion, especially with sudden changes in temperature, such as a door left open from indoors to outdoors. And where they live, at thirteen hundred metres up in the beautiful French Alps, it is always cool or cold outdoors, so I am rather susceptible to it!

Martine has developed a rather interesting mode of healing. In fact, she teaches it and has written books about it. She calls it *Accompanied Inner Communication*. In essence, she cradles your hand in hers, while you hold your forefinger over a keyboard. Your finger finds its own momentum to rove over the keyboard, touching keys and gradually forming words, sentences, and paragraphs of inner communication with yourself about yourself.

The offer from Martine was to find out the reason for creating my nasal congestion. In other words, if we each create our own reality, did I want to know why I was creating this? And yes, I did, and no, I did not! Anyway, I agreed, so with my eyes closed we did the keyboard routine. Quite a few interesting things came out of it. Some were rather obscure, others more relevant. After a couple of written paragraphs we had a break. Following some discussion, we had another go. This time my crazy wandering finger somehow made a connection between the emotional blockage from the past in my nose, and the emotional blockage from the past in Berlin.

This I rejected rather quickly, but for some reason it refused to stay rejected! Okay, it just so happened that Berlin was our next destination, so I had little choice but to take some notice. Martine explained to me that Berlin appeared to hold a collective German guilt for atrocities committed during the Second World War. When I tuned-in with this situation, it came to me rather strongly that Berlin was the solar plexus of Germany, and that indeed this was where the collective negative emotions were stored and held. I also learned that it was possible I could help to release this!

Not the sort of thing I like to inner-learn. Assisting with the release of negative emotions in people during the five-day Intensives—okay. But the very idea of assisting the release of the collective negative emotions of millions of people was seriously off-putting, to say the least. How did I qualify for this? I lived on the other side of the planet, for goodness sake! And I could see no connection between my poor blocked nose and the negative emotions of Germany. Unfortunately, life seldom takes any notice of my grumbles or resistance, so I meekly accept my fate!

When we arrived in Berlin, it made an immediate and strong impression on me. Let me be clear about this: I am not a city person. Why millions of people could possibly want to be crammed into a relatively tiny space is completely beyond my comprehension. But . . . I liked Berlin. And I instantly knew that Berlin liked me. That was new! I had never before felt that a city *liked* me. Another strong impression: Most cities create wealth first, then grow. Berlin is growing first, then creating wealth. The emphasis is on *growth:* growth in people, in human consciousness, and in people living collectively. The emphasis in most cities is wealth first.

Although cities have been around for a very long time, people mostly live their rather isolated lives in the midst of millions. I felt that in Berlin, people were learning to live *connected* lives in the midst of millions. Very different. Energetically, Berlin is alive. All cities are teeming with life, but that is very different thing from a *city alive.*

Anyway, Berlin very clearly let me know that I could be of assistance in her whole unfolding newness as a city—if I would care to be involved. She asked me so nicely I could find no way to deny her.

I had no idea of what I would do, or how I would do it, so a mega-dose of trust was in order. I did know that it would happen during our five-day Intensive in Berlin, and that all the people at the Intensive would be involved. Having never been to this part of Germany before, I was not so well known here, although at the talk I gave, we had a full house. This was mostly thanks to the flyers put out by *team Roads* in Berlin—indomitable Marc, his lovely, capable wife, Janina, and the super-efficient, Elisabeth. However, I knew that the number of people participating in the Intensive would be lower than usual. And so it proved to be with about thirty-five perfect people.

The Intensive began—the players in place, the stage set—I had no clue!

As stated, my Intensives run for five days. I knew that the perfect timing for my attempt to assist Berlin with her emotional indigestion would be on the third day. It felt right. After our coffee break in the morning, I explained about my insight of Berlin being the solar plexus of Germany, and talked about the guilt issues that still prevail. The participants nodded vigorously. A few mentioned their own strong awareness of this, and all agreed about the obvious guilt issue in Germany. I then told them that I was proposing that the morning's inner-exercise would be about our collective guided attempt to redress this issue to the best of our ability. I told them that I had no definite plan, and that I would be flying on the wings of trust.

I would be their guide.

We do inner-exercises twice a day. They are designed to

give the participants an inner metaphysical connection with whatever our subject has been. This avoids getting bogged-down in intellectualisation. Although the inner-exercises follow certain themes to promote inner growth, they are also spontaneous, allowing for moment-by-moment change. And this happens. On this particular, cloudy morning in Berlin, the only procedure I followed was the one at the beginning of each inner-exercise, where I take people through a process to reach a higher state of consciousness. I do not imply that this always happens for every person, I mean that every person has the same *opportunity*. By waiting until the third day, most of the people have surmounted the challenges of maintaining the conscious imagination and clear focus required for the inner-exercises, and all is going well.

❊   ❊   ❊

This was the scenario I faced six months previously while on my spiritual teaching tour.

Things happened that morning, beyond anything I expected. Things I need to look at from a greater metaphysical perspective. Now I am ready to revisit that past event.

Relaxed in my study, I shift away from my physical reality as I bring my focus to Berlin.

With a small sigh, I step . . . *Between* . . . stepping into the Intensive room just as we/they are about to begin. Everyone is sitting relaxed, eyes closed, faces rather intent.

I look around the large room. Michael's energy is calm and relaxed. I am aware that he did not know that he would metaphysically revisit this while it was happening. To be absolutely clear, I am here physically six months ago as a participant, and I am here metaphysically in this present moment as an observer. (For clarity of communication, I will refer to the present metaphysical observer me as I, while the 'me' who is participating is Michael).

Michael is being translated into German by Elisabeth, who has a role in the organisation of Michael's German Intensives, as well as the translation. Together they are taking the participants through the initial procedure of raising the frequency of both body and spirit; this always happens prior to any inner journey or inner work. From my viewpoint, the room is very Light. Michael does not see metaphysically while in his physical body, so I am surprised at the intensity of Light that has nothing to do with daylight. Watching metaphysically, I am easily able to see the changing energy of most of the participants. As they sink deeper into a meditational space, so their auras change, reflecting a far greater inner connection with life than I see in a person who is only physically active. Only a few hover in a state of high mental energy, remaining disconnected. It is always a challenge for people to relax away from mind into inner silence and stillness.

Michael reaches the conclusion of the induction, and auras continue to radiate. By this stage he has taken the people through a procedure whereby each participant is now in their Light-body. He invites them to walk out of the physical room and to proceed to different areas of Berlin. I notice how much greater the human organisational ability of a Light-body person is compared with a physical-body person. If this was a physical process, each person would need to discuss where they were going so that other participants could all go to a different area. And with thirty-five people it would take a lot of time and discussion to get evenly distributed over Berlin. Metaphysically, it was smooth and easy. I admit I really did not fully realise the efficiency of metaphysical organisational abilities. All those involved simply moved into different parts of the city, and the distribution was perfect, without anyone even needing to think it through.

The next step was for everyone to focus on Self as a metaphysical Being of Love and Light, and to visualise and consciously imagine the Love/Light of Self growing larger and larger until it fills the whole city. This was not just connecting the Love/Light of each individual Self, but each individual Love/Light Self filling the whole entire city.

Michael is surprised when the Over-Lighting angel of Berlin makes its presence known. To his inner eye, it towers far into the sky, but to my metaphysical perceptual vision, it is a radiant energy of Light that fully embraces the city while reaching the clouds. In no way does it have a human shape, and yet I feel that it is filled with human compassion, with human Love, with human grace. It may not look in any way human, yet to me it holds the very finest of human qualities. This incredible energy Being deliberately connects its luminescent Light with the Light of all the Light-body participants there. The effect is absolutely amazing. Could the city of Berlin ever have experienced anything quite like this?

I bring a few of the Light-body participants into my perceptual vision, and for most of them the energy of their Light-body is greatly increased and magnified. I suspect that the lingering effects of this will be very beneficial to them.

Back in the room, aware that all is proceeding well, Michael is contemplating his next move. Without any prior warning, in his startled inner vision, the room abruptly fills with scintillating Light. I can more clearly see that which Michael is almost shocked to inner-see.

Near one corner of the room is the Archangel Uriel, Light pouring from him in shades of gold unseen by human eyes. To my surprise he smiles at me, inclining his head while also smiling toward Michael. He knows! In the opposite corner is Archangel Michael, radiating Light in a wide range of electric blues—colours beyond any spectrum I have ever seen. He also is smiling in acknowledgement. Near another corner of the room is standing the Master St Germain, his Light more as pure illumination than any real colour. His Light is not radiating in the way of the Archangels, but rather it fills in all the space around him. His smile at me is far more of a human nature, somehow more tangible. And finally, near another corner is a figure that really catches my attention. Standing in a dynamic, yet completely relaxed way is the Master Sananda. He watches me gravely, yet his energy field is twinkling in a surreal manner.

Michael knows this Being is Sananda. Knowing who they are accompanies their presence, but he had no idea that Sananda is the spiritual name of the Master Jesus. In fact, I learned this only yesterday, so I am not now surprised. Michael has never involved himself with any research into the Ascended Masters, nor has he metaphysically investigated them. What surprises Michael at the moment this is all happening, is that Hilarion is not one of the four Masters present. Hilarion is the one Master that Michael has often had contact with.

Telepathically speaking for all of them, St Germain communicates with Michael. *We are here to offer assistance. This healing is of a human initiation and worthy of our support.*

I watch the expression of surprise cross Michael's face, and he silently voices his thanks.

The Light in the room grows brighter by degrees, and I am aware of the radiance literally penetrating the physical bodies in the room. Suddenly, the Great Beings are no longer visible, but their Light is joining the Light energy of the Over-Lighting angel of Berlin, and connecting /joining with the Light-body Self of all the human Light-body participants.

Hugely empowered, the Light has all of Berlin bathed within it. As I observe this, I am mildly surprised that Berlin is not physically glowing, because it certainly is on a metaphysical level. But no, physically it appears to be just the same: gloomy clouds and patchy rain. But of course, this is about energy and people. When I bring my vision to people, walking the streets, laughing, hurrying, busy talking, I notice that each aura is slightly brighter. Looking at a few energy-signatures, I see that the more aware and conscious the person, the more they are affected by the Love/Light. I look for the generation that is more affected by the memories of the war—the people who feel the guilt, who continue to look for the rights and wrongs of war and life. For many of these people, life is a war, and sadly, they are their own enemy.

Unfortunately, these people who most need it are usually the most resistant to the energy of Love/Light. Despite themselves, the Love/Light is persistently clinging around their rather drab energy fields. A few of them are becoming more open. I can see that guilt over long-past war crimes is strongly connected with personal guilt for many of these people. One guilt has seeped into and connected with another guilt. Guilt is a very negative energy. How can you define one guilt as different from another? You cannot. Negative emotions are negative emotions, and no matter how the intellect may separate them, giving differing reasons and causes for different guilts, emotionally it is all in one hurting bag. Some of these unfortunates are very closed, but a greater proportion of them have varying degrees of openness in their energy fields. And it is into these people that the power of Love/ Light is making a difference. Maybe not now, possibly not even in this incarnation, but in another incarnation the timeless effect of this Love/Light will outwork and re-make these people in many subtle, life-changing ways.

Inner-seeing the incredible radiance that is highlighting Berlin, Michael, who remains in verbal communication with all the participants physically in the room, now suggests that they spread their Love/Light to encompass all of Germany and Europe. It is not like watching a tsunami of Love/Light sweeping over the land; rather, it is as if an incredibly powerful illumination has abruptly been switched on encompassing all of Europe. The healing Light of Love bathes all the land in a higher energy. I become aware that an energy of this level, precipitated by a small, simple group of people, could not have happened on this scale prior to the frequency shift that took place during the time of the 2012 Change. If ever I needed to see the proof of what humanity is capable of in the realms of Light, I am looking at it. Okay, it has become far greater because of the input of Great Beings, but the precipitating Light that preceded the illumination of a spiritual Lighthouse was a very human Light.

Michael has decided to include Britain now, because of its involvement in the Second World War. As he speaks the words of inclusion, I see the vast Light leap across the North Sea, flooding the country in a single moment. I also see that there are people in Britain who, while not carrying guilt, are crucifying themselves on emotional crosses carved during other terrible years of war. The Second World War did not create *new* atrocities, it simply continued the old expressions of hate, of anger, and of bloody-minded self-righteousness that grew and prospered in so many wars. And they have continued in the Korean War, the Vietnam War, and on and on. Hate has no use-by date! If we are foolish enough to learn to hate, then it is our creation until we learn to *Love*. Hate is a human creation, and it is always self-contained. We can sow the seeds of hate elsewhere, and other hurting people can create their own hate, but, I repeat, it is *always* self-contained. Where there is Love, hate cannot exist. I will go so far as to say that even though hate is one of the most powerful of all illusions, when unconditional Love is finally embraced—hate has never existed.

For maybe a linear hour, the Light potential of Change holds all Europe and Britain in its benevolent energy, then slowly and smoothly it gradually decreases in power. I am aware that the Masters have withdrawn. Michael also realises this, and instructs the participants to allow their Love/Light energy to slowly decrease in size, withdrawing it back until once again it simply encompasses only Berlin.

A pause for a few minutes, then Michael guides them to bring their Love/Light energy back to Self, guiding them back into the room of the Intensive, finally bringing them to the place where the inner experience comes to an end. As I glance around prior to my departure, I notice that every person who fully participated has tears trickling down their cheeks—and this was most people. It would be no exaggeration to say that many of them looked emotionally shaken and shocked.

Metaphysically, I step . . . *Between* . . . and back to my study.

*   *   *

The physical me continued sitting with the other Intensive participants for maybe twenty minutes before I felt ready to face the physical world. I was simultaneously shocked and thrilled by all that had taken place, and I gave sincere thanks to the great Beings who had accompanied us. I had been blessed and honoured to conduct a mighty orchestra indeed!

When I left the room, more than half the participants were still sitting with closed eyes. A few were sobbing quietly—a couple not so quietly. I am reasonably sure that some of them had no lunch that day, unable to eat. Marc, who energetically was deeply involved, looked as white as a sheet. I learned later that he had been vomiting, so deeply did the cleansing energy reach into him.

In no way am I claiming that we healed all the German guilt in the solar plexus of Berlin. However, I am definitely saying that whatever actually happened on a metaphysical level in Berlin on that day has created ripples of Change that will continue for a long time. A city of people cannot receive the blessings and benediction of two Great Masters, two Great Archangels, and the Great Over-Lighting angel of Berlin and remain unaffected. Even if, as a group of people, we had expanded our Love/Light over Berlin without any other assistance, this too would have had a very beneficial and healing effect. Never underrate the human power of Love, of which we are all so capable. As it was, not only Berlin, but the whole of Europe and the UK received a rare and wondrous gift of healing energy.

While my involvement with the solar plexus of Germany was certainly unusual, I also had another very odd experience during the Intensive tour the same year. This experience, however, was entirely personal. For as long as I can remember, I have detested the sound of drums. Actually, it is not quite that simple. When I hear the traditional drums on our television broadcast of the annual Edinburgh Royal Military Tattoo, I am thrilled by the blood-stirring sound, especially when accompanied by the bagpipes. But if I ever hear the Native American Indian style of drumming, I get a deep gut-feeling of pain and apprehension. So I avoid it. I walk away.

This unexpected experience came to me on two levels: personal and physical *and* personal and metaphysical. I will share what happened at the time, rather than metaphysically revisit it.

We were in Switzerland doing our Intensive in the mountains at Zentrum der Einheit Schweibenalp. The site of the centre apparently dates back to the times of the ancient Druids. A very beautiful area with stunning views over a glacial lake. Our program begins at nine o'clock in the morning, finally ending at six o'clock in the evening, when we have dinner. The evenings are free to enjoy.

During our travels, Carolyn and I have picked up what we smilingly describe as a fair number of our cosmic children, with the occasional brother or sister. Jerome is one of our cosmic children. While he is a skilled practitioner of Chinese medicine and a martial arts teacher, he is also skilled with—you guessed it—Native American Indian drums! He had announced to the group that after dinner he would be drumming on the fourth evening of the Intensive, and that all were welcome to listen and/ or participate.

As it so happened, that evening Carolyn and I had been invited to a Chinese tea ceremony, offered to us by Oliver, our Swiss translator. Oliver is a river that runs deep, so we were happy to attend his private ceremony. To keep this brief, I learned more about the Chinese philosophy of tea in the next hour than I had ever dreamed existed—and Oliver only skimmed the surface. He was very accomplished in the way he conducted the tea ceremony, and he created a whole new respect and appreciation in Carolyn and me for the ancient Chinese tradition of tea.

When this was concluded, we headed back toward our bedroom. Jerome was drumming in the large seminar room in the same building, so we entered the room and quietly sat to listen. Why I did this I had no idea, for I almost immediately felt very uncomfortable. Naturally, Carolyn loved it, completely enchanted by Jerome's obvious skill. I sat and endured it, wondering why I was doing this, instead of just leaving the room. He soon finished, and smiling at me, asked how I was feeling. He knew of my dislike of drumming.

I told him I was feeling as pained and uncomfortable as always.

Most of the Intensive participants had been listening to him, and obviously enjoyed it. After answering a few of their questions, he began drumming again, and chanting.

I kept telling myself to leave the room, but for some perverse reason, I remained seated. As he moved deeper into the energy of the drumming, gaining in depth and intensity, I closed my eyes, letting myself metaphysically go. I say go, but I felt as though I was strongly taken, not with violence, but with clarity and power. Abruptly, I am metaphysically watching myself as a Native American Indian of maybe a couple of centuries ago. I have no clear identity for the tribe, but it could have been Sioux. I know that I have had several incarnations in the Hopi tribe, but this was a very different people. From my experience, the Hopi were more spiritually focused in life; this was predominantly a warrior tribe.

I was at the beginning of undertaking a warrior initiation. My metaphysical intuition tells me that this initiation was the final step in being a highly graded warrior. It would make me something like a warrior first class, or senior warrior, or warrior chief, something of this ilk. Certainly it was voluntary, and equally certainly only a few extremists like me volunteered to go through such an appalling and gruelling initiation. It was considered the highest honour.

I watched them cut under the muscles on each side of my chest, and force a shaped and sharpened stick under the large strap of muscle and sinew that goes from the shoulder to the pectorals. (Sorry, this is my best description). Following this, they tied long woven leather ropes onto the sticks, and finally connected me in this way to a small tree. The idea was that while standing, I lean my full weight on the sticks that pierced my chest.

As a metaphysical observer of this, I cannot say that I felt the physical pain. I did not. But energetically I connected with that long ago torment for which I had volunteered. In the way of timelessness, I metaphysically watched and connected with the whole process. Physically, I was not allowed to collapse, that was failure. Somehow I kept on my feet, enduring an extraordinary level of pain for the required twenty-four hours. Throughout this whole time a number of the other warriors kept an unfailing drumbeat on the go, along with a monotone of chant! I was aware of having quite a few physical hallucinations. I was able to metaphysically see the hallucinations that my physical self was having. One was of myself as an Indian boy. I climbed to the top of a mountain, eating no food and drinking no water. It took me four very tough days of endurance to make it. It occurred to me as I observe this that my life of initiations had begun rather early.

In another hallucination—or were they flashbacks?—I was a teenager with a teenage girl. We had just finished making young, vigorous, wonderful love, when I saw her father hovering over us, his face scowling like a thunder cloud. I knew I was in trouble, because for some reason this girl was forbidden to me. Next moment, my head was jerked back and my throat was cut. I died convulsing in complete and total shock.

After my time of intense pain was finished, the men cut me down, and laid me gently on some bedding. They extracted the sticks from my hot and swollen flesh, and a herbal concoction was applied to the ugly wounds. I was then allowed to rest and recover. At this stage the drum beats changed. Knowing nothing about drumming, all I can say is that the sound became a bit more upbeat! The chant also matched this, with less monotone and more variation.

This is when, for me, everything went wrong. My wounds became very seriously infected. After a couple of days raving in a high hot fever, my body went very cold. This was when I died.

The metaphysical me of today observed my metaphysical Light-body of then leave the physical shell. We looked at each other, I with enquiry. He shook his head, sighed heavily, and stayed with the body, as though in some way anchored to it.

It was at this moment that Jerome brought his drumming and chanting to a close.

What amazed me was the synchronicity between his drumming and chanting and the way it had sounded in my experience of the past. While not identical, they sounded horribly similar.

I told Jerome what had taken place. He looked very surprised.

"Your drumming and chanting was perfect. It somehow initiated the experience and maybe kept it moving along. A bit like the glue that held it all together."

He replied. "I just followed my Indian guide. He was the initiator."

"Ah, I see. Now I know who pulled me in. You have a powerful guide."

After a few people asked some questions which Jerome

answered, he began again. This time without the drum, he used a rattle to accompany his chant. I found this to be a pleasant sound. After listening for some minutes, I once again closed my eyes.

Immediately, I was back at the moment of my earlier physical death.

The metaphysical me of that time was still somehow anchored to the physical body. Why, I had no idea. However, I was here as an observer, so I trusted that it would all work out. I listened while Jerome shook the rattles and chanted, his voice strongly rising and falling.

As I watched, two large rattlesnakes came slithering out from among the surrounding rocks and scrub, sliding gracefully toward my dead body. Each snake seemed to be in very close coordination with the other, moving almost as though two parts of a single snake. On reaching my body, each snake slithered up and along my outstretched arms, where I lay sprawled on the earth. As they reached my shoulders, they paused, and I noticed that somehow they were now coiled around each of my arms, firmly gripping them.

Wondering what was going to happen, I continued watching. There was no active role for me. I was an observer only. Suddenly, from some unknown cue, both rattlesnakes began to shake their tail-rattles, and I was aware of the sound being in perfect synchronicity with the rattle that Jerome was using. Only then did it occur to me that his rattle was the same sound as a rattlesnake's rattle. I also became aware of a powerful unseen presence, of some energy watching, and maybe guiding, the unfolding events. I realised that this was Jerome's Indian guide.

The snakes rattled their rattles for a few long moments; then again, in perfect unison, they each struck the open festering wound closest to them, one on each side of my chest. Even though metaphysical, I could feel their venom coursing not through my body, but into and around the wounds, and into my heart. I knew I was feeling this through the metaphysical Light-body still bound to the dead physical body, and connected to my metaphysical body of today. There was/is no *true* separation.

From my metaphysical vision, the rattlesnake venom was

like a liquid gold flowing through the wounds and corrupted flesh, and into my non-beating heart. I watched as the rattlesnake venom swiftly killed and destroyed the infection which had killed me. In that moment it came into my awareness that in a Hopi incarnation I had nurtured a long and honouring association with the rattlesnakes in the area in which I had lived. It seemed that I, in turn, was being honoured.

I watched the venom clean my whole body of infection. Even though my physical body was dead, the red inflammation around the wounds swiftly faded, leaving my skin brown and healthy. There came a moment when the rattlesnakes abruptly stopped rattling, swiftly withdrawing. At that moment Jerome also stopped his rattling and chanting.

The metaphysical Light-body which had been anchored was abruptly released, and simply walked away from my dead physical body without a backward glance. I was healed.

I gave sincere thanks to Jerome's Indian guide. He had set me free from a past life bond of disturbance that I had not known existed.

I shared the rest of the story with Jerome and, of course, the other people who were in the room. And I thanked Jerome most sincerely.

"You have a *very* wise and powerful Indian guide," I told him.

I listened to another session of drumming, and all was well. *I enjoyed it.*

Okay, bed time!

Chapter Seven

The Drifting Veils of Light

I have long had an interest in agriculture. By this, I mean soil and animal husbandry, not the modern approach of agribusiness. Most of this is an offence against Nature, an offence that will one day require recompense. For many years now, humanity has been in the process of creating a debt to Mother Earth, a debt based in the detrimental extraction methods of coal, minerals, oil and gas. However, agribusiness is not only the ruthless, negative exploitation of the forests, the soil and Nature in general, it has also become a violation against humanity. The ruthless few have created an enormous debt that is owed to the many.

A debt that will *inevitably* have to be paid . . . consciousness demands balance.

We are not a wise humanity. Homo sapiens we are not! Ever since we unwittingly took the path of separation instead of the path of Oneness, we have become increasingly isolated from Nature, each other, and from our own selves. Spiritual enlightenment perfectly describes that moment when I took the quantum leap away from the subconscious illusion of identity and separation into the conscious Truth of individuality and Oneness. This is why we are here on Earth. It is the journey for every one of us—from illusion to Truth. We can delay the journey—most do—and we can linger along the way, playing our games of illusion, believing this or that, but the journey is always with us, always waiting for our conscious attention, utterly immutable.

I sometimes think about world issues. We all do! Such issues are all based in illusions—but they are illusions that affect us all. Because I am an author with an available electronic profile, I am easily contacted. I get too many links sent to me about the wrongs of people against people, people against Nature, people against . . . ! Just a few of them I read, or watch. I then remind myself that in every moment of our lives every person is creating the content and direction of every moment of our ever, ongoing lives. In other words, while we watch YouTube, or read material that makes us angry, generating thoughts and feelings that are judgemental, critical, and aggressive against other people—no matter who— we will continue to attract negative and exploitative situations into our own daily lives. I describe this as living in the lower levels of unwitting subconscious and sub-emotional creation.

I sometimes wonder what this all looks like on an energetic level. I have questions regarding the fields of energy of Nature and humanity in view of the new energies of today. I wonder about what is energetically happening to all the many people who are in constant self-conflict. What is energetically happening to the negative exploiters of Earth and its people? How does one energetic value mix and mingle with another? We have a well-known biblical quote: "Blessed are the meek for they shall inherit the Earth." My translation of meek is those people who embody and express humility, tolerance, and gentleness. In our present time of huge metaphysical Change, what is the future for opposite types of people, the meek and the ruthless? For ages these two human expressions have inhabited the same Earth, the same cities, the same villages, the same cultures. In view of current Change, how will this be reconciled?

I am a person of inquiry rather than questions. Questions

seek an answer, and answers can become conclusions and beliefs, fixed and stuck. Inquiry seeks more to explore a subject, keeping it ongoing and open-ended. Much healthier! This is the attitude I am going to take: to explore the relevant fields of energy without creating fixed conclusions.

These were my musings one sunny morning. Although I often have my time of musing, I rarely have questions. I tend to muse—and directly know. This morning, however, although I am musing and knowing, I also want to *experience* my knowing on the deepest level that is possible for me, going beyond the intellect into an experiential situation—as is my wont!

Much of this I have been sharing with Pan.

"I started off thinking about our exploited agriculture and how it has become agribusiness, but it all boils down to a small percentage of humanity negatively exploiting a large percentage of humanity. I plan to overview this from a metaphysical viewpoint. Any comments?"

'There is nothing outside Self.' This is one of your famous quotes that you like to use when public speaking. I suggest you explore this on a deeper level.

"Yes . . . I'll go along with this and see what happens. We are each responsible for our own creations in life. But Mr. and Mrs. Public do not see it this way."

Then take your journey and share it with them.

"Mr. and Mrs. Public wear two hats. One hat is new; the other hat is very old. Most people wear the old hats . . . and they do not read my type of books!"

But what you write will be out there energetically . . . yes!

I sigh. "Yes, another undeniable Truth from my beloved teacher."

Your infinitely patient and kindly teacher.

"And humble?"

Oh yes, such is the vastness of my power, I am also an expression of humility.

I laugh. "My gratitude for all you have given me is . . . indescribable."

See to your journey. Trust that you will step between perfectly.
"Yes, beloved teacher . . . always I trust."

         ❋   ❋   ❋

I have learned that I cannot always go where I want to. Mostly, not always. Sitting physically relaxed, my eyes closed, aware of my Light-body, I focus on the energy of agriculture.

Stepping . . . *Between* . . . I emerge over a forest that I instantly feel to be true wilderness.

Hmm, what has this got to do with agriculture?

Hovering in my Light-body over the forest, I realise that I had better let go of my strong agricultural focus. Why I am here, of all places, I have no idea, but it is as it is! Everything will unfold in perfect timing. Sitting in the lotus position high above the forest, I allow life to show me what it is I need to see/perceive, and to metaphysically experience.

Patience . . . very good . . . Mixael. The inner words are a chuckling, faraway whisper.

I sit in the air for a timeless time, observing the forest below and the unusual energy it contains—and which contains it. Moving deeper into the essence of the forest, I am no longer certain if it exists in our normal frame of reality. It has a quality of energy that feels too high, too fine for our everyday reality. I am aware of wildlife in the forest. I cannot see them, but I feel their presence and see their energy fields moving within the forest.

Sitting in the lotus position, I feel very content. Slowly and gently I bring my focus toward clarity, seeking nothing, needing nothing, content with the fullness of nothing. This is a state of being that is truly dynamic. I feel as though I am sinking deeper into . . . what? A knowing? A seeing? Maybe it is the gathering of clarity? I feel . . . something . . . hovering around me, flitting in and out of my awareness.

I do nothing. If possible, I relax even deeper, both physically and metaphysically.

Very slowly, it seems as though I am seeing/perceiving more than is usual. I am aware of veils of Light-energy draping themselves over the forest. They stir as though from some gentle wayward breeze. I sigh very softly—and the veils in my vicinity ripple gently. Hmm?

I have learned there are two states of waiting. The most common waiting is passive, mostly accompanied by boredom. Then there is a dynamic waiting, fully active, fully involved. When younger, I was familiar with the passive, boring waiting; with the wisdom of age, I am more familiar with dynamic waiting. Now I am discovering another expression of waiting. This is not easy to describe; I will call it *creative waiting*. I am waiting for the energy of the forest—the energy of the forest is waiting for me. Each is aware of the other, and that awareness is creating the potential held within the waiting. Neither wishes to impose itself on the other; each is content for the unfolding energy of the moment to reveal the newness the moment is creating. Those in my family who tell me I can be rather impatient should play *this* game of patience!

I focus on the veils of energy. It seems obvious that they are made of Light—the Light of creation, not sunlight, or such. As far as I can see, all over the forest, the veils are rippling. This is not stationary rippling—they are rippling as they move, slowly changing their positions in relation to the forest. Thoughts of 'why' struggle to be born, but I pay them no heed. As I focus on the veils, I feel my focus gently moved by some energy to refocus *behind* the veils. These veils are only visible to metaphysical sight, and even then they are not obvious. And apparently even this inner-seeing needs its own education. Despite the veils of Light catching and holding my attention, what is beyond them or behind them is what surprises me.

As the veils of Light move across this forest, every leaf on every shrub, tree, and tiny plant is Changed. I can feel it and energetically see it. Every blade of grass, even the mosses and lichen and fungi, all are subtly Changed. Not changed in a way obvious to human sight, but in the way of energy. As I become more and more attuned to the creative moment, continuously releasing wanting to know, wanting to understand, in fact, releasing wanting—so clarity is drawing back my own veils that hide a deeper inner-seeing. I see what appears as an energy radiation in colours of such subtlety I have no names for them. My best attempt is a complex range from indigos to violets. I feel the radiation of these colours as fragments of soft Light, somehow tickling and caressing my deeper metaphysical senses.

On the impulse of a half-born insight, I take myself considerably higher into the sky, making visible a bigger view of Earth. And everywhere I see the moving veils, intangible to all of Earth's people except for the most exquisite of evolved human sensitivity. Insight reveals that the forest over which I linger is, indeed, of a higher than normal Earth vibration. By this, I mean that it is a forest seldom visited by people, seldom disturbed by any human energy.

I attune to this knowing. Now I am watching frames of time as pure energy held in the moving veils of Light. Rather than seeing the illusion of linear time—which is real for physicality—it is as though time is a pack of cards being shuffled into a new order by some invisible sovereign hand. Some of this forest is changing to a finer and higher mystical level, while simultaneously some of it is plunging deeper into the density of a physical realm. I get the feeling that, for me, this forest represents the Change that is taking place on Earth. The forest of a higher frequency will now be unavailable to hunters and back-packers. It will be more elusive to find, somehow turning people away from these remote areas of a higher energy. They will more easily find the availability of the lower frequency forests. And yet, paradoxically, both will also occupy the same places. And if that sounds crazy, so be it. It is all about the compatibility of human and forest consciousness!

New Age people talk of a higher frequency Earth; it is easy enough to speak of this and believe its truth. However, this higher frequency is still in the process of re-creation; it is a process of Life, a reverent process, no matter how powerful or destructive it may appear when it becomes volcanic. As I have often written, destruction is the de-structuring that invariably precedes a re-structuring. These physically invisible, intangible veils of Light, drifting over the Earth, are fully attuned to appropriate Change. They *are* Change. They are Change in communication with consciousness. Where the Earth frequency holds strongly to an old energy, the old is reinforced; in another area with a higher energy, the new is given birth. No right, no wrong; it is as it is.

This is also happening in people.

I am watching a couple of hunters moving through the forest. I can easily read their energy-signatures. One man, young and idealistic, is not emotionally involved in the hunt. He is here under the pressure of emotional obligation. Spiritually, he wants nothing to do with killing animals, and is determined to make enough noise to indicate his presence. The other man is the uncle to the younger man. He is determined that the centuries-old family tradition of hunting shall be passed on; it is his duty to ensure this. He is a caring man, sensitive to shoot for a clean kill. Emotionally he is fully involved. And herein lies the difference between the two men.

I get the impression that the veils of Light are aware of the two men. While I can see no differences in the Light-veils, I can see that they have very different effects as they energetically pass over the land and forest. A veil moves up behind the younger man, enshrouding him in Light for a brief moment, then continues to move ahead of him. Everything living is affected. He is now of a higher frequency, in an area of higher frequency. Unbeknown to him, in that moment his life is forever changed. Already he feels deeper emotions, touched by the veils of Change, but mentally he is bewildered by these deeper feelings that are new to him. As he continues forward, a perfect deer steps into a clearing ahead of him. The perfect shot. His rifle has been held in the orthodox, relaxed, 'at ready' position for quite a while, and his honed reflexes bring the rifle smoothly to his shoulder.

The young, yet mature stag stops in the clearing, still as a statue and stares toward him.

Without hesitation, the young man unslings his rifle and puts it down. Kneeling on one knee, he watches the stag, his breath held in awe. How many stags has he seen at death? Too many. This is the first moment that he actually connects with the *life* in a stag. He feels the energy of life, he feels the touch of life, and for the first time ever, he consciously connects with the *life* in himself.

He recognises the connection, the Oneness.

Humbled, he bows his head in gratitude, continuing to kneel in silent wonder. He *knows* that he is Changed—and he embraces it.

Not far away another Light veil moves through the energy of the older man. He pauses, feeling an odd moment of—something—then with a shrug, dismisses it. Change passes him by. His forests will always carry the old energy that supports the person he is. His life will continue in old patterns, old habits, and he will find it difficult to accept that his favourite nephew will never hunt again. He was offered Change, briefly felt its creative touch, but he could not embrace it.

I sigh. It was not yet the right moment of timing in his consciousness. We each create this timing, and not being aware of this slows down the process.

I watch one probability of their future unfold. We each carry our probable past and our probable future in the moment, but we are not aware of it. The young man never forgets his forest experience. He meets and marries a woman of equal insight and passion for the newness of life and, skipping the details, his life goes in a completely different direction than if he had shot the deer. One simple action of non-violence in perfect timing has a profound long-term effect on his life. I see Change rippling through all his past, changing it—and on into his future which is now the result of Change. And yet, past and future are simply words of reference demanded by linear time. In a greater reality—which I am seeing—the past and future are held in perfect collocation in the ever ongoing moment. You cannot affect the moment without equally affecting the past and future.

The uncle, a good, kind man, continues with more of the same. Not once did he ever feel that a moment of opportunity passed him by. He and his nephew remain as friends, but with the nephew moving into a new wave of energy, a higher frequency, they gradually find that they have less and less in common.

I am aware that Nature is conscious of Change, and consciously changing. As I scan a wider picture of the veils of Light as they drift across the Earth, I see that the whole planet is lifting its frequency. What a paradox! The whole of planet Earth is moving with a new and higher frequency, yet many huge areas of Earth will not reflect this Change. They will continue expressing the old so that more-of-the-same humanity will be able to continue. If all the Earth and all its expression were on the new, higher frequency, only the humans that are of that frequency would be able to live and thrive within it. It is worthy of note that the emerging, new frequency more strongly expresses the consciousness of Love.

In truth, none of this is actually new to me, but I am seeing/experiencing the effects of Change in a powerful, new way. I watch change in the actual way that plants grow, moving from a more physically induced growth to a more metaphysically induced process. I marvel at how a forest can hold both the new, higher frequency of life and the old, lower frequency simultaneously. Lower does not mean bad, or negative, or wrong, it simply means that it is a lower frequency of energy, allowing for the synchronisation of similar energy to continue its usual expression. And that is the key; usual—not new.

I briefly wonder if the veils of Light move randomly, but I realise that nothing is by accident or chance—or random. Life is the purposeful expression of consciousness.

With this insight, I cast my vision to a farm of the near future, where a farmer knowingly uses a new form of control— no, not control, but dominion. Very different. A farmer cannot take dominion of the land before he or she takes dominion of self. Self dominion comes first. In a modern dictionary, dominion and dominance now mean virtually the same thing—typical of the modern intellect. Modern life is about controlling by dominance. My mid-century *Chamber's Twentieth Century Dictionary*, links dominion with sovereignty. I agree. Energetically, taking dominion over self is literally the same as taking sovereignty over your life. Controlling is an expression of force; dominion is an expression of power. Very different. Dominion stems from the higher frequency of life, dominance comes from the lower frequency. Aware dominion is born from the intelligence of natural cooperation. It has absolutely nothing to do with control or dominance!

I am watching this farmer during his time of inner change. By this I do not mean Change induced by the veils of Light, but by his observations and common sense in his life as a farmer.

The veils do not really induce change, they accentuate Change that has, or is, taking place in a person. The veils act in accordance with the expressing consciousness. They affect Nature according to either its natural state which is compatible with a higher frequency, or its chemically induced growth which is compelled to a lower frequency. This farmer has observed that the further he goes along the chemical path of agribusiness, the more money he is required to spend on ever-increasing problems in his crops—more persistent weeds, more resistant insect pests, far more fungicides required, and on and on. He can also see that the quality of his land is on a very expensive downhill spiral. The structure of his soil is becoming increasingly fragmented with very low humus levels, and the organic matter content is steadily moving toward zero. He realises that this is also reflected in the diminishing health of himself and his young family.

He is a courageous man. He steps away from the confines of modern agribusiness and begins to explore other ways of farming. He finds many other answers; all were obscure while he was in denial, yet they are all too obvious when the mind is open. He reads about the various modes of organic and biodynamic farming and visits a few bio-farms scattered around in his area. He is shocked and amazed by the differences between their soil and his. They have a topsoil depth of about sixty centimetres. On his farm, only a few kilometres away and virtually the same soil type, the topsoil depth is about six centimetres. And he knows the implications of this. While the structure of their soil is improving each year, his soil structure is rapidly deteriorating. And this soil deterioration is accompanied by the failing health of his livestock and crops.

He attends meetings, talks to the farmers and soaks up new knowledge like a sponge. His whole position as a farmer is quickly changing. Less obvious to him are the inner changes taking place within: a new openness, new insights—and the new recognition that a farmer and his/her land are deeply linked in consciousness. The full extent of just how deep and real that link, is still waiting to be discovered in his future.

Now I see what I have been watching for.

As he begins to apply the principles of Steiner's biodynamic farming, so he is attracting the Light veils of Change. As I inner-knew, they do not move randomly. They are attracted by people, or repelled by them. I have yet to see how this works within Nature. Can Nature attract or repel the veils of Change? With the veils sweeping over his land, a higher frequency is invoked. I wonder if he is the attractant, or if this is all about synchronicity? Even as I frame the question, I see that *he* is the magnet to the Nature of his land.

I suspect Pan may be over-lighting my experience because as I watch this transformed farmer, I see his energy-signature is changing significantly. And as this changes, I am seeing right down into the profile of his soil structure. This is new! The micro-organic life within the soil is also changing its own minute energy-signatures. As his energy-signature changes individually, so it changes the soil life en masse. And as it changes, so it proliferates rapidly within a soil that is now treated in a way that respects and nurtures soil life. All these Changes are not instantaneous; they are taking place over a matter of a year or three. I am observing this from a metaphysical frame not based in linear time. Even the farmer's wife is affected. The change in her husband's farming was first seen as a change in techniques, but she gradually sees that his farming is reflecting the change in him. Not the reverse.

She finds that she likes the changes in him, finally realising that these changes are also positively affecting her. She, too, embraces newness. The crops are affected, all farm life is affected. And this is not just the farmer's crops. Everything that has life on the farm has a new and higher energy. The farmer has taken to walking his land with bare feet, feeling the pulse of life within the soil moving into his own heart, his soul. He marvels at the difference that unfolds with each passing year. His state of consciousness is now a new nutriment for the land—an enrichment.

Only very slowly does he comprehend that he is now *connected* with the pulse of life. And with the dawning of this awareness comes the discovery that most of humanity is *disconnected*. He visits other bio-farms, slightly disconcerted to find that for some farmers, biodynamic farming is a successful technique, yet they remain disconnected. He finds others who, like himself, are clearly connected. He visits many regular farmers of modern agriculture, finding that almost all of them are completely disconnected from the pulse of life. He learns to know the *feeling* of connectedness in people, and is saddened to encounter it but rarely. Happy as they are together, even his wife lacks it. He turns to public speaking, attempting to raise an awareness of being connected *with life*, as opposed to disconnected *from life*. He looks for understanding of what, for him, is profoundly obvious. He finds ridicule. He finds scorn. He finds derision. He learns that he is now a radical. He slowly learns that while he has discovered a Truth, this is a Truth that can only be recognised and accepted in perfect timing. He has created his own timing. Speaking a Truth to people outside their timing, and then expecting them to understand it and live it, is rather like talking to a fish about breathing air, and then expecting the fish to live out of the water.

Several years have passed by now, and he quietly acknowledges his new insight. Like some others have before him, he transforms his farm into a teaching centre for those new people who wish to learn new ways. And in the trickle of their own perfect timing, people come.

This farmer is by no means the only one to go through the transition of Change, but they are the few rather than the many. And *real* Change *is* a transition. It is virtually a transition from one reality to another. Just as a dormant acorn holds the potential of growing into a huge oak tree, yet it remains dormant until the conditions of germination and growth are induced. And so it is with humans. Unlike an acorn, however, we are the triggers of our own growth. The prime factor is whether we are *open* to change and growth, or attached to the repetition of more-of-the-same.

Shifting my position away from above the forest and farm, I relocate over a small city.

My intent is to see if the veils of Light, of Change, are as active over cities and industries as they are over the forests and land, where there are relatively few people. I scan the energy over the city. This is very different from the rural areas! I am familiar with city energy, having described its Chaos—the engine that drives, and Order—the stability of structure, in my previous trilogy of books. But this is my first in-depth investigation of city energy since the end of 2012—that time when nothing *appeared* to happen! This is a city of approximately two million people. It is nothing like as speedy, stressed or hectic a city as those with ten million plus.

The veils of Light are here—nothing can deny their reality— but people can certainly avoid being affected by them; it only requires a closed mind. But to be clear, it is all about our personal states of consciousness. What is happening in this small city is very similar to the forest. The whole city area now has the duality of a new frequency energy field in collocation with the old energy field frequency. It is very obvious that each and every person, by their thoughts, emotions, and actions, is choosing which energy field they are now living in, or will very soon live in. There is no good or bad, right or wrong. It is as it is—we are as we are!

I also see that every person's energy field and energy signature is strengthened. The newness in the aware people is strongly empowered, while the more-of-the-sameness in other people is equally strengthened. Those of the new become more open, less attached, while the reverse is true for the others. As I look into the so-called future, I can see where this is taking us. As I so often state, all that which we call the future is a probability based in this moment—which also changes our past! Why? How? Let me explain this. We have two basic linear directions, the past and the future. Both are malleable, constantly changing under the stimulus of our moment-by-moment living. History and memory records only a distorted version of our physical past, and never our *meta*physical past! Interestingly, reality and creativity record only our metaphysical moment, never our physical past! And it is the metaphysical moment which is always in flux and change. We place very grave limits on ourselves when we use our memory to recall our physical past, thus recreating our new moment in the image of what is actually a false representation of our past. Generally, it is a sub-emotional attachment!

As people of free will, we are now in the process of creating two probable futures—the burgeoning new and the stagnating old. It is most probable that the many will journey on the old subconscious, sub-emotional path, unwittingly clinging to their past history, to their sameness. The few will travel the path of newness. Neither path is better nor worse; each reflects the person's developing priorities, gleaned from their many physical incarnations. Even now, people are moving from the old to the new as they increasingly empathise with the higher frequencies, the new impulses.

I watch as the veils of Light sweep through shopping centres, through huge office buildings, through outlying industrial areas. I see the energy fields of the buildings take on this strange, shifting duality. Just as there will be forests that repel the hunters and backpackers, so now many people who work in some of the buildings will unexpectedly be made redundant, sacked, laid off!

I can see that many people whose energy-field is a reflection of the new, will no longer be able to fit into the workplace of the old energy fields. For some, this will mean instant and abrupt dismissal, with a very poor excuse for being dismissed. Others will clearly realise they are heading toward a use-by date, and they will know this without being overly concerned. Some will fearfully resist change, and their fear will push them more toward the old, even though their hope and dreams take them toward the new. While Nature flows easily *with* the new energies, humans attempt to understand them, to rationalise them, to explain them—rather than trust and flow *with* them.

I see large, multi-level office buildings where some levels are becoming a mix of the old and the new, both with the potential to progress or regress, while some levels are purely the new, where the sameness consciousness will no longer be able to fully express. Equally, there are buildings where sameness prevails throughout, and all those people who are expressing the new will be unable to work in such places. I can see plenty of resistance to all this both from the old and the new, but Change is happening and there is no turning back. And, of course, I see office buildings where the reverse is true, and the old consciousness will surrender to the new.

Watching people thronging the streets it becomes obvious that insecurity issues are now rising to the surface in our human population. In a system dominated by a strong focus on intellectual development in school, university, and continuing in adult life, with almost a complete disregard for the same level of emotional development, it is hardly surprising that emotional issues run amok, with emotional insecurity a forerunner. We were never taught that our emotions are the powerhouse that writes the script of our lives. Intellect does nothing more then read the script and then spend forever arguing about it, trying to rationalise and understand what is written. The intellect is becoming so confused that it has yet to discover that rationalised emotions have little to do with the actual emotional content of a person—emotions stretching way back into the distant subconscious, sub-emotional past.

With the current Change, all the millennia of suppressed sub-emotional junk is rising in the human consciousness like a thick mist rising from an over-saturated soil. How people will deal with it depends entirely on their current relationship with themselves. The new will manage it without too much inner conflict, the old will fight to understand, while clinging to everything they need to release. I see some people's energy-signatures changing, synchronising with the veils of Light that unites them with the consciousness of the new. I also see energy-signatures taking on more shadow, as anger and rage surges ever more easily to the surface after contact with the Light veils. Light is the precipitant. I see it precipitate spontaneous joy and laughter; I see it precipitate suppressed anger and retaliation. The old digs deeper into the program of sameness; the new touches new feelings of wonder and appreciation. Where does all this come from? It comes from the deeper layers of consciousness that each person has developed over our aeons of incarnations.

Years ago, when I physically visited New York City, it seemed to me like a patchwork quilt of cultures. Walking along a street in Little Italy, I crossed a road and was suddenly in Chinatown. Outwardly, they all appeared to live in harmony, but a few locals revealed that this was a false perception. The patches were not in harmony with the whole, the quilt was fragmented. *This* city, over which I sit in a lotus position, has a similar expression. This is all about to change. Not so much change in the continuity of the patchwork effect, but in the residents. Some of the residents in one patch of the quilt will soon find a greater affinity with some of the residents in another patch. The cultures will be less adhesive, while like-consciousness will make new and lasting connections.

I notice that people are still clustering. (I have described this in my trilogy.) Angry people cluster with people of aggression, critical people cluster with judgemental types, and so on. There is nothing new in this except that with the empowerment that accompanies Change, the negative energies are clearly more negative, more angry, more aggressive, more critical, more judgemental—on and on. I notice that people compatible with the veils of Light seem to automatically avoid people of the lower energies as they walk the streets. They walk around them with more focus, more care, yet most are not fully aware that they are doing this. They feel bad vibes, and act accordingly. The clusters are also becoming more defined following Change. Not all critical people are violent, so I now see non-violent, non-aggressive clusters of critical people, and people in clusters who are inclined toward aggressive, even violent criticism. This inner violence is not necessarily expressed as physical violence; it is more mental and emotional, consisting of thoughts and feelings filled with heavy swearing and cursing aimed at the people they are criticising. This is a dangerous condition, for I can see the energetic breakdown of molecular cohesion in several of the body organs. Few people seem to realise that violent mental and emotional energy is probably more damaging to their own body than the effects of being beaten in a fist fight. You can see and treat outer damage, but the inner damage goes undetected and untreated until often it is too late.

I see a developing cluster of people who are each locked in their own individual self-conflict. They are walking within a shopping centre, each unaware of the same energy-type in the other people gradually clustering around them. It seems that so often inner conflict is waiting for an outer expression. Even as I watch, one person carelessly nudges another, and the nudged person, off-balance, catches their hip on the corner of a display cabinet. And it *was* completely unintended, even if careless. People preoccupied with heavy negative thoughts are very often careless, generally to their own detriment. The nudger apologises to the nudged, but the nudged explodes with anger, swearing at the other about being more careful. Feeling confused and intimidated, the nudger backs off, then turns around and hurries away. However, the nudger now has more self-conflict than ever, muttering and grumbling about the other person's rudeness.

I cannot help but reflect on how we attract to ourselves all that we need to show us our own inner state of consciousness. But very rarely does anyone look within to honestly see their inner emotional turmoil. Unrealised, they are the very person who creates the situation; a situation devised to reveal to themselves their own inner state. What do they do? They ignore all that they could learn about themselves and, looking outward, they project the blame onto someone else.

As I watch, I see that those people who respond positively to the veils of Light are making the inner shift from self-conflict to self-confidence. And it is obvious that, for the majority of them, this was an aware process they were already involved in. The Light of the veils finalised their inner shift. I realise that this is huge Change. Those with self-confidence based in a degree of self-love are on a journey into the new. Yet there are people whose self-confidence is based in their ability to exploit other people. I smile as I perceive this. There are many levels and expressions of self-confidence. It is not so much about self-confidence as it is the person's state of consciousness which is expressing the confidence in self!

Scanning the moving crowds, I look to see if negative self-confidence is creating a cluster of people. At first, I cannot see any, then I notice a few people sitting at different tables in a rather up-market coffee shop. Their energy-signatures indicate a higher than usual degree of self-centredness. For these people, they, themselves, are the centre of their world. And this need not be negative. But for these few, it is clearly to the detriment of their consciousness. This is a cluster of people who exploit other people with a carelessness similar to the way that agribusiness carelessly exploits the soil. They are uncaring of other people, uncaring of their feelings or their lives. Each one of these few is obviously very wealthy and full of self-confidence. On a sudden whim, I rise higher above the city to see if there are others of this type in the locality.

Yes, there are a few others, but they are scattered across the whole district. These few in the coffee shop are the only actual cluster of them in the inner city. I wonder, why this particular coffee place? I scan the interior for the owner's energy signature and sure enough, it is similar to these few. There are other self-confident people in here, and clearly they are all in the bracket of considerable wealth. However, their energy fields hold no suggestion of money obtained at the detriment of other people — just the self-centred few.

Selecting a well-dressed, stout, fairly bored-looking man of middle age, I view his probability future. I have no wish to see his past, for I am being careful not to make judgements of him. I like to think that his past would not influence me, but I have no intention of testing myself. He is as he is. I am merely curious to see where the exploitation of other people will take him. He is actually a good representation of the extreme wealth in this city. He is a very ruthless exploiter of people, including the people who work in his large company. All this is obvious in his metaphysical field of energy. Mind you, he has attracted others like himself to his business, men and a few women who are intent on learning all they can from him. As I scan his probability future — which is not fixed and stuck — I see that a small group of these other, younger, rivals are collaborating to ruin him. They have been badly treated by him, and being his own type, they are out for revenge. His probable future is not pretty. A scam they concoct ruins him, his board of directors overthrow him, and his wife leaves him. Not that this is any great loss in a loveless marriage of convenience. The old adage will probably unwind into reality—what goes around, comes around. Cycles keep on recycling! Maybe this will be his eventual salvation. I hope so. He is not a nasty or deliberately bad person; he is a product of his own upbringing.

All this indicates that as we move onward, year by year, the two long-interwoven states of consciousness in the two paramountly different types of people are rapidly unwinding. For the first time, we, of humanity, are on two different journeys. These two journeys will always continue to be interconnected— one humanity—but they will no longer be so strongly inter-influenced.

From my position high above the city, I look into the probable future to see where all this is taking us. I watch the strands of interwoven humanity coming apart over a period of several years, then it becomes a rushing blur of probable probabilities—again! I sigh. I get only a fleeting sense of a few of these probabilities, but nothing that stands firm, other than the two differing directions. I get a sense of intervention, where our greater intergalactic family comes home to deal with the wayward kids! I also get a sense of ascendency, where the meek inherit the new Earth that has long been awaiting them. I get a fleeting sense of drama and catastrophe, where the long-expected polar shift takes place. I get another fleeting sense of a very changed Earth landscape, with plants and animals from a bygone age flourishing once more. This one puzzles me, but like all the others, these are fleeting sensory experiences which might or might not be based in a future reality. I also get a sense that the very unexpected is as likely to happen as the commonly predicted future scenarios.

Within all these fleeting impressions, I sense that the consciousness of each and every person will determine their passage through it all, no matter what the scenario. Whether it be rather adversarial for the many who cling to the old, or a rite of passage for those people who are ready for adulthood, we are each responsible for our own direction and content.

I smile. Oh yes, Change is here, and the unseen, mostly unrealised veils of Light are working their metaphysical magic on our metaphysical world.

*　　*　　*

Abruptly, within my metaphysical viewing and speculation, I have a profound insight. Without any hesitation, I step . . . *Between* . . . realities to emerge among the photon Light-flakes as they were falling to Earth. I watch as they all seem to be absorbed by the people to whom they are attracted, and by all that is natural in Nature. But long, long after I stopped watching, the photon Light-flakes continued to fall. It was not that I did, or did not, expect it, I just never got around to following it through. As they continued falling to Earth, the Light-flakes gradually took on an organised cohesion—rather like the cells in a healthy body—and they formed these rather wonderful and mystical veils of photon Light which are now sweeping across our planet. I see that those people, who first energetically attracted and connected with the falling flakes of Light, are more easily able to continue the Change and development when they now encounter the veils of Light.

I feel delighted. Everything connects. I know this, but somehow I did not see the obvious connection between the Light-flakes and the veils of Light. Sometimes one cannot see for looking!

*　　*　　*

I step . . . *Between* . . . back to my previous time, but to a different location.

We are all aware that there are many great men and women on this planet. Their elevated state of consciousness lifts the overall human consciousness far more than is ever realised. Few of them are advanced on a metaphysical level, so they seldom see their energetic effect on humanity. If we use Jesus as an example of greatness, he was a man who *was* aware that while he was speaking and consciously connecting with the few, he was raising the consciousness of the many. He did not need television exposure to ensure this. While I make no claims to the greatness of Jesus, I have learned that while I consciously share with the few in a country, I am touching the consciousness of the many in that country who are open to the new. And so it is with many other—hopefully, all— spiritual teachers. Paradoxically, of course, just as the *many* were the *few* long ago, so this continues. The many of the few will read these words, while only a few of the many ever will!

Paradoxes, the spice of human communication—don't you just love them?

One of the greatest of the great men of our time recently quit his physical body. He was also one of the angry men of our time—with good reason during the years of apartheid. For his stand against apartheid he was imprisoned for twenty-seven years. I write, of course, of the late, great, Nelson Mandela. It is worthy of note that the shame of apartheid in South Africa lasted from the election of the Afrikaner National party in 1948 right up to 1991.

I have moved my metaphysical location to Cape Town in South Africa. I have also shifted from our present time to the time of Mandela's imprisonment. I am curious about this man. I have heard it suggested that the Mandela who left prison was a walk-in. Certainly his incredible change from anger to acceptance while imprisoned, then, on his release, to reconciliation, was a massive Change for any person. Metaphysically, I look back on that time. I am not watching a physical man; I am reading the field of energy that we all leave as evidence of the story of our lives. Human bodies may come and go, but human energy continues and we all leave our metaphysical mark! I have not read Mandela's book, so I have nothing to guide or influence what I am seeing. Energetically, I see Mandela moving through a period of deep introspection lasting from about the twelfth to the fifteenth year of his incarceration. During this time, his anger is basically released and he takes a considerable leap in consciousness. This growth in consciousness continues steadily up to, and after, his release from prison. I see no evidence of a walk-in.

As I view his energy signature, I see Mandela as the perfect example of a man who is spiritually enlightened with absolutely no conscious knowledge of this state of ascendency. It could be said that his mission was not to understand his enlightenment, but to powerfully express it. This he did—brilliantly. For me, Mandela's greatness is in that over the years of his imprisonment, he released the corrosive force of his anger. How justified and easy it would have been in a harsh prison system for him to have grown his anger into an even greater and destructive rage. He did not. His greatness lay in his ability to transform the negative aggression of *force* into the positive healing *power* of Love. Given the circumstances of his life, that transformation was *beyond* remarkable. For me, this is his greatest measure of greatness.

I shift my viewing time slightly, watching his final funeral. I say final to differentiate from all the previous ceremonies and viewing of the body. It is not surprising to me that the Light-body of the soul who was Mandela is also viewing his own funeral. But he surprises me. During the week he has been out of his body, his soul awareness has grown and expanded enormously. He stands with the Light-bodies of other aware friends of his, who have previously left their physical bodies. There is quite a group of them. There are also great souls of Light in attendance, honouring a human who rose from tragedy to triumph. The Light-body of Mandela is almost luminous, glowing strongly. Although I am sitting in my lotus position well above the funeral area, attempting to be unobtrusive, Mandela glances up toward me with a wide smile and a nod. I can see in his energy field that he is not sure who I am, but he recognises my energy as one of Love.

*　　*　　*

Once again, I step . . . *Between* . . . realities, emerging over rural Europe.

In this time of the photon Light veils and a higher life-frequency, I am here to get a brief agricultural overview. Like many cities, rural Europe also has the patchwork quilt effect, although I am looking at the patchwork of agricultural energies. From high above Europe, I cancel out the energy-fields of large towns and cities, so that only the rural areas are in my metaphysical vision.

The energetic effect is quite startling. Rather like phosphorescent fungi in a forest at night, all the biological and organic farms are softly glowing with a vibrant, luminous, living energy. And this is in full daylight!

This energetic Light is not physically visible. It would seem that although a photon is a particle of light without mass, the effect within the balanced environment of the bio- and organic farms may possibly cause the photons to somehow glow, creating the effect of mass—and this is what I am seeing. Or, who knows, maybe in these times of Change, the photon Light particles are responding to a new and higher order. It occurs to me that this Light effect was not showing in previous metaphysical journeys I have made over Europe. Times they are a-changing! Conversely, the majority of the land, which is farmed with a complete disregard for the soil-life, has a shadowy quality that I have never before observed—or noticed.

I am not defining this as good and bad, or right and wrong, or even positive and negative. What I am seeing is the effect the veils of photon Light have had on the energies of the farms as they drifted across the land. Everything that connects with the way each farm is managed is involved in this effect. Nothing stands alone. However, every farm is soil-based, so responding to my feelings regarding the micro-organic life in the soil, I take my vision deep into the soil profile of a biological farm. I inner-view the root profile of farm crops and pasture where the soil-life is abundant, and multiplying prolifically. It is here that the photon glow seems to find birth. Certainly, the glow is also affected by the primary farmer of the land, as I have witnessed and described earlier, but the soil is always the nucleus of a farm.

The micro and macro soil-life on the majority of the farmland, which I see as cast in shadow, is not abundant, nor is it proliferating. The life in the soil is struggling for survival. A sand desert appears as the word describes—a desert. It appears deserted of vibrant life, yet it has developed specialised methods of survival. Micro-organic soil-life in a desert has an ability similar to animal hibernation, although far surpassing it, sustaining a state of suspended animation for decades, even centuries if it becomes necessary. The desert waits for the rains that will trigger explosive new growth, and a proliferation of the soil-life, along with the germination of the huge abundance of specialised seeds awaiting the same stimulus. All this has evolved over millennia. But exploited farmland is not like this. These farms are on soil that once had an abundance of soil-life which fed on the organic matter which created the rich fertility of humus. No matter how lacking some of the early agricultural practices may have been, the land was not subjected to chemical devastation. The farmyard manure that accumulated each winter, when cattle were kept in sheltered yards, was carted away and thrown into large dung-heaps, there to mature and mellow for a season. It was then spread onto the land, thus feeding the soil-life. When a teenager, I spent weeks involved in such work. To this day I enjoy the smell of mature, fully ripe, farmyard manure.

As I hover over the land, I see what must be the complete opposite of that early practice of fertility — almost its nemesis. The Netherlands has a unique situation inasmuch as a large percentage of the land is below sea level. Like many other countries, they have huge dairy, poultry and pig enterprises, along with the enormous amounts of manure these produce. Unlike other countries, they have a far higher water level in their soil, hence the abundance of dykes and drains. To be clear, I am no authority on Dutch farming methods, but energetically I can see that deeper in the soil profile the accumulation of the endless quantities of fresh pig effluent that is sprayed onto the land is causing ever-compounding soil complications. For many farms, the problem of chicken and dairy manure is added to this. The complications seem to stem from a soil that is unable to convert such huge quantities into humus, owing to a chemically complexed and highly disrupted soil-life. Add to this the adverse complication of fluctuating high water levels in much of the land.

In the rich, older, fertile soils of much of Europe this situation is not as bad, but as with the Dutch farms, it is a problem that will one day have to be reckoned with. Without knowing the techniques used, I can see from their energy that the bio- and organic farms do not have the same problem. They have a very different approach to farming, including the management of pig effluent and poultry manure.

However, it is not my intention to get into an agricultural discourse. I am simply over-looking the European agricultural scene to get an idea of the effect of the veils of Light. And this I am seeing on an energetic level. Although the energy translates into a physical reality within the soil, most of it is beyond my comprehension. Enough to say that soil complexities are increasing on the chemically stimulated and controlled farms—the majority of farm land—and this will surely have repercussions on the quality of the meat, grain and vegetable food that they produce. When I refer to quality, I am not so much referring to the physical properties of the produce, even though this is affected to the detriment of the consumer; I am referring to the *energetic* quality. When we consume food, we *ingest* it all. Our own field of energy extracts the energy field of the food we eat, then we excrete practically all the physical material. In other words, we are Beings of energy that live on the energy of what we consume. With the advent of Change, food grown under chemical control will have considerably less energy, while the bio- and organic food will have considerably more.

Compared with the vast broad-hectare patches in Oz, the European landscape is a very complex patchwork, yet with some pleasing aspects. Although it is still the minority of agricultural land, there are far more bio- and organic farms than I expected. This is good. The overall energetic effect is a quilt of many very small patches of farmland, much of it with different qualities of shadow, while the bio-farms and organic farms are also composed of different qualities of Light.

Without realising it, every farmer and land owner imprints their own energetic quality into the energy field of their farm. Taking chemical farming as the common practice in these times of agricultural exploitation, some farmers use the chemicals simply because they are told to do so by the Department of Agriculture. These are functional farmers, not really connected to the land at all. Their energy field adds nothing of quality to the land. Then there are the fearful farmers, watching all agricultural sensibility go down the drain, and unable to combat this. There are also the greedy farmers, who have no feelings for the land beyond their bank account. There are the angry and aggressive farmers, where their exploitation of the land is in harmony with their attitude to life. There are the non-farming land owners. Some are businessmen, their land a tax write-off. Some have inherited a farm, but have no interest in it. Some landowners have almost nothing to do with the land, simply handing over to a farm manager. And while a few land managers are obviously very connected to the land, doing their best to nurture it, a great number of them follow their orders to make as much money as possible, regardless of the workings of a vast and complex soil-life.

Without making judgements, all these many differing farmer-types have an effect on the holistic expression of their farms, and from my position, it is all metaphysically visible.

I sigh. I have had enough of viewing a basically lack-lustre agriculture.

Without more ado, I step . . . *Between* . . . back into my study.

Chapter Eight

Mental Astral Worlds

We are in very strange, yet dynamic times. The energetic qualities, or lack of such qualities, within all life forms are being strongly accentuated. I have seen this in both agribusiness and organic agriculture. I have seen it in forests and in wilderness. I have seen it in domestic animals, farm livestock, and wild animals. I have seen it in people. The old expression of life as we know it is breaking down. Mind you, this will take time. Chaos and Order are recreating different values. Chaos, the engine that drives, is driving Change in a direction of newness. Order, the structure of physical form, is less able to hold the old together. Balance, the place of greatest potential, is being redefined. A higher potential is becoming ever more available.

Nature will find its own way through our time of Change in a natural flow. No intellects to mess it up! We have a choice. We can flow with Nature, and with the nature of Change, or we can resist. As already stated several times, it will all play out according to our own personal states of consciousness. Without mental or emotional attachments we can move easily into the new—or by staying attached to our mental and emotional programs, we stick with more-of-the-same, going nowhere. The choice will be less intellectual than emotional. Emotions make the final choices, while the intellect attempts to understand. If we are emotionally free, we will find that our thoughts and actions easily define the newness we are expressing. If we are emotionally fearful, we will find that we are unable to release the program of our past. Choice made!

It could be truthfully said that the ultimate choice comes down to Love or fear. We cannot fearfully Love. And if we truly experience *unconditional* Love, then we do not—cannot—experience fear. I used to think that fear was a negative emotion, but I have learned that fear is a very, very powerful illusory emotion. Certainly there are emotions attached to fear, but the cause is illusionary. Fear has absolutely no basis in reality. All fear is based in the power of very strong, but *false* beliefs—illusions. Death is one of those false beliefs, along with its attendant fears. If we can accept that fear is self-created, and if we can accept the truth of fear, we are no longer compelled to create it. Conversely, if we believe that fear is natural, and our fears 'naturally' belong to us, then our fears will, as now, continue to control us.

About thirty years ago, when I was considerably less wise and compassionate than I am today, I woke up in the night to be confronted by three Beings with bodies of Light. They were human, yet they were different. They told me that they came from a mental world, and that they did not take on physical incarnations because they were too fearful of physical pain and suffering. Memory indicates that I judged them a bit too harshly at the time, and they departed. Apparently they were attracted to me for some reason, but I never did learn why—or I forgot!

However, I never forgot the incident. It was peculiar, to say the least. Later I regretted my lack of compassion for the obviously very nervous Beings. I recognised later that it must have taken great courage for them to somehow enter my physical reality. It has long been my intent that one day I would find a way to return the visit—and treat them with the respect they deserve.

With this in mind, I have decided that I will attempt to step out of my familiar physical world reality, and into their mental world reality—assuming there is one, and that I can do this. Nothing ventured, nothing gained!

I debated with myself about informing Pan of my latest plans, but decided that as he always knows my intent and whereabouts, there was no need. If I was out of order, he would intervene.

Sitting in my study, relaxed, I wondered where to focus. Focus is rather like when you shine a beam of light from a flashlight onto something in the dark—you visually connect. When I focus into a metaphysical journey, it is as though I am sending a beam of my Light-energy to connect with where it is I intend to go. Mostly it works—with the odd reservations! There are times and places that seem to have a connection-timing, and I can only go *when* it is appropriate.

To focus on a place is easy, even focusing on a 'when' or 'where' is simple, but the mental world is purely astral, so I am not quite so sure about my focus. Oh well, nothing ventured . . . !

Focus is an essential aspect of reality hopping. Focusing into my metaphysical Light-body, I then focus on my intent. Stepping . . . *Between* . . . I step out into . . . ?

＊　　＊　　＊

Hmm. Where am I?

I seem to be in a thick fog. Maybe in, or on, a cloud? The mist is very white and very fine, but even metaphysically I cannot see anything. However, I get the feeling that I am not alone.

"Er . . . anybody around? Anybody here?"

No. Last time I looked there were no bodies.

The voice is telepathic and humorous, and I do not recognise it.

"Okay, you have me at a complete disadvantage. I don't know who you are or where I am. I appreciate your humour, but who are you, and why are you here?"

I am definitely a who so there must be a why!

Despite myself, I chuckle. "If we ever get introduced we

should get along very well."

Abruptly, the thick mist vanishes, and I see a Light Being. He appears to be quite human, but I get a strong sense that this Being is *very* ancient, and that he has not had a physical incarnation in a *very* long time.

"Wow . . . er . . . hello. Who are you?"

My name is Patch.

"Patch! Seriously? That's a strange name for a . . . !"

Strange Being, perhaps. The very human looking Light-Being smiles at me. *And might I ask your name, oh lost and wandering traveller?*

I chuckle. I like this person. I find it difficult to think of him as 'a Being'.

"My name is Mixael."

Mixael! Seriously? That's a strange name for a . . . !

"Wandering traveller!"

We both laugh out loud—albeit silently!

Okay, let's give the funnies a rest. I was told about your intended journey, and asked if I would meet and accompany you. I was also told that you have two aspects, the fifth-dimensional Mixael, and the more playful and impulsive three-dimensional Michael. I think I have met both.

"Okay, Patch. Did Pan put you up to this . . . or perhaps *volunteer* you?"

Well, we could say that Pan is indirectly involved. It was suggested that you might get completely lost in the astral worlds without a guide. I, who had never actually met you, have nevertheless heard about you. When a guide was requested, I volunteered.

"I thank you, sir. However, whereas I am known to easily get lost in the physical world, I have had no trouble negotiating the places of a greater reality. Despite this, if Pan thinks I need a guide, I am sure that once again he will prove to be correct."

I stare at Patch curiously. With a smile, he stares back at me. His field of energy suggests a very ancient human indeed, far older than any I have met to date. Yet he also has an energy that is youthful and vibrant, radiating an exuberant humour. I like him.

"I suppose you also can read the thoughts I broadcast?"

Of course. Naturally enough, you like me. I was told that you are an open book. Do you never close the covers?

"No. I was never taught. And, to be honest, I don't mind. I have nothing to hide. Like it or not, I am who I am. Patch, am I reading you correctly? Are you as ancient and as youthful as you seem to be? Please, tell me a little about yourself."

Of course. In linear terms, yes, I am ancient. I am also ageless. In some ways I am a bit of a paradox. Although I could have remained on Earth as a physical immortal, I chose to finish my physical incarnations on Earth in one of the advanced civilisations several hundred thousand years ago—a civilisation your history seems unaware of. Yet I have retained the ability to incarnate physically, if I so choose, into any age of humanity. This is unusual, even though easily possible. I have spent some of eternity exploring the astral worlds, of which there are countless numbers. This qualifies me to be a perfect guide.

"I'm not sure if I am worthy to warrant a Being such as you. In human terms you sound overqualified for the job . . . although I am truly delighted to have you with me."

To be clear, without me you might not be allowed to wander the astral worlds. You have a well-deserved reputation for . . . provoking or disturbing . . . certain situations and Beings. The repercussions of these, to you, minor infractions, continue long after you have forgotten the incidents. In some of the astral worlds this might not be wise.

"Hmm, well . . . okay. I admit, I have . . . perhaps . . . acted a *tiny* bit rashly at times. But it's all very minor stuff. However, when you mention astral worlds, it sounds like there is quite a lot involved. Oh, one other thing. You say you are ageless, but aren't we all metaphysically ageless?

I will elucidate. If I choose to physically incarnate again, I will be physically ageless. As I said, immortal. Now, regarding the astral worlds, yes, there is a lot involved. It was obvious that you would eventually be ready to journey to astral worlds, rather than stay with the multiverse of greater realities. The distinction between both is not easy to describe, and the differences are subtle, for one collocates within the other. But, differences do exist. I am to be your teacher and your guide. And, may I say, I consider it an honour. Your comment of your not being worthy of me, is not worthy of you.

We both chuckle.

"Thank you. But seriously . . . Patch is an odd name for an ancient Being. I mean, whatever happened to names like Socrates, or Aurelius, or Winnie the Pooh?"

Pooh! Common names. Patch is my choice of name while I am with you.

We laugh. "Well, my friend, I really like your sense of humour."

Do not think that I cannot be serious, firm, and capable of reprimand, if needed.

"And do not think that I will not appreciate it. Okay, enough of all the flimflam, where do we go from here?"

Actually, now that I really focus on it, 'here' is a place of nothing, nowhere. Once the thick mist was removed, nothing was left except . . . space. Truly, it has no 'where' or 'when', it simply *is*. I should also say that, like my metaphysical human friend, Ben, I see Patch as both metaphysical and human, even if considerably more ethereal than Ben. I relate to him as an aware, advanced person.

We will visit the mental worlds. This was your original, clueless, intent.

"Okay. As long as I'm clueless I'll follow you."

You will need to. Stay close. Better still, take my hand.

Patch reaches toward me and I clasp his hand in mine. Hmm, odd. It feels very much like two physical hands clasping.

$$* \quad * \quad *$$

We both step . . . *Between* . . . emerging into a world that looks somewhat similar to the world of my reality.

"How can this be an astral world? It looks perfectly normal."

What is normal? Who defines it? The astral worlds can be like this . . . or like this.

As he speaks, he grabs my hand. The world spins a few times in a gut-churning wrench, and we are standing in a valley that looks so ethereal that it is almost wavering. It takes me long shaky moments to realise that this is exactly the same place as the more solid version—and that I like the more solid place a whole lot better.

The valley spins once again, and then solidifies.

"Did you ever teach kids how to swim?" I ask.

With my thoughts carefully blanked out from him, he stares at me in bewilderment. *That's a very strange question.*

"If you did, I bet you threw them in the deep end."

He smiles. *Point taken. But it did save a lot of explanation.*

I agree, it did. Astral reality obviously comes in a wide range of physicality. As a human I am used to just the one. Not for a moment did I consider physical reality was anything other than our familiar physicality. Obviously, metaphysical reality is not physical! Apart from the density or porosity of an object, it never occurred to me that there were gradients to physical substance as a whole. Yet this valley went from substantial to insubstantial.

The mechanics of substance is not as fixed and rigid as is believed. If you take a substance from one dimension to another, energetic changes occur at a subatomic level.

"Yes, of course. The mental world cannot be my normal physical world."

Oh yes, it can. This 'is' your normal physical world. When you are physical in your world, you basically see what you expect to see, because human eyes are conditioned to a physical reality. But within this world of yours are mental worlds and emotional worlds, interacting in your 'normal' perception of physicality. Both the mental and emotional worlds are in perfect juxtaposition with your world.

"Obviously there is more to this than I expected."

It would help if you let go of all assumptions. Be open to newness.

I smile. As a spiritual teacher, I am having my own words quoted back to me.

You will notice there is a path winding through the valley. We will follow it.

So saying, Patch and I stroll silently along the path. He is about my own height, looking rather as I do in my Light-body. We could fly, or float, or instantly relocate, but strolling is a very nice thing to do, especially with good company. It also allows me time to regain my scattered wits!

Be aware that all your thoughts will be broadcast throughout the mental world. I suggest that mental silence will be appropriate.

"Hmm . . . so all our communication will be broadcast?"

No, only yours. I send my communication directly to you, not to all and sundry.

"Okay . . . so will you kindly teach me how? Please."

Patch smiles. *Focus on your thoughts, and on me, simultaneously. Imagine we are in a conversation in a crowded room, and you particularly want only me to hear. You focus on me, speaking clearly and distinctly. Your words are pitched just loud enough for only me to hear, and they are projected to me, not to other people.*

I nod. "Yes, that makes good sense."

So saying, I project my silent thoughts to him only. "Do you have any idea where we are going? Are we just strolling through a valley?"

You see. That was perfect. No broadcasting. I, alone, am the recipient of your thoughts.

"I'll need practice. I repeat, are we going anywhere?"

Indeed we are, my friend, indeed we are. Ahead of us is a small town. This town is a non-physical town, within the physical valley. The town does not exist to physical people; it has no reality, but in the astral world of the people who live here, it is very real. This is where one of your long-ago visitors from an astral mental world, that triggered this journey, came from. When we arrive, be aware that two very different realities coexist. Okay, enough cruising, I will speed up the distance to be consumed.

Sure enough, although our stroll is the same speed, at his will, the scenery flashes past us as the distance to the town is rapidly reduced. Neat!

The town is now quite close, and even to my metaphysical vision it appears to be very insubstantial. I can see the physical valley, firm and substantial, but in the place where the town is standing, it seems as though the town is no more than a hazy hologram in the valley.

"When we enter the town, will we actually be in it? Are we metaphysical enough?"

Oh yes. Don't concern yourself about that. The people will see us and probably treat us as one of their own.

"So, if physical people walk this path, going right through the town without even seeing it, do the people of the astral world in this town see the physical people?"

No, they do not. The mental worlds interact with the physical worlds, but for most of the people in both worlds there is no awareness of this at all.

"You say most of the people. Some physical people are actually aware of the astral worlds?"

Yes, but there are two categories of people in this group. Some have the intellectual knowledge of astral worlds, but neither see nor interact with them. The other, fewer, people are highly developed spiritually. They can, and do, consciously interact with astral worlds. Oh . . . then of course there are the people who, while physically sleeping, connect with astral worlds. Some of these are aware of their astral travels, and consciously guide them, while the huge majority have no conscious awareness of anything, other than a jumble of dreams when they awaken.

"Yes, I know of astral worlds, but I do not see astral towns while physical."

Very few do. Nor would you want to. But you did see the astral world in London when you metaphysically visited there. You saw the generations of people who are disembodied, yet with no awareness of it. This is a part, or aspect of the astral world.

"Not only were they not aware of a physical reality, but each spectral person was unaware of the lost, disembodied generations that remained from before them. They were only aware of the incorporeal people in their own time frame. Ghosts, not aware of untimely ghosts!"

Patch laughs. Good one! As I was shown the story, you put a very considerable shock into three rather negative and unpleasant ghosts while you were in London.

"*Shown* the story! How could you be *shown* it?"

Very simple. You should know this. A story can be shown or viewed by interconnecting with the moment the story was/is taking place. No linear time! Get it?

I nod. "I didn't think of that. Our reality does not allow such luxuries. Anyway, to describe them as *very* unpleasant is putting it mildly. They were deceased heavyweight hoods. And they deserved it. (*Through the Eyes of Love, Journeying with Pan, Book Three*). They were terrifying and seriously draining the life-energy from my friend, Anne. And as for what happened . . . I didn't think it through, I just acted. Who, er, showed you?"

Oh . . . such incidents get around. You have the makings of a non-physical fan club!

"Ha ha! Anyway, all's well that ends well. The hood-entities are being rehabilitated."

Rehabilitated! That's one way of putting it.

We are smiling as we reach the town, our thoughts placed on hold.

We walk into the town, glancing at its signposted name: Sunrise.

"Well, that seems to be normal enough! Now what? Do we just wander around, or go to one of the . . . shops? *Shops!* What do you buy in a mental world? Like . . . ideas?"

The whole concept of a mental world acting in accordance to our physical world is difficult for me to grasp. Surely mental projection will create mental objects. I mention this to Patch.

There are many levels of the mental astral worlds. Beings in higher astral worlds can, indeed, produce almost anything they need by mental projection. This is neither a higher nor a lower astral world; this is somewhere between both. We will visit a few of these worlds to give you a more complete insight into them.

A group of people are coming toward us. They look just like normal physical people, except they are not. These people are a mental projection of physicality.

I focus carefully and project my words to Patch. "Why do they look physical? Why not just float around like ghosts? That is what I expected. It almost seems that the physical world creates the criteria of how they should be, or should look."

You are correct. The physical world does create the criteria for this, shall we say, more moderate mental astral world. Quite a lot of these people have had physical incarnations. This is also a fairly well-populated astral level, balanced between extremes.

"Would I like to see the extremes?"

Probably not, but I suspect we will need to.

I sigh. "Override me if I make rash decisions."

A young blonde woman has approached us. "Hello, you're strangers to our little town."

Does she think that we are both perfectly normal to look at? Whatever happened to our metaphysical appearance? However, she *is now* clarifying her perception. I had a false impression.

"What realm do you come from?" she asks me.

I glance at Patch helplessly. "What do I say?" I project.

You tell her the truth. She lives in a mental world, not an idiot world.

"Well . . . to tell the truth I am a wandering metaphysical human from the physical world, taking a look at some of the astral worlds. This gentleman is my guide, Patch."

"We thought you both looked different. We welcome you. I had an older brother who visited your world long ago. He found it very frightening. Tell me, is the physical world constantly full of pain and suffering, or is it more occasional? But before you answer, come in off the street and have a cup of tea." She smiles sweetly. "That is, if you are able to."

We follow her into a home that is as normal a small-town house as any in my reality. We sit in comfortable chairs with no trouble, while she makes the tea. A small girl watches us, giggling. "What's your name?" I ask her.

At that moment the woman comes back with a teapot. "I'm sorry. My name is Pedra, and this is my daughter Petra. My husband is at work in his shop."

"My name is Mixael, while I am metaphysical. In my physical world, I am Michael."

Pedra looks at me enviously. "You can obviously live physically, and also be metaphysical. I wish that I could live mentally and also be physical. This is my dream."

I am surprised by her accurate description of me. And she knows the nature of our differing realities. Her knowledge is impressive. But her dream? That puzzles me. "To be honest, not many physical people move into their metaphysical Light-body as easily as I do, or travel in this way. But surely it would be impossible for you to take on physicality . . . and then return to this."

"Oh no, that's not what I mean. I mean that when I leave this body and incarnate again, I would like to do so into the physical world, with all my mental abilities. I believe your reality combines the physical, emotional, and the mental. Wow! That is so amazing."

I stare at her in astonishment, then at Patch. Something that I take so completely for granted, as we all do, is a dream for this woman living in a mental world.

"What is to stop you?"

"Fear," she replies. "Overwhelming fear."

"But fear is an emotion. Oh . . . no . . . it is not an emotion. Fear is based in a set of false beliefs, creating a negative energy that we harbour, get attached to, and *call* an emotion. Thought precedes emotion. You are right. Fear comes first from the mental world. But surely you can set aside such fear, knowing it is false information not based in reality."

And can you walk on water, knowing that if you create a strong belief that you can walk on water, then you can walk on water? It has even been done . . . and it still is! But . . . can you? Or is the illusion of your lifetimes of conditioning so strong that you cannot walk on water?

I sigh heavily, and nod. "You're correct. It is exactly the same for Pedra."

"Pedra, I can assure you that pain and suffering is not *all* that physical life is about. For many, in what we call Third World countries, suffering is really bad, and yet they laugh, and smile, and Love, and truly value life. In many other more fortunate countries, the people only occasionally encounter physical pain and suffering, mostly as they get older. Yes, I do live in a world of hardship, with a measure of pain and suffering, but it is also a world of compassion, of Love, of respect for life. It is a world filled with all the good things that we nurture and value. Fun and laughter abound. And so much Love. In our world, we create our lives. In every moment we are creating the content and direction of every moment of our lives. But to be honest, not many people accept, or believe, or live this Truth. This alone creates suffering."

Pedra smiles tremulously. "All our concepts of your world are frightening."

"But what do *you* feel? Beyond concepts and thought, what do *you* feel?"

She looks puzzled. "What do you mean, 'feel'?"

Inspiration. "What is Petra to you? What do you *feel* for her?"

"I love her, of course. This is only natural. But what are feelings?"

Now I am puzzled. "How can you Love without feeling? How is this possible?"

It is possible because this is a mental world, not a feeling world. You claim that one cannot Love without feelings. I can assure you, very many millions of people of your physical realm, who blithely talk the words of love, have absolutely no feelings *of love.*

I sigh again. "Yes, I cannot dispute that. What a terrible thing. It simply confirms that our relationship with Love is based in our varying levels of consciousness. So in this mental world they are able to *talk* the words of Love . . . but that's it? Nothing more?"

Nothing more, but this is enough. It is their reality. Your Love feelings are an impossible concept, an outrageous dream, completely unreal for them. Even if they do not feel *Love, be assured that Love feels them. Their relationship with Love is as deep as they can manage and are ready for. As you say, it is a consciousness issue. Incidentally, where do you think the people in your reality who have absolutely no feelings of Love are eventually going to incarnate? Every issue in our lives that we create has to be addressed. And separation from Love is one of these issues.*

Deep inside, I am shocked. I feel an inner complacency that I did not know I had being shaken like a rat. Good, shake it out of me. Oh God! What is life without the inner melting into Love? Without the feelings of joy and even grief that accompany Love. When I think of Carolyn, my thoughts are accompanied by Love, turning mundane feelings into something magnificent. Love transforms, uplifts, makes whole. Does it do this for these people? Oh . . . am I broadcasting?

You are not fully broadcasting although I am picking it up, but take care. Be aware that in the higher *mental realms, the mental relationship with Love is deep and meaningful. But not here.*

I had no idea that there are so many unrealised aspects to multidimensional life. And this is just the beginning! With a smile, I find that I cannot drink a cup of tea with Pedra and Petra, although Patch is having no trouble at all as he enjoys his second cup.

"Is it me?" I ask him, indicating my cup.

No, it is not quite possible for you. It could be, but it is not.

I decide to let that pass.

A group of men come into the room. One, a tall, lean dark-haired man addresses us in a challenging voice. "I take it you are the newcomers in town. Not quite normal."

Patch and I both laugh. "Yes, that's us," I reply.

He looks surprised that we have laughed at his remark. "So, what are you doing here?"

We are cosmic tourists. You and your town are on our schedule.

To my surprise, the group of men babble away at each other in the most confusing, crazy mishmash of conflicting nonsense and idiot concepts I have ever heard. Nothing they say adds up to any sense. And they go on and on, dispassionately spitting out a torrent of mental garbage.

"Is this a joke?" I ask Patch.

This, my friend, is regular normality at this level. Petra is well advanced. She will incarnate away from all this before too long.

"Will she go to a higher mental level, or may her dream be realised?"

That decision rests with her. She needs to focus on her dream of physicality.

One of the men turns toward us. "You will have to come with us. We will lock you up until we decide what should be done with you."

Patch and I stand up. Definitely time to go!

"Petra, your dream will come true before too long. Just hold the focus."

✳   ✳   ✳

Each holding a hand of the other, we step … *Between* … emerging in a wispy, wraithlike place that has an instant bad feeling.

"I take it this is a lower mental world. Let's make this a quick visit. If those men were normal in a moderate world, heaven help us here. I already don't like it.

Be careful with your feelings. The mental worlds do not nullify them, they tend to accentuate them, and bad feelings here have a mental translation which is definitely not advisable.

I sigh. "What does that mean, exactly?"

Feelings in a higher mental world become like soothing music. Feelings in a middle astral world are interpreted according to the individuals, but in the lower realm feelings are received as an energy of anger and aggression.

"This visit is not a good idea. Do we have to stay?"

Yes. It is important for you to be fully cognisant of the negative creative ability of lower mental thoughts, and to share this in your books and Intensives.

"Are you suggesting that lower thoughts can lower a person into this place?

This place, as you call it, is exactly the same place. We are still in the town of Sunrise, but in a lower mental astral realm.

"But are you saying that people of my reality can be here if they have low mental thoughts?"

What is this realm if it is not lower mental thoughts? Of course people can touch-in here when they descend to the base levels of their thinking.

"So we can be physically in one reality while mentally in another?"

Look at it like this. All realms occupy the same moment in no-time and in no-place. Time and place are illusions.

"Whoa, whoa, whoa! That's ridiculous. Time is an illusion, yes . . . but *place*? Everyone lives in a *place*. All Beings, you included, live in, or have a place."

Let me explain. Yes, we all live in a place, but in eternity, place does not exist. Thus we have the illusion of time creating the illusion of place. Take the planet Earth as an example. We could say that this is your place, along with billions of other people. And within the frame of linear time this is true, it is your place. But Earth has no permanence.

In a few trillion years of no-time it is/will be gone. If you consider 'place' as permanent, it is an illusion, for there is no such thing as permanence within the context of linear time, only within the context of eternity . . . which is changeless. If you see that 'place' is temporary, then you live in, and with, illusion, but within the framework of a greater reality.

"Gee! Okay, I grant you this . . . but what mortal Being is ever going to consider their own planet as an impermanent residence? I mean, really!"

All the many races of the many species that have had to leave the place of their permanent residence because its time in space was finished. And all the species that have died on their planet of residence because they could not leave and it had reached its use-by date . . . to quote you. And all this before Earth was born. All this, countless aeons before humans ever reached Earth.

If a metaphysical mouth could hang open, my jaw would be touching the ground.

"Phew! You certainly think on a larger scale than I do. Okay, I concede to your superior knowledge. So . . . how did we start this discussion?"

You were asking if we can be physically in one reality and mentally in another. And I was saying, all realms occupy the same moment in no-time and in no-place. Yes, you can physically be in a physical reality while you are mentally in a different astral realm. I will show you.

"This implies that my physical reality is also an astral realm."

Well, of course it is. What did you think it was? An exception to all reality?

"No, I actually thought it was an astral reality, but I was never quite sure."

If you want me to be really provocative, I will point out that even your 3-D reality has a fair variety of physical density. I know that you are aware of the many levels of 3-D reality, but are you aware that not all those levels share the same experience of physicality, even if some are only a few degrees different from others.

"No, I did not realise that. Is the difference significant?"

Meaning what, exactly?

"Do the degrees of difference give a physical advantage for one reality, as opposed to another? Or does it make a biological difference regarding Nature? That sort of thing."

No, not really. Some 3-D realities could be said to be comparatively tougher than others, but it makes no significant difference to the holistic 3-D reality. No more so than different shades of visual colour, according to the sun's intensity, in whatever country you live in.

"That's a very good analogy. I get it. Okay, oh guide, why are we here in Sunrise, in a lower astral level?"

Because I have something to show you.

"Hmm . . . I bet I'm not going to like it!"

Watch carefully . . . and don't ask immediate questions. I will explain it.

So saying, Patch slowly waves both of his hands in front of him in a large circular motion, each in an opposite direction. Within the circle that he elegantly frames, a picture quickly forms. I see a normal-looking person, completely drunk, staggering along a street. I realise that I am looking into a frame of my own physical world reality. It also becomes obvious that this man is a regular drunk, a full-blown alcoholic. I am able to see his energy-signature. His relationship with himself is one of the deepest, most base loathing. His self-hate is clearly visible in his energy-field. He is living on the lowest base level a person can reach on alcohol, or so it would seem. As I watch he screams in terror, wildly punching the empty space before him. He futilely swings his fists at nothing until, sobbing, he curls himself into a foetal position on the pavement, moaning fearfully in a low monotone.

Now look around you in the town on this lower astral level.

Wrenching my gaze away from the pathetic drunk, I almost freeze in shock. We are both surrounded by a crowd of the most diabolical monsters I have ever seen. Grotesque serpents, giant deformed toad-like creatures and other nightmare creatures. As I stare at them, I realise that they are completely unaware of us. But they are not unaware of the drunk. The astral body of the alcoholic is actually here, screaming at these awful multi-coloured monsters as they cluster around him. Base connects with base. The astral body of the drunken man is here, in this town, connected to the monsters he has created, and continues to create, for other monsters are literally forming in front of us.

"How is this possible?"

Astral matter can pull, or call forth, etheric matter with which to create. In this case the drunk is unwittingly pulling his own etheric creation into a lower astral realm. Remember what you teach; you each create your own reality. He is doing this right now, with all the same complete unawareness of those who are not drunk.

I sigh. "Your words give this terrifying scene a whole different angle. If regular, normal sober people do not know or believe that they create the direction and content of their lives, how could an addicted alcoholic be expected to know . . . and not create this? He might not be here physically, but he is here mentally. This is obviously his mental reality now, and I assume it will eventually cause his insanity. When I think of all the mentally disturbed people in our reality, I shudder. Currently, we have a new case of dementia every seven seconds . . . and it is steadily increasing. Could any of those people end up here mentally?"

Dementia has many different emotional and mental causes. To keep this simple, many do touch base with a lower astral reality, even if it is not inhabited by monsters. It takes a high degree of self-loathing to create loathsome monsters that continually besiege you. Those with dementia, who are expressing extremes of anger, aggression and/or violence, certainly plunge into some grim lower astral realms.

"Such as?"

I should not have asked!

Another quick circular wave of his arms, and we are surrounded by a mob scene of anger and aggression. Men and women are screaming at each other. Men are fighting, while women seem to be intent on tearing the hair off the head of their opponent. Everybody has an opponent. All are engaged in fighting and swearing in the street we are standing in. Actually it's the same place as the drunk with his monsters, but it is a different level of astral reality. The scene of violence changed so fast it caught me unprepared. I stare in horror at normal-looking people, not addicts. No, I am wrong. These *are* addicts. They are addicted to their moral issues. Addicted to being right. Addicted to arguing. Addicted to inner aggressions. Addicted to anger.

Yes, as I focus into their energy fields I realise that every one of these people has a constant and dangerous addiction.

"I take it that everyone in this crowd has a metaphysical connection with their physical counterpart in my reality frame."

Yes. You have stated it perfectly. All of these are strong, base-mental, negative creations. In this way the creators and the created are connected. It is a similar scene in an emotional reality frame. But we will visit that later. As creative Beings, humans continually create.

I shake my head sadly. "I know this does not represent all humanity, but we are a sad and sorry bunch, aren't we? People are so much into the illusions of success and making money that every life they live is a spiritual failure. A failure to Love. A failure to Truth. Just . . . failures!"

A spiritual teacher whom I rather Love speaks of success and failure as two very powerful illusions. Could he be wrong?

I smile, and sigh. "No, he is correct. But he is also human and he occasionally allows the human addiction to illusion, and all its suffering, to hurt him. He will recover."

Beloved friend, Love cannot fail, nor can Truth. Vast spans of linear time illusion may need to pass for some humans to develop wisdom and insight, but pass it will. Light will always triumph over ignorance. And Love is as endless, as eternal, as constant as is God. For, ". . . they are One."

They are indeed. Listen to my words and embrace them.

It is good that you feel hurt when others are hurting, but let not hurt be your focus.

It is good that you can cry for those who are crying, but let not tears be your focus.

It is good that you feel the feelings of those who are lost, but never let loss be your focus.

It is good that Love can truly touch your heart with grief, for then the grief is resolved.

This, beloved friend, is why you are a great spiritual teacher.

I say to you, as you say to many others, you are far more than you think you are.

I look at Patch in surprise—and with a passing touch of embarrassment. If a Light-body can blush, mine is blushing!

"Well . . . thank you, kind sir. Thank you, indeed."

And will you embrace all that I have said? Yes, I see that you have. Very good. Allow me to show you another aspect of the lower astral realms.

Once again his hands create a circle, but this time nothing seems to form in it. I hasten to add that each new manifestation banishes the previous one.

As I watch the new, unfolding scene in the same town, I now see people walking the streets alone, while muttering to themselves. Seems normal enough.

Watch, listen, learn.

Hmm. Sounds like a familiar mantra!

The mutterings are intense, even if very quiet, so I metaphysically connect with the words they are muttering. Every single word is negative. The mutterings are a reinforcement of how unfair life is, of how no matter what you do you cannot succeed, of how the government is out to get you, of how all the people in your office laugh at you behind your back, of how you are considered a failure, of how there is never enough money, of how your spouse is probably cheating on you, of the neighbour who continually persecutes you, of your relatives who hate you, of the relatives you hate because they are so nasty, of how terrible the state of the world is, of how the environment is polluted and all our food is toxic—and on and on and on with almost endless negative drivel.

"So these are the astral bodies of the physical people who live with an ongoing litany of complaints and grumbles about life and everything in it. Am I correct? In other words, where we focus our energy flows . . . and recreates itself on many unseen levels."

Yes and no. This is an astral world of worry and anxiety. These people around us live in this reality, and this is their lives. Their astral bodies eventually fade away from mental exhaustion. However, each one of these people connects with a counterpart from your physical world reality. This continuous complaining negatively feeds and bolsters the fault-finding and grumbling of the counterparts, thus making it a negative habit that is very hard to break.

"So to break away from this, they would need a change in consciousness?"

Yes, absolutely. Every astral level is maintained by the consciousness of the physical people who are connected with it, no matter how low it becomes.

"What happens when a physical counterpart dies?"

Good question. On this lower level, the astral counterpart literally fades away, but it does not die. It accompanies the late physical counterpart on their continuing metaphysical journey.

"Do the astral people have lives of their own, or are they simply the metaphysical counterpart of physical people?"

Another good question. Both are true. Given time, while connected with a person on this lower level, the astral counterpart may take on a life of its own, even while it has a physical connection. At the more moderate level we saw earlier, the astral people have a life of their own, independent of the physical people with whom they may, or may not, connect.

There is another way to understand this. You are aware of the shadow selves that accompany many negative people. You have spoken and written of these shadow selves. As you know, the shadow self survives the death of the physical body simply because the person's negativity does not come to an end. Those shadow selves are of an astral reality, connecting with the physical world but also living in their own astral world.

"I have to admit, these astral worlds have given me a whole new insight into my words regarding focus. While I know that we are always creating, I did not quite realise the full depth, content, and consequences of our creations. It is massive when you consider the astral levels on which we are creating, with no awareness of it, or the repercussions derived from it. Living in a basically physical world, we have no thought or regard to the astral impact of our unwitting creations. It gives a whole new meaning to the illusion of separation and isolation."

As you have learned, there is nothing outside Self. To understand the full impact of such a statement you have to realise that Self, at One with the consciousness of All, contains the physical world and all its astral realms. You are where you create, or, you create where you are.

Same truth, different angle. Humans think that what they personally create only happens at the level they can see and relate to. This is the view through the window of ignorance. In reality, their personal creation also happens on many other levels of non-physical reality.

"This must mean that if a person starts off their young adult life in a state of worry and anxiety, with low self-esteem, they are connecting and interacting with a similar astral realm. Let us say that they become spiritually aware, and bring meditation and self-awareness into their life, thereby growing in consciousness. They then grow away from the lower astral connection, and are now connecting with a mid-astral level. They continue to grow in consciousness, and they now feel inner peace. Worry and anxiety are no longer part of their life, replaced by serenity and wisdom. They are now connected to a higher astral realm which is supportive of higher consciousness. Am I correct in this summary?"

Yes, you are correct. Each astral realm correlates with the state of consciousness with which it is connected. A low astral consciousness correlates with a low physical state of consciousness. On the other end of this, a high astral consciousness correlates with a high physical state of consciousness. It could be said, truthfully, that the astral worlds are neither with you nor against you, although on the low end of consciousness the correlation works against you, while on the high end it works in your favour. But this is simply the mechanics of consciousness. It is not a reward or punishment system.

"It obviously works this way physically, as well."

Yes . . . a regular low energy punch to your lips is far more damaging than a regular high energy kiss!

I laugh at his metaphor. "I'll take Carolyn's high energy kiss!"

We both chuckle. "I never thought I would suggest this, but may we return to the realm of the monsters and addicts? If there is a public house (hotel) in the town, I would like to see how our physical pubs connect, or interact, with astral pubs on a structural level, without involving human consciousness."

Patch once again creates the circles with his waving hands, and the colourful monsters of a really low astral world appear within it. Taking my hand in his, Patch leads me into the reality he opened to us, so we are no longer onlookers. We are involved.

Before we reach the pub, let me say that it is not possible to have a public house where human consciousness is not involved. It is where people drink. A pub with no people is not a pub. I am not sure of your plans, because your thoughts are now shielded . . . I taught you too well! If you mean the connection between each building on its own physical and astral structural level, this could be interesting.

"Yes . . . I think that's what I mean! I'll know when I see it."

The town is considerably larger than I expected. Being in it gives a greater perspective than looking into it. As we walk along a street I am surprised to see astral cars and bicycles—which is ridiculous; streets mean cars, right?

"Astral cars? I never even considered such a thing. And yet, I suppose it makes sense."

There are very many astral worlds . . . to put it mildly! Some, many in fact, are connected with humanity, perfectly reflecting life in the physical world of humanity. This means that physical technology has an astral counterpart, working perfectly in astral conditions. Many astral worlds have little or nothing to do with humanity, other than reflect the human impact on Earth. And there are astral worlds that have absolutely no connection with humanity.

By this time we have reached a building that is obviously a pub. Even the name is a commonplace pub name: The Pig and Whistle. We must have hundreds!

"Before we go in, can we see or visit the exact physical counterpart, or is that difficult?"

No problem.

*   *   *

I take his hand, and we step . . . *Between* . . . walking out into our designated Pig and Whistle's physical counterpart.

"Is it possible to see the two pubs merged, so I can see the astral pub in the physical pub? As I understand it, they occupy the same space in the same town."

All you need do is change your perspective of viewing . . . and it is done.

The change in viewing is easily accomplished. As I look

around, I now see the physical pub with a number of patrons scattered throughout. A few are drinking seriously, even though it is early evening. Some patrons are having a meal, some are chatting over a beer; all is casual and quiet. A view of the astral pub shows an almost identical scene. Looking keenly at the astral pub, I see a few areas that indicate serious astral disturbance. The energy is distorted, disrupted, very different from the rest of the area. When I look at the physical counterpart, I see the same disturbance, yet there are no people in these few areas. Walking over to a disturbed corner at the end of the bar, I *feel* the energy is as disturbed as it looks. Each area of disturbance has an energy-signature imprinted into it.

"Okay, now I would like to see the cause of this disturbance."

Patch smiles at me, nodding. Abruptly, it is later in the evening, and each disturbed area has a person who is drinking heavily. They perfectly fit the imprint of their own energy-field. Even as I think about asking Patch to roll the clock back a little bit, time rolls back as more people, singly and in small groups, enter the pub. Every person avoids the disturbed area, except for the people who have left their imprint of disturbance. Even in a public house, normal drinkers feel and avoid the disturbance. But I doubt that they are aware of doing this.

Those imprints contain more than a drinking addiction.

I focus on the energy signatures, and, yes, they contain high levels of anxiety, deep layers of despair and hopelessness, and more than a touch of suicidal tendencies. The astral counterparts have exactly the same energy scenario.

"This helps me to realise that a person who wants to end their alcohol addictions really does need to go to a clinic, or a place where they have no prior imprints of their disorder. A rehabilitation clinic is not just a clinic; it must be an energetically clean place. My gosh, what must a doctors waiting room be like?"

We are instantly in the empty waiting room of a group of doctor's. Energetically it is not clean. Although it is completely different from the pub energy, it has an energy of complaints, of emergency, of real sickness, of demand, and a strange energy of dissatisfaction. Not at all what I expected. However, because I am really observing what I see, I am aware that this energy, like the physical pub, is heavily encumbered, not only with negative thoughts but also negative emotions. The astral counterpart in the mental world does not have this.

"It would seem that to get the whole picture I will eventually need to visit the astral worlds of emotion . . . but not just yet."

We can do that. Have you learned what you wanted to learn from the pub?

"Yes. I was wondering about the energy of the building itself. I feel that it was clean when it was first built, but human energy is very pervasive, and the building soon developed its pockets of disturbed energy. Insight also suggests that if one of those people of disturbance die, rather than simply fade away, the empty pocket will attract a similar disturbed consciousness."

This is the way it works: like attracts like.

"Thank you, Patch, for showing me all this. Would it be possible to find and visit the astral mental spokesman who came to see me all those years ago? I am aware that it is no accident or chance that we walked into the town he came from, and I would like him to know that his visit was appreciated. Hopefully, I can return the favour."

Of course. Goodbye physical Pig and Whistle. Hello astral Pig and Whistle.

*   *   *

Taking his hand, we step . . . *Between* . . . and back into the astral Pig and Whistle!

CHAPTER NINE

MORE ASTRAL WORLDS

Of course, nothing appears to change at all. The astral continues to reflect the physical.

Even as I think about this, a man walks into the room where we are standing.

"My sister, Pedra, told me about you. Apparently you are a physical human travelling in a metaphysical body of Light."

I nod. "That about sums it up."

He looks considerably older than Pedra, almost old enough to be her father.

"Nice to meet you. I'm Mixael. My good friend and guide is Patch."

He stares at me intently. "I can tell by your energy that you are the man in the physical world I visited many years ago, although your energy is very changed."

"Oh! Then you are the person I came here to see. I have long regretted my rather brusque manner with you at that time. I was shocked, drowsy from sleep, and impatient . . . but that is no excuse. So I am here to make amends. I never forgot your visit, although I could never quite comprehend all that you represented and your courage in visiting. Only now am I learning about this. When you told me that you were from a mental world, I thought maybe *I* was going mental!"

He smiles. "My name is Gilbert. I am sorry if I disturbed you, but I was involved in an experiment to see if I could consciously enter the physical world. I, too, was rather shocked while it was actually happening."

I wave toward a chair. "Do you sit down to be comfortable?" I immediately regret such a stupid question, considering we were surrounded by chairs!

He laughs. "We certainly do. We get tired, and our legs can ache just like yours."

I still trip over the concept that only physical substance can get tired. I need to remember that this astral reality reflects ours: aches, pain, sickness and tiredness . . . and fears!

I wait until we are all seated. "When you came to see me, you mentioned the fear within your mental world. Can you explain a little more about this?"

Gilbert nodded. "In your physical world, the only manifestation of fear is within the thoughts and actions of the people. This is the only way you can see physical evidence of fear. Mob panic, people frightened and shaking with fear, etc. You never see the *substance* of fear."

"That's because fear does not have any substance. It's an illusion."

"Yes, there we have it, an illusion in *your* world. This is the big difference between a mental world with mental substance, and the physical world that only has physical substance. I can show you the substance of fear in this world."

His words really shake me. "Really! I never even imagined such a thing."

An illusion in the material world takes on substance in the non-material world. This is because it is based in human creation. It's all about subconscious focus. Patch chuckles. *Illusions do not mate and give birth to baby illusions. Illusions come from disconnected people.*"

Gilbert frowns. "Disconnected . . . in what way?"

189

"All consciousness is One. We call it a unified field of energy. A minority of people are consciously connected with this; the majority are not . . . hence the illusion of separation."

"But if you all live in a unified field of energy you cannot have separation!" he replies.

"That is the reality. Being *conscious* of that reality is true spiritual awareness."

"Amazing. I thought life was easier in your physical reality."

"Nothing could be further from the truth. Homo Stupidus makes life as difficult as possible, while Homo Sapiens makes it far more enjoyable. The majority make it *v-e-r-y* difficult."

"Homo . . . what? Is this a joke?"

Patch is laughing. *The 3-D aspect of my human friend has a great sense of humour.*

"On a more serious note, I would really like to see the substance of fear," I say. "I confess to a pinch of disbelief!" We follow Gilbert as he beckons us. At a complete loss as what to expect—not that expectations are *ever* a good idea!—we accompany him out of the Pig and Whistle and into the street. Together, we walk along like the Three Musketeers, off on a new adventure to right the wrongs of the world—in this case, a *mental* world!

He takes us to the town centre where a series of wide, stone steps lead deep down into the ground. There is nothing to signify where the steps go, no signpost—not even a gate or doorway—just the bleak, wide steps with a *really* bad energy. As we descend the three-persons-wide stairs, I notice that Gilbert is becoming increasingly agitated. Down we go, ever deeper. Soon, all daylight has gone, replaced by what appears to be electric lighting. It is very bright, almost in defiance of the increasingly *very* bad energy. Gilbert is visibly sweating, with a tremble to his hand that clutches the railing alongside the stairs. Patch appears totally unperturbed.

By now, I am aware that the bad energy is fear. In my own reality I am able to choose not to create fear, thus I very rarely feel it. Although most people believe that situations or people create our fear, we actually create fear by misusing our powerfully conditioned, negative imagination. Despite this, right here, right now, I am feeling fear as though it is a ferocious beast waiting to pounce on me, a beast with which I am strangely familiar.

We continue descending the now narrower, single-person wide, spiralling stairs.

The feeling of fear is growing stronger and stronger.

"This is incredible. Can you feel the fear, Patch? Can you feel this?"

Yes, I can feel it. However, I am also aware that this is not my fear.

"Oh, my gosh. You're right. It isn't mine either." Knowing this, I am able to dissociate from the terror content. I still feel the fear, but it no longer affects me. "Thank you, Patch."

"What do you mean, 'not your fear'?" Gilbert asks in a shaky voice.

How much of the content of fear that we are approaching is yours?

"At the moment it feels as though it is *all* mine. I'm terrified. Despite my logic saying that nothing can happen to me, I am experiencing almost overwhelming terror," he replies.

"You are a very brave man," I observe.

Are you able to take your mental imagination to a scene of great happiness?

Gilbert is now shaking so violently he is literally stumbling down the narrow stairs. "No . . . no . . . too, too m-much t-terror."

"We don't have to do this, Gilbert. I don't like to see you in such distress."

He collapses onto the stairs, shaking like a person with a raging fever. Then he indicates for us to continue. "K-k-keep g-going. Y-you'll s-s-see it. I-I'll g-g-go back."

As he attempts to pull himself one-step-at-a-time back up the stairs, we continue down.

I feel the fear growing ever stronger, ever more powerful. How can you store fear? Why would you? This is weird. I feel malevolence in the fear, and shades of screaming pain.

"Never in my wildest dreams, would I have thought that this is possible."

You are broadcasting. They store fear because this is a world without true emotions.

"What do you mean, 'true emotions'?"

Let me finish. They have rudimentary emotions, but not developed emotions. Their mental *relationship with fear is very different from your* emotional *relationship with fear. To retain all the mental fears they create would be totally overwhelming, so they have found a method by which to shed fear; I assume in an underground basement, leaving most of it there. This enables them to function reasonably well, without their handicap of crushing mental fear.*

I shake my head in amazement. "Absolutely astounding!"

We are still going down the now steep and narrow stairs. Despite the bright lighting, the air has become murky, like a dirty fog. This must be a manifestation of the stored fear. The steps end abruptly and it seems that there is a great hole in the floor of the large room we are entering. I am becoming very cautious as I approach. It is a *really* huge, deep hole.

"Surely I have nothing to fear down here. I'm a metaphysical Light-Being."

I think I am attempting to reassure myself!

Caution is wise. This astral reality is as metaphysical as you are. Just keep your focus away from fear and all will be well. We would not be here if I did not think you can handle it.

"Well, thank you. That's encouraging. I admit, some tiny part of me wants to scream and run, but it is very tiny, and way down deep."

We are now standing on the edge, or brink, of a large pit, set in the floor of a very large man-made, rock-lined room. Within the pit, the murky, dirty fog is a dense, seething mass.

"Oh, jeepers! It's *moving!*"

I stare in fascination. I can only attempt to describe the feelings I am getting. I feel as though this horrid, compacted, filthy fog is going to emerge from the pit and engulf me. I feel as though it will slowly tear me apart, sucking me dry of all substance, of all life. I can feel this, but I refuse to give it credibility. I refuse to connect with it. This is *not* my fear. This is the dense, awful, mental manifestation of fear from the inhabitants of this town, which has been shed over the centuries. It is not my fear. I do not have any. Oddly, it does not feel truly evil; angry, aggressive, violent, totally horrible maybe, but not truly evil!

"How do they leave it here? I mean, how do they shed it?"

Patch turns to me and creates those circles with his outstretched arms.

Within the picture that forms, I see a man close to where Gilbert collapsed. He, too, is a trembling, shaking heap on the steps. As I watch, I see a small segment of the murky, fog-like substance drain from his body, and slide down the stairs as though animated. We watch its progress as it slithers and flows down the steps until it reaches the pit room. It flows easily into the pit.

I stare into the pit. "So . . . this is the substance of fear!"

Patch lowers his arms and the picture disappears.

You have done well. This is a tough test. Even I feel the grasping energy of fear. I feel it as a huge and terrible serpent waiting to strike. Have you seen enough?

"Yes . . . I've seen enough and *felt* enough. Thanks for trusting me. Let's go and help Gilbert, if he is still on the stairs."

We go up the stairs, fast. Sure enough, Gilbert is a trembling heap, only a few steps higher than where we left him.

He looks apologetic. "I'm exhausted. My legs have no strength. Did you see it?"

We assure him that we did, indeed, see the mental substance of fear.

I take his shoulders, and with Patch holding his legs, we carry him like a sack of chaff to the point where the stairs widen enough for three people. We rest briefly while Gilbert makes a rapid recovery. We take our time moving up the remaining stairs.

As we emerge into the sunlight, a strange thing happens. It is as though all memory of the awful fear is being erased. I retain the emotional impact of the huge store of fear, but I am struggling to retain the mental memory. I fully focus my thoughts on the memory. Moments pass, while I feel a deep inner struggle, then abruptly, like a light switched on in a dark room, the memory is back, as strong and terrible as ever. I realise that in regaining the memory, it will always be with me, but I am not concerned. This is my choice—and it was never *my* fear.

Patch is aware of my struggle with memory. *Yes, I agree with your choice. Because you are unaffected, it is wise to retain the memory, otherwise you cannot share or record your experience.*

"Do you remember what happened?" I ask Gilbert.

"We, who live here, are aware of losing the memory. It has always been so. I have no memory of the experience at all. I remember going down the steps a little way with you, and I remember the last few steps before we emerged into the town square . . . but that's all. And it is more than enough."

Of course. Very clever. It is only by losing the memory of fear that enables you to return, and not returning would erase the whole exercise.

"But you both remember all the details?" Gilbert asks.

I nod. "Yes, we do. Would you like me to share it with you?"

As we walk toward Pedra's home, Gilbert frowns as he thinks it over. "Yes, part of me would like to know the details, but no, most of me is frightened of knowing. I told you that I would show you the substance of fear, yet I have never seen it, nor has anyone I know . . . until now. All I would like to know is if the actual substance of fear truly does exist."

"Yes, Gilbert, it really does exist. We saw the substance of fear, just as you said."

"Thank you. It is enough. I may regret not asking you to tell me more after you have gone, but for now it is enough."

Gilbert is fully recovered before we arrive at Pedra's home, but with no memory of fear, his quick recovery is natural. My own thoughts are that had he not collapsed on the stairs, and had he reached the pit alone, he would never have been able to leave it. But as the vision of Patch showed, nobody ever reaches the final step. As the fear drains from them, when they collapse on the stairs, the energy of the huge, horrible, collective pit of fear easily attracts and magnetises the small personal fears the rest of the way down into the pit. Astonishing!

Pedra wanted to talk and talk, and she wanted all the details, while Gilbert begged us not to tell her. We deemed it wise not to go into it. After lingering farewells, we made firm moves to depart.

As we swiftly speed-walked away, I reflected on all that I had experienced.

"What an utterly incredible experience. Had you ever seen the mental substance of fear before this?"

No, never. Like you, I never considered such a possibility. There is no state in our evolving consciousness where we are beyond learning and growing.

"I agree. Okay, wise and noble guide, where to next?"

It seems fairly obvious to me. You have seen a glimpse of the lower astral realms, and a slightly larger glimpse of the mid-astral, but so far we have not visited the higher astral realms.

"I also figured it like that."

✳   ✳   ✳

Taking my hand in his, we step . . . *Between* . . . and out into paradise.

I look around in surprise. The town of Sunrise is gone. Instead, we are in a huge city with great parks and gardens liberally scattered among the startling and incredible buildings.

"Holy moly . . . this is something else! Beautiful doesn't get close."

I have a sudden insight. "This astral realm is the place that spiritually-advanced physical people come to at so-called death, isn't it?"

My dear friend, every level of astral reality is where physical people go in their astral body at their so-called death. The lower astral, with a few hundred more gradients, the mid-astral levels being the same, and this, one of the lower to mid-gradients of the higher astral levels. Remember, the reality you describe as your physical reality would more truly be described as astral, despite most people's complete unawareness of this. All the many zones of human reality are astral.

"Because I have a dense physical body, there is a limit to how far I can metaphysically travel into the higher astral levels, correct?"

Correct. This is close to your limit.

"Amazing! If this is a lower mid-gradient of the higher astral, all I can say is that the highest of the high astral must be out-of-this-world."

In some ways it is. If you were there with your current consciousness, you would see and experience absolutely nothing. But, of course, you could not be there.

"Have you been to such a level?"

No. I am told that it is a level of beauty beyond anything you can imagine. But equally, while we are discussing this, there are also lower astral levels that you could not visit. You have too high an energy. It works both ways.

"Phew! That would be serious stuff! Talking of lower astral, I would like to clarify one other point. If people in my physical reality reach a mental base level, connecting with the astral zone which has the pit of fear, would the people from our reality leave fear in the pit?"

It is possible. Using the analogy you so often use in your public talks, all realities are the pages of a single book. The writing on one page is exactly the same writing as on every other page, even though it may describe very different situations and images. If such people deposited fear in the pit, then it will remain, but it has a connection to them. It is up to them whether they sever the astral connection, or retain it.

"So to sever it, they choose Love. To retain it, they continue with more of the same. Yes?"

Exactly.

"The quandary is, of course, if they were able to choose Love, they would not have created fear in the first place."

Exactly.

"Okay, that's clear. The more I metaphysically learn, the more I find there is to learn about what I think I have already metaphysically learnt. I think!"

This is a new experience. Patch and I are hovering about a hundred metres above the city, both of us sitting in the lotus position. Usually, I am the only person doing this. But no longer. I see a dozen or more other astral Beings sitting as we are above the city and parks. As we arrive, they slowly look at us, a few wave serenely, then continue with their own inner contemplations.

Patch smiles at me. *You no longer have an exclusive. Have you ever wondered why you like to sit a hundred metres above whatever it is you are viewing?*

"That's obvious. To have a wider, much further ranging view, of course."

Wrong answer. Think about this. You sit up high because in your physical reality you would, indeed, have a wider, further ranging view. This is logical. However, in your metaphysical reality, you could sit in a hole a hundred metres deep, and still have a wider, further ranging view, if you chose to. Your metaphysical viewpoint has nothing whatsoever to do with your location.

I stare at him, dumbfounded. He is right. Of course he is right. I have been taking my normal everyday logic and applying it to a metaphysical reality.

"Jeepers! Obvious is not so obvious after all."

This is not all. Negative energy is, indeed, very heavy . . . as we witnessed with fear sliding downward into the pit. Your lofty position is often over a city. This not only distances you from it, because you are not overly fond of cities, but it also distances you from the immediate and heavier negative energies. This is your automatic, metaphysical instinct at work, under the stimulus of your everyday logic.

I gaze at him, amazed and amused. "I was going to ask how you know I'm not very keen on cities, but undoubtedly you read energy-signatures better than I do. So metaphysically, I am attracted to the higher level for a very basic reason. Well . . . it does make perfect sense."

Indeed it does. I am merely sharing observations with you, a few you have overlooked.

"By the same token, I assume that higher energies find a stable level at around a hundred metres above the city. I wonder how many other observations I've managed to overlook."

Oh . . . you will find them all in perfect timing. Now you know why we have company at this altitude. Even in this serene atmosphere, the serenity is more tangible at a hundred metres.

"Thank you, for furthering my education."

My pleasure. Any ideas of where you would like to go, or shall I be your guide?

"Lead on, O guide."

He points to the heart of the city and we drift down toward it. I quickly realise that airborne traffic is commonplace in this higher astral reality. Most people are lazily floating/flying to their destination, in defined levels or layers. Nobody is moving fast. If it appears that two people are on a collision course, both of them move far enough away from the other to safely pass, even if very close to each other. This appears to happen without any apparent awareness on the part of the travellers. It is as though there is an automatic, non-collision program that safeguards them.

We, too, are drifting *slowly* down. I realise that this slow speed is happening *to* me, rather than me choosing it. We must automatically be in the automatic program! As we drift lower, I notice that there are no roads—there is now!—in the city. No mechanical traffic exists here. This, I like! A level below me, I see that several people are transporting large, truck-sized objects from one building to another. The objects float. Very convenient! Unlike ours, the atmosphere in this city is as pure and fresh and clean as it could possibly be.

As I look at the buildings, I realise with a sense of surprise that there are many levels, or qualities, to what I often describe as ethereal. These buildings are ethereal, but they have a quality of ethereal structure that I have never knowingly encountered. Every building, every home in Sunrise had an ethereal energy, but only now, as I experience the ethereal contrast between there and here, do I realise that ethereal is not simply ethereal. Ethereal substance has many levels of quality. As an example, consider the range of woods from the very cheapest soft-wood, for making crates, up to the most seasoned hard-woods, for making the very best, hand-crafted furniture. The former will last a year or two, the latter many lifetimes. The range of ethereal qualities far exceeds this.

A good observation, Mixael.

"I feel as though I am back to basics. I should have known about ethereal qualities."

Experience teaches . . . and you are learning.

I smile at him. "Do you realise that when we reach the ground, the very first Roads will be in the city! Traffic-less roads, that is. Roads that lead to the Light!"

Patch laughs. *Good one!*

198

Puns aside, it is odd to walk in a city without any streets. Wide footpaths abound, all having equally wide borders of beautifully maintained plants. Some of the borders appear to be natural vegetation, while much of it is cultivated. Flowering plants are everywhere, almost enticing the walking person to see more and more of what lies ahead. This is the effect it has on me! I like it, especially when the path I am walking has plants that are new to me. Traffic-less and quiet, this is *definitely* my kind of city.

"I would be delighted to come here when I transit away from my physical reality. I would be happy to be a gardener here. I'm the gardener at home . . . when it is growing . . . when it rains! I can never quite decide whether I am a gardener who is a spiritual teacher, or a spiritual teacher who is a gardener. But I do know that gardening came first, and it has been a great teacher for me. A garden is the meeting place between Nature, the teacher, and the gardener, the student, if the gardener has the wisdom for this."

You had the wisdom from an early age to become a student of Nature, even if you were not actually aware of doing so. In truth, your metaphysical journeying began at a very early age . . . even though you had no idea you were doing so.

"I guess you are saying the intellect spans a single incarnation, whereas intelligence continues on forever. My childhood intelligence continued an old journey that my intellect, in not understanding it, disclaimed."

Patch gives me an admiring glance. *Very well and succinctly stated.*

"Are we here for a particular reason, or just to look and learn?"

We will just take it as it comes. Who knows who may chance along!

We walk along the pathway that we are following, simply to see where it goes. For a while it takes us alongside a huge building on one side, and flowering beds of plants on the other. I confess, my attention is more on the fascinating plants than the building. There is a mixture of plants I am familiar with, along with plants entirely new to me. The familiar plants come from my reality, but where do the others come from? I stop to touch a leaf of one of the new plants. As I do so, it alters very slightly. It now seems to have another identical plant superimposed on the original—two in one!

Patch calls my attention to the corner of the building, which we have just reached. He is gazing intently at something on, or in, the building, but I have no idea what.

"What am I supposed to be looking at?"

He glances at me in surprise. *You don't see it?*

"I don't see what? I can see the corner of the building. I can see the tree close by. I can see a hazy reflection in the glassy material of the building but . . . that's it."

Hazy reflection . . . really? I suggest you look again. Reflection of what?

Hmm, that's a good point. I stare at the hazy reflection, trying to figure out what it is that is being reflected. Is it me? No. Is it Patch? No. So what is it? I stare some more, moving position as I try to figure it out. Oh! Maybe it is not a reflection!

"Okay . . . I was a bit hasty. It now seems as though there is a . . . ghost, trapped within the very structure of the building itself."

Touch the building. You are metaphysical. Try to push your hand into the structure.

I attempt to do as he suggests. When my hand touches the surface of the glassy building, it feels as firm as glass. I push on my hand, but the surface remains unyielding. However, now that I have my hand flat on the surface, I see a ghostly, human-like Being that appears to be as flat as a sheet of paper, moving toward me, placing its hand, palm to palm with mine.

Reality explodes.

I am spinning over and over, round and round, completely disoriented. For a brief moment I feel a touch of panic, then it is gone. I have no idea whether I am standing or spinning, but I attempt to focus on the only reality I have: palm to palm with an astral Being.

Slowly, reality quietens. The spinning slows gently to a standstill, and I am standing at the corner of the building, my hand touching the glass-like substance, palm to palm with a flat astral Being. Nothing is hazy anymore. I can see into the structure with utter clarity.

(For the reader's clarity, I now enter a strange duality).

I see a metaphysical Being standing on the pathway at the corner of my structure. He has his hand on my surface, his palm touching mine as I place it with his. I beckon to him. He is clearly unsure of what to do, and I am hesitant to draw him into my structure in case he is overwhelmed. I watch him carefully, beckoning again, but he does not know how to join me. I smile at him sweetly, then very slowly and gently I begin to pull him into my structure. For a few moments he struggles, but his companion speaks to him, and he relaxes. Now he is more than halfway into my structure, and the rest of him is sliding easily into me.

Yikes! I get the sense of a feminine energy Being wanting me to enter the structure of the building. Is she crazy? I can't do that. I'm still giddy. I call out to Patch, and he tells me that I am perfectly safe, to just relax. It's easy for him to say! He is not being invited into the structure of a building. Oh my gosh, I'm being pulled in. Now I'm sliding in. Wow! To my astonishment, the flat Being who has pulled me in is not flat, but she is definitely a she. She is actually rather voluptuous! Her energy field is very powerful, but although she looks human, she is not human in her energy.

I have the male human with me. I am intrigued that he is a physical male, yet he is in his metaphysical Light-body. How did he get into this reality? I will try communicating with him.

"Who are you? How did you get me in here? Ouch! Your telepathic questions are blasting into me. Too loud. Ouch . . . don't shout! Ah, that's better. My name is Mixael. I am a metaphysical traveller. I am with Patch, my guide, and we are visiting a few of the astral worlds."

He can hear me, and he is replying. In all my time this is completely new to me. An astral traveller who knows nothing of our realm. I speak to him very softly. "My name is Raeeele. I am the Energy Being of this building. The building is my energy. I am the building; we are One."

"How is this possible? You are a Being? You cannot be a Being and a building. Are you trapped in here? Can I help you escape? And how is it possible that, within the walls of the building, it is so huge . . . with so much depth, so much space?"

*"You know nothing . . . but you mean well. I do not need to

escape. I am the building. Listen, while I explain. When this building was created, I was born with it. As I peer into your psyche, you might understand if I say that I am the spirit *of the building. The external of this building is in the city, where you are. However, the inner structure, which is the building, is in multi-dimensional space. What you see from the outside, or from within the rooms, is but a fraction of my greater reality. Can you comprehend this? I now realise this is way beyond your reality."**

"Thank you for explaining. Yes, I do comprehend even though I don't understand. How utterly amazing." I gaze around inside the space of the structure. It is unlike anything I have encountered before. The nearest impression I have is of galactic space. "Why does this feel a bit like being in space . . . when you are a building?" I sound ridiculous!

*"Come with me, I can show you my world. I am not a prisoner; this is my choice. What you call the building, is me. Let me show you what none in your realm have ever seen."**

Raeeele takes my hand in hers. She looks human, but she is something else altogether. Her fingers are hotter than is possible. If my hand was physical, it would be charred. I even feel the heat metaphysically, but it is not painful. She steps upward as though we are walking up stairs, taking me with her. As we ascend— to where, I have no idea—I see thousands of small fuzz-balls whirling around us. It is not a dense cloud of them, but they seem to be thickly everywhere. They also appear to be animated, but with no apparent will of their own. I point this out to her. "What are they?"

*I am learning that the reality I see and experience is not the same as Mixael's. He appears to see everything as disconnected, whereas in my reality, all is One. I suspect that the apparent space between what he sees as separate objects is where he bases his reality. I send out an impulse of pure thought, and all the space momentarily appears to disappear. The feeling is probably one of suffocation, but it is not real. I have created an illusion to identify his illusion.**

Oh my God! All the fuzz-balls have come together into a solid cluster, and we are right in the middle of it all. I can't move. Luckily, I don't need to breathe in my Light-body. This is really suffocating. Raeeele must know what she is doing—obviously! "What is happening?"

"I am attempting to give you an idea of how this space would appear in your reality. It would be dense. Like you are now feeling. You can move, and breathe if you wish. This density is an illusion. Just focus on reality the way it was. Project that reality."

Okay, this is not new—focus! I project my memory image of the inner-space of Raeeele as strongly as I can. Instantly, it is as though the density explodes away, and we are once again in her bizarre and wonderful space.

"Very good. You are stronger than I expected."

"Yeah, dumb but strong." With my words the most incredible, unearthly music I have ever heard suddenly bursts all over me. Celestial harmonies of delight. "Wow, what is that music?"

For a moment there is complete silence.

Then the music sweeps over me again, pealing and echoing through this inner-space.

"I realise that you are hearing my laughter. You make a joke, 'dumb but strong'. I am laughing at your effort to let me think you have misplaced your sense of self. You make a joke."

Truly? This incredible music is Raeeele's laughter? I could listen to it forever. "Raeeele, your laughter is beautiful music to me. How far will our journey into your reality take us?"

Fresh music/laughter, with a new dancing lightness, washes over me.

"You make another joke. Our journey is as long as it takes to go nowhere at all. We are always here, journeying here."

"Okay, you've lost me completely. Our realities are so different I think understanding might be impossible. So . . . while we ascend the steps, we are not ascending at all. Is this right?"

"Steps . . . what steps? Mixael, it would appear that as entertaining as this may be for both of us, we have little reality compatibility. Is there anything you would like to ask me?"

"The strangeness of your reality is beyond my ability to frame it into a cohesive thought. This makes it impossible for me to comprehend, or even question. I can experience your reality, but in the way that fish out of water would experience mine. It humbles me to realise that as you have evolved to the consciousness of a reality where you can reside, create . . . and be the creation, so too, your intelligence must go through enormous growth and expansion."

*"*That was very well expressed. Yes, as consciousness grows, intelligence grows; they are One. As intelligence grows, so a greater reality grows; they are One. As a greater reality grows, so the multiverse grows; they are One. As the multiverse grows, so everything within grows; they are One. As the All grows, creativity grows; they are One. This is eternal."*

I nod, as I gaze at her in wonder. She is deliberately coming apart. The rather lovely, human-looking body is disintegrating, and as the cells slowly drift away in their billions, I see they, also, are the fuzz-balls that are floating all around us. I see them as larger, simply because this is how I see them. Soon Raeeele is part of the inner-space in which I stand.

*"*Goodbye, sweet, human Light-Being. I enjoyed your company. Please do not feel in any way diminished by the differences between us, for I am hugely impressed by your courage and audacity. It took a large measure of both to enter the structure of a building where you could only trust that you would ever emerge. And never underestimate your intelligence. Remember, as your consciousness grows, intelligence grows; for they are One. Farewell, I will never forget you. I will create anew in your honour."*

As she inner-speaks to me, I am being slowly ejected from the structure of the building. No, I am being very gently evicted from a space that is a beautiful intelligence named Raeeele.

"Thank you, Raeeele. It has been my honour, and my pleasure, to be with you."

Patch is waiting, sitting in the lotus position about three metres above the path.

Welcome back. You look both bemused and in awe, simultaneously.

"That's because I am both, and more . . . simultaneously."

Together, in unspoken agreement, we rise up to the hundred metre zone. Sitting in the lotus position with a few other people in the vicinity, we do not speak. I am almost lost in awe. I need to regain balance.

A . . . space . . . of . . . silence.

I have no idea of time passing. I do know that in my no-time of silence, I have regained my balance. My thoughts flicker toward Raeeele, but they are unable to hold to any image.

How are you feeling now?

I share with Patch some of my experience as best I can. It has the feeling of a dream that keeps slipping away, but speaking of it is also stabilising it in my memory. I do not want to forget, so I detail as much as I am able to him.

A very great privilege. She very rarely draws an astral person into her domain, and generally those few find it more incomprehensible than you have. And they live in this reality!

"Hmm, that's good to hear. I felt a bit like a total primitive with a great sage. It's nice to know that I did okay . . . under the circumstances. Right now, I feel like walking in one of the parks among the trees, standing by water, immersing myself in Nature. Is that okay with you?"

Sounds like an excellent idea.

We come gently to Earth. Because we hold an image of trees and water in our focus, we settle next to a stunningly beautiful lake, surrounded at its edge by graceful trees. As I gaze on the water's surface, I realise that it is unlike any water in our reality. But how can I describe it? If you compare the energy of a vibrant tree in full Spring growth, with the energy of a long dead tree, you get some idea. The energetic quality of this water makes all our water seem energetically dead. I almost wish I had not seen this! Beauty is an energy within itself. The beauty of this stunning lake brings tears to my physical eyes and a lump in my throat, as I sit in my study. I thank God that I am able to see the beauty in the Nature of my world.

As I gaze spellbound at the scene of tranquil, living beauty, at the tall sweeping, pendulous trees that stand watch, like so many sentinels over their lady of grace, the lake, I feel immense gratitude that this is possible. I feel gratitude to Pan, to Patch, to Raeeele, to Seine, to all the Beings who willingly stretch my reality from its meagre, mundane roots, into something ever-growing and magnificent. I feel immense gratitude to Carolyn, my beloved wife, who lives by my side. Her unfailing, unflagging Love for me, for life, for every human, for every animal and bird, and all plants, is a constant reminder of the very best qualities that are inherent in humanity. By example, she teaches me. I am so blessed.

Raeeele certainly rattled your cage. Such an experience is always beneficial.

I burst out laughing. At certain moments, Patch can be incredibly irreverent. He has shattered the moment, and maybe it is just as well. I do not want to get too introspective.

"Okay Patch, I take your point. How about we do something completely different? How about we go to an astral world of emotion. Somewhere around mid-level to begin with?"

He holds out a hand to me with a smile, and I take it.

Chapter Ten

Astral Worlds of Emotion

Once again, we step . . . *Between* . . . coming out on the edge of a large country town.

You need to be prepared for this. This is basically a world of emotions.

"It feels very different from our recent astral visit."

Of course it does. As I just said, this is an astral world of emotion. Just as in the mental astral worlds there are rudimentary emotions, so here, also, emotions are accompanied by a very capable but rudimentary mentality. One is not entirely exclusive from the other, nor can it ever be.

"That is very true. I was once shown that in a sixth-dimensional reality, the emotional, mental, and soul bodies all fuse into one. This is when I learned that the mental and emotional bodies each have, and develop, their own states of consciousness. However, regarding this astral world of emotions, could it be compared with left-brain dominance? This does not mean there is no right-brain activity, but simply that the energy directed from the left-brain is strongly dominant?"

Yes, that would be a good analogy. In the mental worlds, thoughts rule. Here, the emotions rule. Just as people in the mental world experience fear mentally, here, fear would basically be an emotional experience.

"Right, got that. For myself, I feel that I have a balance between my emotional, mental and physical experiences of life. I honour them all, equally."

That one word 'honour' for your emotional, mental, and physical bodies, says more than an hour of talking would do to convince me. So, let's take a stroll!

And stroll we do, the metaphysical way, gracefully, effortlessly—holistically.

This is a very much larger town than Sunrise. People are casually aware of us as we stroll along the pavement; maybe it's because we take care to give all passing cars on the street a wide berth. Although the cars could not hurt us, I am sure that it would be disconcerting for the town folk to see a car pass through us. We are *not* of this world, but the risk of being hit by a car is very real. Traffic is a bit erratic and careless; not much order. Not that it is chaotic, but it is rather on the wild side. I glance at a bank. Yes, they have banks and money! This is obviously a small bank, with a sign hanging on it: The Bank of Balm. I can only assume this is the name of the town. A nearby shop, Balm Pharmaceutical, confirms it.

"Hmm, interesting name for a town, Balm. It's wild enough here to need some sort of a balm, even if it is only a word."

Yes, it certainly lacks order. This usually accompanies emotional rule. After all, this is a mid-emotional astral world. The people will have either fairly wild, or rather controlled, emotions.

"This suggests that a lower emotional world would be very chaotic, with almost zero order."

Yes, Chaos and Order would be very imbalanced.

"In that case, I will happily give that world a miss. I don't need it. I wonder how well the emotions mix on this mid-level. It sounds like a volatile combination to me."

As I speak, two cars came into collision at one of the roundabouts. Most crossroads here appear to have a roundabout, rather than traffic lights. From my observation, there seems to be no 'give way' road-rules, which would be sensible. Or, if there are any, nobody bothers. The roundabouts are very chaotic, with people beeping car-horns and waving fists. Very emotional, but not very effective!

Two people jump out of one car, and three out of the other. Nobody is hurt, even though the cars look a bit crumpled. Then the screaming and fist waving begins as they confront each other. I listen, but find it difficult to follow what is shouted. It seems not to make sense. One woman manages to smack her opponent on the side of the head—and all hell breaks loose. Now, everyone who had been watching wades in, fists flying and voices screaming as it becomes a free-for-all.

Of all the spectators, only Patch and I are not involved. We look at each other and smile.

"Wow, if this is a minor altercation, I wonder what a serious situation would evoke?"

Well . . . you said it was a volatile brew. If we watch, I think we will see the people who are more emotionally controlled disengage from the melee very soon.

Sure enough, temporarily deserting their battered car, three of the people move away from the scene. They march determinedly up the street and enter into Balm Breakdown and Towing. This makes good sense. Let them fight it out!

The three people soon come out of the service yard and, crossing the road, they enter a small coffee shop with a cute, old fashioned entrance.

Let's go and introduce ourselves to the natives. These three are not quite so emotionally volatile or, at least, they controlled it more quickly.

"Good idea." I sigh. "How I would enjoy a nice cappuccino."

We enter the cafe, and it really is cute. Very tastefully furnished and classy. Our three potential friends—hopefully!— have just finished ordering. We walk over to them and Patch politely asks if they would recommend the coffee and cakes here.

"Oh yes, we always come here. Top spot in town," says the man.

One of the women agrees. "Are you new in town? I cannot

recollect ever seeing you." She laughs apologetically. "Country town, you get to recognise people after a while." The other woman nods in agreement. We gradually learn that they are a husband and wife, and her sister. At first they are not very chatty, but with a bit of encouragement they open up.

"We saw the collision at the roundabout," I mentioned. This was the encouragement!

"Did you, by gosh? Did you see the way that other car deliberately ran into us? My name is George, by the way, and this is my wife Ethel, and her sister, Elaine."

"So very distressing" said Ethel. "I'm shaking inside . . . and they were so rude. The very first thing they did was to blame us, when it was obviously their fault."

"Really shook me up," Elaine agrees. "If only they had been more careful."

I decided to play the devil's advocate! "We are strangers to this part of the world. But from our viewpoint, the traffic does not flow around the roundabout in just one direction. People seem to go any direction they want. It's no wonder cars collide. You have a crazy system."

George immediately bristles. "That is hardly our fault."

"I'm not blaming anyone. I'm simply saying that your rules of the road are flawed."

George harrumphs. "Yes, well . . . we have had many town meetings over that very point, but we can never agree about which way the traffic should flow. So nothing changes. Most people think that if they simply want to turn right, it is stupid to go all the way round to the left. Or vice versa. So they turn according to need."

"And collide with someone coming the other way." I murmur. "This is what you did."

George turns red. "Are you blaming me?" he asks in a loud voice.

I ignore him. "Where I come from, all the traffic on a roundabout gives way to traffic on the right. Everybody knows this, nearly everybody does this, so collisions are rare. In most other countries, they give way to the left. This also works perfectly.

But here, you have endless confusion over who will give way to whom, so nobody does. The system is ridiculous."

George leaps to his feet, slamming a hand on the table. "How dare you, sir. You come barging up to us at our table then do nothing but insult us. Get out, before I throw you out."

Smiling, we both leave the coffee house.

That went well. Now I have seen your meddling and interfering in action. I'm sure you enjoyed yourself, but what were you trying to prove?

I laugh. "I wanted to see how quick they were to anger. Or if they could accept that the system is flawed. Or if they might concede that both cars collided, not just one. That sort of thing. I wanted to see how they would emotionally react. It is obvious that anger and blame are high priorities. I wonder if their emotional encumbrances allow them to embrace forgiveness."

You certainly got one emotional reaction. I thought Ethel was going to whack you.

"Yes, I noticed. She would have got a shock." We both laugh.

"I find it interesting that they have no overall county-wide rules of the road. From what George said, it seems that each town works it out for themselves. What total confusion. Anyway, it was good for a lesson and a laugh, but I would like to meet some spiritually aware people in this world. A bit more like Pedra. She was open and aware. Is this possible?"

Patch holds out his hand. *We are in an astral world. Just as there are people with many varying consciousness in your reality, and in Pedra's reality, so in the emotional world there are many differing states of consciousness. Now, focus on people who are spiritually aware.*

*   *   *

We step . . . *Between* . . . and into a busy bustling city.

I immediately glance at the traffic, smiling as I see it flowing smoothly and orderly.

"Ah ha, now I see what it was all about in Balm. We were immediately confronted with the chaotic energy reflected in the traffic and the people. Emotional chaos was dominant. Here, by

211

way of contrast, there is more order."

A good observation.

I point to Crestridge Real Estate. "This would appear to be the city of Crestridge!"

Without heading upward a hundred metres, cast your metaphysical vision wide to see if we are, in fact, on a hilltop ridge.

It takes me mere moments to confirm that although the city is not on the highest part of the long range of hills that I can see, it *is* located on a high, wide, stable, rocky ridge. Crestridge it is! "Okay, so where do we go from here?"

Maybe we should bypass 'go' and be ready for 'come'.

"Meaning?"

Meaning that while we focused on spiritually aware people, I also held a focus that they are now looking for us . . . so we wait for them to come.

"I'll try not to be sceptical."

You don't like waiting!

We both chuckle. We are in an area of the city where it is very busy. I have no idea how anybody will find us among such crowds of people—or where! I have enough trouble finding myself! There is a large city square nearby. This purely pedestrian area is covered with paving slabs of varying soft autumn colours. They are laid in such a way as to create an overall flow of soothing colour. It looks and feels very attractive, somehow creating a soft, inviting sensation. I like this place. A city square offering an emotional invitation! Neat. We walk over to the square and stand under some leafy trees near the road, well away from the crowds.

Moments later, a taxi pulls up near us. The rear door opens and a voice calls out, "Come along then. We got your message and we are dying to meet you. Hop in."

Patch smiles at me triumphantly. *See!*

"Okay, I admit, I'm both surprised and impressed."

This is a first. I have never before been in a taxi while purely metaphysical. Odd, I get a strong sensation of physicality, as I sit in a back seat. We have two companions. A tall, older man is sitting in the front seat next to the driver, while Patch and I are in the back with a slim, middle-aged woman. The whole feeling is so strongly like my physical world, I have to check that I am, indeed, purely metaphysical.

"Hello. My name is Pat, and that's Tom in the front. Welcome to our world. This is so utterly intriguing . . . and so unusual. We have so much to talk about."

"Are you familiar with Beings such as us?" I ask.

"More familiar with the concept, than the reality," Tom says from the front.

"Thank you for meeting with us. My name is Mixael. I often journey in my metaphysical body to other reality frames, although this is my first deliberate visit to an astral world of emotional reality. My companion's name is Patch; he is my guide. He is also far more than he appears to be."

I notice that as we travel in the taxi, there seems to be far less traffic than in my reality. I mention this, commenting on how nice it is to have a city this big which is so uncrowded.

"We have a traffic-flow system that produces this level of order. If all the traffic was able to be on the streets at any time, it would be complete chaos. Actually, it would come to a standstill."

"We call that a gridlock. In the most basic terms, how does the system work?"

"In brief, each vehicle has its own allocated days it can be driven in the city along with an *urgent need* travel system. Abused, it would not work. Respected, it works as well as you see. It is to our mutual advantage to ensure that it works, otherwise . . . traffic chaos. Finally, to ensure that people can move around the city, we have a super-efficient underground transport system for normal public transport, and also for the delivery of heavy goods."

"Hmm, I'm impressed. In many parts of my world, no matter how good the system, it would be subjected to such abuse and misuse, it would be ruined."

The taxi pulls up in front of a large house in a spacious, leafy suburban area. I notice that each house has a large, rather nice garden. We all get out and the taxi drives away. I see no sign of the driver being paid.

"Come along in," Tom says cordially, ushering us toward the house.

I could spend time describing the house and garden, but it is very much like any top-quality home that is not overly lavish, and in a good area. Just the same as in my reality. Remarkably so. In fact, this similarity to our reality is so strong, I am wondering if I have my wires crossed!

When we enter the house, several other people are waiting for us. All the usual niceties are observed, and the perennial tea and drinks are offered. I actually try a tea, but, as usual, it is impossible for me to drink. Why this is so I am not sure; it seems to be a frequency incompatibility. Ah well, at least this confirms the difference in realities!

Tom and the others have a lot of questions for Patch and me. Patch answers the questions put to him by not really answering any of them. But only I seem to notice. He appears to give brief, unexplained answers, while I stare at him in astonishment. As he glances my way, I get a strong message not to interfere. So I don't. Despite this, they all seem perfectly satisfied with his replies. Okay—this *is* a different reality!

When they question me, I answer as truthfully as possible. However, all the loose ends I leave are never followed up. They are content no matter how I reply. I even try avoiding answers that have any complexity at all, and one or two people lightly applaud me. The more simple I keep my replies, the more admiration I seem to attract.

I send a tightly controlled beam of thought to Patch. "I don't get it."

He, knowing exactly what I mean, beams back to me. *It is not so much the words they are listening to, as the feelings they contain. Emotions are what speak and explain things here.*

"Oh, of course! It never even occurred to me. So similar in appearance, yet so different in the energy of communication. They use the emotional energy of words, not the mental content.

Turning to Tom, I ask him to explain something. "When I asked you in the taxi if you were familiar with Beings such as Patch or me, you replied that you were more familiar with the concept than with the reality. If, as I understand it, this world is predominantly an emotional one, how can you have strong

214

mental concepts about . . . anything?"

Tom looks surprised. "What makes you think that concepts are mental?"

Now, *I'm* surprised. "But a concept has to be mental. What else could it be?"

"In our world, concepts are emotional," Tom says with a smirk.

I am flabbergasted. But—of course! It *must* be so. It never even occurred to me that a concept could be emotional. I try to grasp that—an emotional concept. "In our reality, a concept is mental, although it can have emotional energy with it, such as if we like or dislike the concept, but a purely emotional concept, this is new to me."

"Likewise, we have a mental connection with our concepts, giving the concept an objective mental viewpoint, but it is rather basic. How interesting that we each take our realities so much for granted. It seldom occurs to us that an opposite reality lies alongside our own reality, separated only by . . . by what?" Tom frowns at his own unexpected question.

By levels of consciousness, by restricting beliefs, by attachments to perceptions, by a lack of openness, by habit and repetition, by the conditioning of consensus reality, by lack of enquiry . . . to name just a few.

"Tom, do you experience and perceive your world as physical? Or do you have a different term for the materials and substances of your world?"

"We experience our world as physical. We, ourselves, are emotional Beings, but, of course, we think to some degree on a mental level also," he replies.

"So people here are never overwhelmed by depressive thoughts?"

"No, but many people are overwhelmed by depressive feelings," he says emphatically. "So how does this work in your reality? You apparently express the physical, mental and emotional all in one combination. Is this true? It sounds like an overpowering, even uncontrollable mixture to me. I find it difficult to imagine."

"I'm sorry Tom, I will answer your question, but you just mentioned imagination. Surely to imagine you must have, and need, to use a degree of mental visualising?"

"Not so. Imagination is strongly emotional for us. We emotionally visualise what we are imagining, with only very little mental input," he said.

I nod. "Yes, as you explain it, I understand. For us, if we mentally imagine something while deliberately adding strong emotional feelings, what we imagine will materialise much more powerfully. However, on the occasions of unrealised subliminal emotions, such as depression, anger, or self-criticism—all negative emotions—then life seems to go all wrong. Ironically, it is our *emotional* creation that we manifest, rather than the desired *mental* one. But we mostly blame someone or something else. We are not good at taking personal responsibility for what we bring into our lives . . . unless it is nice!"

Pat looks sympathetic. "I have quite enough problems with emotional imagination. I would not want to add mental energy to the brew. It must be tough in your reality."

"Quite honestly, I am learning a whole new appreciation for the people in my reality world. For us, our mental and emotional energy manifests its creation in our daily outer reality, as well as in our physical bodies. Unfortunately, very few people truly recognise this, or act upon it. This self-creation can be very physically liberating, or it can . . . and frequently does . . . cause physical disease and death. Right now, in my world, mental and physical diseases are rapidly escalating, with mostly unrecognised emotional causes behind all of it. I would not recommend consciously incarnating into our physical reality until, or unless, you have mastered this one."

Pat shudders. "And I thought *this* was difficult."

"Anyway, I've probably already answered your question, Tom, about the physical, mental and emotional blend. Here, obviously, emotions rule. In a mental world, the intellect rules.

"In my reality, people consider our world to be one of physical substance. While in the mental world I saw the substance of fear, but for us, that would be an unheard of concept. It can be confusing. Your physical substance is as physical to you as ours is to us, yet if a physical person from my world came in their physical body to you here, they would see nothing of this world's substance, other than, perhaps, a world of mist. They might *feel* it, but little more."

"We do get astral visits from your people," Tom says.

"This intrigues me. You know of our reality, and you recognise an astral visitor. Yet, if you were to visit us, nobody would know. Ah yes, the penny drops. Our energy field is much denser than yours. That would make the difference. Only a comparatively few people in my reality would be aware of, or even open to, astral worlds of just mental or emotional realities."

Each has its own developing states of consciousness. Inter-exchange between these worlds is possible—as you are proving—both metaphysically and by incarnation. In my observation, the so-called physical world is the most difficult to master, but it also offers the greatest rewards.

"In what way?" asks Tom. "And what do you mean by the so-called physical world?"

Patch looks at me. *I'm sure this is your question to answer.*

I smile. "I'll do my best. In any world of spiritual Beings, self-mastery is the stage that takes us out of illusion into a greater reality. This happens when the injustices of the physical world no longer imprison us. We see through the illusion. In this state of consciousness we experience the profound depth of Peace. Peace becomes a spiritual substance and a reality within the soul Being we are. This Peace cannot be adequately described. The 'physical' world Patch mentions is so-called because people see and relate to our world as physical, but it is *actually* spiritual. As metaphysical Beings, we each have a physical, mental, and emotional body through which the soul-self expresses. Physically, we see only the physical body. This is the weakest body we have; very easily disrupted. Next weakest is the mental body, vulnerable and rather fragile. Then we have the emotional body, vulnerable also, but by far the most powerful. In our reality, emotions rule, but most people don't recognise this because they basically relate to the world as physical. Physical bodies come and go, while the metaphysical, mental and emotional bodies are permanent. We have a world of people who believe only in what they can physically see, hence, the *so-called* physical world! Of course, they are very aware of thoughts and emotions, but it's still deemed a physical world."

"It sounds far more complicated than in our world reality," Pat muses.

I nod. "It probably is. However, people here, like yourselves, who seek to become more aware and more open by following a spiritual path, must find life easier than those who just blunder along without giving any feelings to such things."

Pat and Tom both nod, along with most of the others.

"It is the same with us. In my younger years, I was the victim of all my many emotional insecurities. Most people are! The next stage is to gain a measure of emotional security, and this helps. But the real answer, found by considerably fewer people, is when you learn that security and insecurity are no more than the positive and negative of the same illusion! Once you let go of the false and deceitful security/insecurity concept, and find balance . . . you are on the path to emotional completeness. Life becomes easier . . . it is as it is."

"Now that is *fascinating!*" A girl in her late teens almost explodes the words. "Oh, yes! Oh, yes! Thank you, thank you, thank you . . . yes, I get it! We have exactly the same . . . concept. We *feel good* if we are emotionally secure, and we *feel bad* if we are emotionally insecure, and it just goes on and on forever. But . . . emotional balance, *that is it.* Let go of security and insecurity, and find balance by simply *accepting* the way *it is as it is* in the moment. *YES!* Thank you so very much."

I laugh. "You are very welcome . . . and I feel in your energy that you do, indeed, get it. *It is as it is* in the moment, sums it up. In my reality world I am a spiritual teacher; I teach emotional completeness. When the emotions are balanced, life is balanced; we are the creators of our lives."

"I knew I had to be here tonight. When the *feeling* went out that we might get some off-world visitors, I knew I had to be here. My name is Lizzie, by the way."

"Happy to be of assistance, Lizzie. Did you say when the *feeling* went out? In our reality it would be the *word* that went out. And probably electronically!"

"Oh no, not here. Tom and Pat powerfully projected the feeling, as I said. A feeling full of excitement and promise, I might add. But you have exceeded all my expectations!"

So many subtle little differences, yet they add up to a completely different reality zone.

Okay, I, personally, have had enough of watching people drink and snack, including Patch. While I never truly feel metaphysical thirst or hunger, I can reach a limit on watching other people enjoying gastronomical delights of which I cannot partake!

"Time to go," I project to only Patch.

Well, beautiful people, it is time to depart. We thank you for your kind hospitality. My metaphysical friend has learned much from you, and happily he has given much in return. It is time for us to move on, before fatigue snatches my friend back to his reality.

Okay, when you put it like that, I am not yet indefatigable. But, I'm getting there!

We exit their home, accompanied by waves, well-wishes, and a few 'come agains'.

Where next, my friend?

I sigh. "I've had enough of mental and emotional *stuff*. It's really tiring and I need a change. I like the idea of the astral worlds of Nature. Now, that would be interesting."

Patch smiles fondly at me. *This is where we say farewell. You focus onto your own world of an astral Nature, and it is most probable that Pan will do the rest.*

"Who are you, really, because Patch . . . !" I shake my head. "That's not your name!"

Oh, it will come to you in the right timing. Anyway, we will meet again.

We embrace — and he vanishes!

CHAPTER ELEVEN

ASTRAL WORLDS OF NATURE

Instead of stepping into an astral world, I focus on my very physical world at home. Stepping . . . *Between* . . . I am back in my study. Patch was correct. The edges of fatigue are definitely creeping in, and I know when a rest is needed.

I slept very deeply that night. The mental and emotional worlds were much more tiring than I expected. Mental and emotional *stuff!* It is not just tiring, it is exhausting.

I tap the barometer, as I do every morning, on my way into the kitchen. We are in another drought, and no matter how many times the barometer indicates a change toward rain, we have had no more than a few occasional showers in eight months. It is known as a green drought. On the coast, the grass is green from the showers, but it is not growing. I have not cut our lawn in eight months! On the inland farms it is literally — *what, grass?* The bush (forest) is very dry and wilted, literally dormant. Several gum trees around our garden are dying, and it is really tough for all the wild life. Plant growth in my garden is stunted and shrivelled, and with no mains water, our water tanks are at their lowest ever.

And so we wait . . .

A few days pass and I am ready for the astral world of Nature. I hope it is ready for me!

*   *   *

Once again, I step . . . *Between* . . . and out into a cloudy area of an abundant Earth.

I am standing on the edge of a forest. For some reason I instantly recall a memory, from a few years ago, of lower astral entities. I saw them in the destruction and ruin of a once beautiful forest, just like this one. As usual, it was caused by the money-hungry people who plunder forests for their own financial gain. This forest, however, is vibrant with health. Maybe this will be one of the forests where most humans will be subconsciously steered away by the veils of Light. I hope so. Equally, it may also be a forest that attracts a few people on the vibrational level of Love. An open, aware and loving person has an energy field that is fully compatible and energetically supportive of the forests of a new consciousness.

I ascend to my favourite hundred metres to feel if the energy is, indeed, better up high. I smile. In this serene location, it makes little noticeable difference. Nevertheless, I assume my lotus position while I briefly review some of my recent experiences. While in the mental and emotional astral worlds, I noticed that the energy of Chaos—the energy that drives, and Order—the structure of form, along with Balance—the place of greatest potential, were all very low key. I saw Balance in the higher mental world, and also in the spiritually aware level of the emotional astral world; but it was not the same as in our reality, a mere echo of our more powerful, holistic energy. Equally, the Chaos of the lower mental and emotional worlds was pale and weak, compared with our physical world. However, it was certainly powerful enough for them. If they had our magnitude of Chaos and Order, their realities would be devastated.

Here, on the edge of the forest, I again see Chaos and Order in the way that I am now used to seeing/experiencing them. And this forest has Balance. The torus of the forest, as a whole, is stunning, vast and magnificent. I recognise that, metaphysically, I have missed this emotional language that I have with Chaos, Order, and Balance. The reds of Chaos in this forest are vibrant, fresh and crisp with newness, while the black of Order easily blends with it, creating the harmony of Balance. It is the world of energy in which we live: subtle, yet hugely powerful. If only humanity would release its hypnotic illusion with the physical world and perceive that, as real as the physical world seems, it is no more than a physical reflection from a far greater, metaphysical mirror.

I am not sure where this forest is located, although it feels familiar. It is an evergreen rainforest and, I am fairly sure, it is in a cold/temperate climate. This suggests that it has a high rainfall which is well distributed throughout the year, rather than a seasonal inundation. I can hear harsh and strident bird song drifting on the light breeze, along with the constant sound of rushing water bubbling along the many, stony creeks within the forest. Hmm, feels familiar. Platypus country, maybe! When I was a farmer, platypus lived in the creek that ran through my farm in Tasmania. I even got to handle some young ones who were washed into my paddock in a flood. They were okay! So—I am somewhere in Tasmania! As I allow my vision to zoom into the forest, I recognise the magnificent great Southern Beech trees, a relic from ancient Gondwana.

I find that I am comforted by the familiar energy of this island state. I have been in some strange places recently, but only now do I recognise how different the energy was in those other worlds. I lived in Tasmania for over a decade, and loved the energy of the island. On the down side, Tasmania has been heavily plundered by the timber industry, and many a battle was fought here, in the South West, between conservationists and the industry workers and police. Guess whose side the police were on? Nowadays they leave a forested strip along the roadside to hide the devastation just beyond it. And for most people, this deceit works. Out of sight, out of mind! This beautiful forest, like all true natural forests, should belong to the people in perpetual trust, a trust that is impregnable by law. I sigh. One day! Okay, enough of my musings. Time to be here, now.

Briefly wondering if Pan is going to accompany me, I inner-hear/feel nothing of him, so I descend gently into the forest. The view from above, looking downward, is very different from when I stand beneath the huge, majestic trees, looking upward. The trunks and thick branches are densely covered with epiphytes, vegetation that uses the trees as a host, like an abundance of mosses, ferns and lichens. For a while I allow myself to drink in the physical splendour. Any description would be totally inadequate to describe this forest. Suffice it to say, only a walk in a cool, wet, strikingly green, great Southern Beech forest could reveal its true and complex beauty. As is usual in most rainforests, it has begun to drizzle, but cold or wet makes no difference to my metaphysical self. Nor do the ever-abundant leeches and mosquitoes—thank goodness!

Sitting in the lotus position, poised just above a boulder in a creek, I watch where the racing current is throwing a permanent, splashing spray of water over the boulder, nurturing the proliferation of dense moss. Even the boulders among the trees are green with moss, or yellowish-grey with liverwort.

As engaging and bewitching as it is, I am not here for the physical forest. I am here for the metaphysical astral levels of life that coexist with the physical.

I hold out my Light-hand, watching the creek spraying and splashing water through it.

You are a very rare sight to behold.

I feel the silent words coming from behind me.

Without moving, I allow my vision to fully encompass all that is around me. Sitting on a damp boulder quite close by is a small, green, human-like manikin, around a metre tall. He/she/it has their long-fingered hands wrapped around two, stick-thin, green legs.

As a courtesy, I move so that I am facing the manikin. "In the reality world that I come from, you are also a rare sight to behold. I am honoured to meet you."

I look to see whether Chaos or Order is the dominant energy, but I see neither. To me, this diminutive Nature Being has the appearance of a small, extremely thin, green, human manikin, with a pointy nose and chin, and a very, *very*, ancient energy.

The Nature Being bows its head in acknowledgement. *You consider me as ancient, but we have no relationship with your linear years. To us, your people appear as the leaves on a tree, here for a season . . . then gone, blown away by time.*

I nod. "This is true. We focus on our mortality, thus provoking it."

The Nature Being chuckles dryly. *Is this wise?*

"We humans are not noted for our wisdom. The opposite would be more true."

You are very forthright and honest.

"It is the simple truth. We are as we are. Would you judge a child for being childish? I am learning not to judge humans for being child-humans. We all have a lot of growing-up to do. And in the fullness of time, it will happen."

You are wise, and if you are wise there will also be others of wisdom. Is this not so?

"It is so. There are many wise and wonderful humans, we are a prolific species."

And a destructive one.

I sigh. "Yes, that too. Our negatives are plentiful, but our positives rise far above them."

You are a good representative for your people. You see them in a fair and balanced way.

"I am not a representative for my people. I am no more than a person who has learned how to use my metaphysical body to journey into other—and sometimes greater—realities. I also enjoy a long and privileged association with Pan, the enigmatic Spirit of Nature. But you probably know this."

The tiny manikin stands and stretches to his—I feel a masculine energy—full height.

Your energy confirms your Pan connection. But whether you are aware of it or not, in a greater reality, you certainly are a representative for your people. You are here in this forest to connect with the astral world of Nature. But . . .

"How do you know this?" I interject.

He gazes at me from tiny, pitch black eyes, each a beam of fierce energy boring into me. He ignores my question, almost daring me to interrupt again. *But this is not a one-way exchange. When any conscious connection is made it is always two-way. True, this is not always known, but that does not negate its reality. To assist you in this interaction, I will be your guide.*

I am startled by this. "Were you waiting for me?"

No, you were waiting for me. I was waiting for you to register this.

Hmm! "My name is Mixael. Do you have a name for easier communication?"

His face creases into a tiny, sly, enigmatic smile. *You may call me Patch!*

I stare at him silently, keeping a lid on boiling words and bubbling emotions. I nod calmly. "Okay, I'll call you Patch. It's as good a non-name as any. Did Pan send you?"

You make this sound like one human instructing another. It is not like this. Within the fields of energy that are continually in motion, I have a sense of beingness which involves you.

"Er, okay . . . what do you normally do?"

The human world is one of doing. The natural world is one of being. I do not do, I be!

"You are not making this easy," I say, jokingly.

Humans always want 'easy'. Everything easy. Human resistance to life creates difficulty, yet you want easy. Do you see this? Doing creates resistance, being allows flow.

This is considerably more profound than I expected. I am *not* broadcasting, but he knows my every thought. What is going on?

"I know what you mean. I have written about *being-with* while *doing-to* in my book, *Conscious Gardening.*"

Patch—weird! No way. He has got to be kidding me—or somebody is!

The manikin begins leaping from one small, smooth, water-washed boulder to another, as he heads downstream. *Come along, keep up, you have much to experience.*

Keeping up is easy in a metaphysical body. Physically, no chance! He heads downstream with the ease of a thistledown carried by a friendly breeze. Within moments he stops by a waterfall, one of many in the rushing forest creeks. Spectacular! It has a three metre fall. I love waterfalls; they are all spectacular to me. They live, they communicate, they invite.

Be with the waterfall. Allow beingness to open you to experiences of the natural world.

I hover in front of the waterfall, open to engage a different level of life. I know that by the term 'natural world' he means the world unseen. I can only allow by being fully in the present.

Very slowly, as though a curtain is withdrawn, I see that the waterfall and creek are filled with many types of spirits of Nature. Some of them use the physical water; others act as though there is no waterfall or creek. Hmm, levels within levels, perhaps? Within the waterfall, moving smoothly up or down equally easily, I see long, silvery, nymph-like Nature spirits, maybe a metre and a half in length. As I watch, they seem to change shape, one moment appearing like beautiful, slender, lustrous girls, and the next as elongated streams of silvery energy, then merging the essence of both simultaneously.

A group of small brownish Beings, looking vaguely like dumpy little old men, are sitting in the creek bed, apparently oblivious to the rushing torrent. They seem to be using a gnarled and submerged root as a knobbly table, while they bounce tiny pebbles from it into the waterfall. Surely, this is not 'being', this is playing! As expected, there are huge numbers of tiny Nature spirits, no bigger than a spark of Light. Unlike any that I have seen before, each of these is a spark of brightly coloured Light. They fly in coordinated rainbow clouds, both within the water flow and outside it. Add to all this, a number of tall Nature Beings, also well over a metre, who have human characteristics while being completely unlike a human. They seem to be engaged in conducting an unseen orchestra, with arms waving in the manner of a human conductor. I hear no music, or do I? When I intently listen, I get the vaguest sense of ethereal sound, but it is completely overwhelmed by the gushing, gurgling noise of the rapids, as they cascade down the waterfall.

As if this overwhelming reality is not enough, within it all, somehow blending, but seeming to be on a slightly different level of reality, I see what appear as platypus spirits, water-rat spirits and the spirits of other small water animals and creek-side birds that I am not familiar with. Spirits that seem to energetically represent their species.

Mystery — to be embraced.

I sit in my lotus position, just observing, making no attempt to understand.

Something very different is happening to me. Metaphysically, I am sitting in the lotus position, but on another level, I am being drawn out of my metaphysical body, literally, like a spiritual essence from my metaphysical body. I am aware of myself as Light, leaving my metaphysical body! I was not aware that this could happen or, if I once knew, I'd forgotten. Rather like a misty white vapour, yet in my own shape, I join the Nature Spirits near the base of the waterfall. Now, for the first time, they all become aware of me. I am now in *their* reality zone.

Hey . . . over here. Come and join us. Can ye play the game of bounce?

As if it is the most natural thing ever, I float toward the small, odd, dumpy Nature Beings. Acceptance fills me, as though this is an everyday event. "No. I have never played."

Ye humans, ye're a bunch of misfits if ever there was one. Take heed to what I show ye.

The dumpy, brownish speaker is vaguely human-like in appearance, but he is utterly different energetically. Holding a small, bright red pebble, he flicks it with a dextrous finger movement and the pebble hits the root at an astonishing speed, bouncing into the water at the top of the waterfall. I watch it fall in the water flow, then, within the creek it returns to him like a trained homing pigeon. Meanwhile, he has sent another small black pebble bouncing off the root to the top of the waterfall, then another red, then another black, all being propelled from him and returning endlessly. While this is happening, his four small companions are also flicking pebbles off the gnarled root to the top of the waterfall. Each of them has pebbles with two strong colours: red/black, green/orange, yellow/blue, violet/purple, pink/white. To me, this is incomprehensible.

Come along then, ye give it a try, the infinity game of bounce.

Could I be trapped here for infinity, bouncing pebbles into a waterfall?

He gives me two of his pebbles, a red and a black. I am able to hold them, but they do not feel like pebbles. They feel like drops of thick water. I make an attempt to flick away the red pebble, but it falls to the creek bed. I try again and again with red and black, to no avail. For me, it is impossible to flick fluid pebbles!

Ha ha ha! I knew ye could not do it. Ye think we are playing, but the pebbles carry our energy into the waterfall, charging it with energy from our inner-realm. This is essential for the very essence of water in your physical world.

I feel very humble. He is so much more than I expected, for his words echo with truth. I have the feeling that the red and black have to do with Chaos and Order, but with the other colours it is clear that more is involved. Could they be chakra colours of the Earth? I ask this question.

Good, ye got the rights of it. I am a Being of energy. I, and my fellows, create and transmit energy across the realms of Nature. On one level there is this creek bed, but on another level we are in a pure flow of planetary energy. This is where we play bounce.

"That is amazing. Thank you for your tireless work. Do you ever stop?"

Why would we stop? This is what we do. Do you ask the creek if it ever stops? It can be stopped, but that would not be natural. Go ye now, and learn more.

I am dismissed as he fully focuses on pebble-bouncing.

Moving over to the nymphs of Nature, I watch them in their flowing beauty. And as they flow with the water, they change to the slender, gleaming, girlish shapes, and watch me watching them. Their eyes are large and expressive, but seeing them melt away as they become elongated silvery energy is rather alarming. The girlish shapes fool me into attempting to make a human-based connection with them, clinging to the familiar is my undoing. As I peer at them, a dozen or more gleaming girlish forms, suddenly leap out of the waterfall, pushing me down into the flow of the creek. For an instant I struggle, then I relax and surrender to the moment. As they again become elongated, silver energy, so also, do I. The waterfall and creek are suddenly changed. The dumpy brown Beings flicking their energy pebbles have vanished, and I am in a huge river. In this river are multitudes of Beings of Nature, unlike and beyond anything I could imagine. The nymphs are with me, a dozen or more clustered around me, urging me to flow ever faster with the World River. I resist them. I wish to *connect* with the World River.

They are ever the scatterbrains, even as they are my beloved children.

The inner-words come from the World River. I had no idea that there is such a thing as a World River, but this is my present *knowing.*

"Where do you come from? Where do you flow to?"

From and to are meaningful in the physical world, but when you are One with the energy of the world, your question becomes meaningless. Flowing is my Beingness. This is considered to be a world of land by land dwellers, but it is truly a water world.

I struggle to remember. "We have a drought where I live . . . in a water world?"

Drought is not the absence of water; drought is the absence of energy flow. Humans do nothing but interfere with flow, rarely facilitating it. Want impedes flow. Human greed interferes with flow. Human corruption interferes with flow. Control interferes with flow. Ripping open the skin of the Earth interferes with flow. Destroying the forests interferes with flow. Killing each . . .

"Enough . . . I get your meaning."

Where your people live . . . ownership of a place interferes with flow. If your humanity was nomadic, you would all grow in consciousness at a greatly accelerated speed. Nothing to own, to possess, to cling to . . . all these interfere with the flow.

"Many people have no homes . . . neither do they have flow."

Child, they lost flow long, long before they lost their homes. Losing flow is why they lost, and are losing, their homes. Do you not see this?

"Yes, I accept your wisdom . . . but humanity will never again be nomadic."

Wrong. Certain reality frames of wiser, more advanced humans are entirely nomadic, as will your people be in the not too distant future.

Your human way is working against you, not with you. Nomadic does not suggest more primitive. It is fluid and flowing, rather than fixed and stuck.

"I agree. The idea of a nomadic life holds much appeal. What a relationship with the natural world it would be."

Exactly. No cities, few industries, but a flow with Nature where all your needs are naturally met, rather than needs and wants created, and then destructively manufactured or worked for.

"You create a vision for humanity I have never even imagined. I confess, I love my home among the forest trees, but to be free in the way you describe would also be wonderful."

As she communicates with me, the World River touches energies in me, creating inner vision and revelation that is neither mental nor emotional. Some sensory energy that is more basic, yet is far more evolved, and involved, than any of the normal senses we use for daily living. I cannot explain, but she opens me to a newness beyond any human newness I have experienced. And yes, I feel her energy as feminine!

I see/experience/perceive a humanity moving in large families, or tribes, over the face of the Earth. These are a refined and beautiful people, and their relationship with Nature is far beyond anything of our current humanity. I watch a large family of maybe two to three hundred people, who are following a wide highway through a forest. This highway is not designed for mechanical traffic. It is for humans, and whatever wild animals might care to use it. These highways are not made by people, nor are they permanent; they are created by Nature to conform with natural law. It appears to be compacted soil, yet when it rains there is never any mud. Equally, if the hot sun beats onto a highway on the open plains, there is no dust. Every few years the highways disappear as the forest, scrub, or plains grass swiftly re-grow over them, while new highways re-form close by. When a highway is being created by cooperating with the great devas of the Earth and Nature, it is as though the Earth moves itself, taking trees, boulders, or any other obstacles with it, and all the vegetation continues growing undisturbed. Thus the basic highways are created.

As I watch this large family group travelling through a forest, they stop for the night. They have transport without wheels. Transport that seems to simply float, silently and efficiently, with no size limit. Futuristic homes travel/float with them, looking rather like house-sized, flat-based, opaque bubbles. I have no idea how the technology works, but it is obvious that these people have mastered the use of anti-gravity. Wherever they stop, there is always waiting an abundance of trees laden with fruit for these vegetarian people to eat. There is no farming of the land; the land willingly gives forth its bounty, and this bounty is always available. They live in cooperation with all the Beings and energies of Nature, and the offering of the people is one that honours a sacred trust. They bless the food they eat, they bless the land on which they travel, they honour the whole planet with a benign dominion. These are not a people who drop a casual "thank you." They *live* their Love and regard for Nature. Nothing is exploited. Nothing is wasted. The people maintain an aspect of themselves that holds an awareness of the Nature that surrounds them, and even while in laughing conversation they maintain this natural, easy vigilance. They are consciously connected to their physical world and its environment, but more importantly, they are connected to the holistic spiritual world, embracing its spiritual environment.

The old cities of the Earth are no more. The numbers of people living on the planet are in complete harmony with the Earth's capacity to feed and nurture them. Many people have moved to other outlying planets that support life. They too, live at One with their home-world. Humanity has learned a different way to live, a different way of being; they have found the Way of Harmony. Sickness and illness are almost obsolete. Lives are considerably longer. Harmony has become the genetic pattern of a more efficient human DNA, and each physical body reflects this change.

However, above and beyond all these amazing changes, humans are no longer alone on the planet—and they have learned that they never were. Yes, there are quite a few visiting Beings from other worlds, studying the marvellous symbiosis that the people of Earth have with their planet, and with Nature. But above and beyond this are the natural denizens of Nature that do not have a human physicality. The people live with a joyful awareness of, and a meaningful relationship with, the many and varied devas, and the throngs of the mystical spirits of Nature.

This family group is gathered around the fruiting trees and shrubs, picking and eating and blessing. These fruit trees and shrubs will always be bearing fruit when a family or tribe arrives with need of nourishment. Their production is no longer linked to seasons and weather, but linked instead to human need and the common, sacred bond they share. It is the same with water, with natural springs bubbling out of the ground wherever they are needed. These food/water stations could be likened to service stations for cars on our own highways. Naturally enough, these people also carry food and water.

As I watch, I see a vast, devic Being of Light containing the whole family group and much of the forest in their area. I am surprised, however, as I watch the Light dissolve into a number of Light Beings, all interacting with the human family. They connect in telepathic communication, even holding hands and occasionally embracing during these profound moments.

"What I see is so *wonderful* . . . is this our future?"

It is a future, one of many probabilities. For the people you are observing, it is their current life on Earth. This is real. They have a consciousness at One with the All, yet they are individuals of a higher order of individuality than your people have presently attained. For many people of your time, this is their future, for others, their path of consciousness will take different directions. It seems so difficult for your people to grasp that they are the absolute creators of their lives—their past, present, and future. Not the creators of their spiritual essence, but of the lives they live.

"This is what I teach. As insufficient as it may be, I give it my all."

When you give your all, you touch into a higher order. Give it no thought, but know that it touches and ignites an order of magnitude far beyond the endeavours of a single person.

Her words touch me with a reassurance I was not aware of needing.

As I observe this nomadic family, I am aware of a multitude of these large family groups, and also other groups travelling the world, and everywhere they travel it is with the cooperation of a revered Nature. The scene changes and I see many groups converging at what appears to be a huge seaport. Here, indeed, there are very large, permanent, futuristic buildings. Even these permanent installations have only the lightest contact with the Earth. Made with some super-tough, lightweight substance, a few enormous pylons with incredible bird-like, widespread feet, hold the buildings which hang suspended in huge, web-like nets of some gossamer-thin substance. It all has a vaguely spider's web appearance, yet is stunningly beautiful in the overall flow and curvature. I am grateful that my observations are accompanied by an inner-knowing of what I am seeing—courtesy of the World River.

There is no air flight. Not because this is impossible; it is a choice. Nobody is in a hurry. The world of hurry, hurry, hurry does not exist here. Travelling across the world, from one country to another, is by ocean transport. Countries are no longer owned; no passports are required. People can travel whenever, and to wherever they choose. Just as transport on the land hovers, so also it hovers on the seas and oceans. The ships are wide, huge, and very comfortable. They have similar shipping lanes to ours, but the behaviour of the weather and the oceans in these many shipping lanes, is always calm. The devas of the oceans and the devas of the winds, cooperate with the humans for the benefit of all. Naturally, the oceans are filled with sea life, while whales and dolphins abound.

I am thrilled to see that a new order of intelligence is rapidly arising in the oceans. With the encouragement, guidance, and assistance of humanity, the octopi are making a great, quantum leap in consciousness. The awareness of the many octopus species is growing swiftly under the stimulus of their own unique, almost alien intelligence. Many people have established community homes in the oceans. Some have moderated their bodies to breathe oxygen from the water; other, less permanent or visiting people, use small, unobtrusive, artificial breathing devices. The people who have moderated their bodies have chosen to spend most of their lives guiding and inspiring the larger octopi species in their evolution. They have already created a complex, yet reasonably complete, communication between their two species, despite their utterly different environments and totally different concepts on the nature of reality.

I watch a hovering, sea-going vessel crossing an ocean. It is not as high as our largest are today, but it is much wider. Wide enough to comfortably hold a village. The few thousand people who are being transported live in rooms the equivalent size of our luxury hotels. There are no upper or lower classes, no richer or poorer, in fact, no currency other than goodwill and blessings. I need to emphasise that blessings are not a few muttered words of prayer. Blessings are a focus of such intensity of the Light from one person to another, or to wherever it is directed, be it Nature, the devas, whatever—that the people, or Nature, or whatever is being blessed, actually glows with a soft illumination. Blessings are a very powerful gift of high impact, strongly focused Love energy. They are a soul gift, healing, harmonising, and extremely beneficial.

As I watch this crossing, I see that the ocean, no matter how rough or stormy it may be, becomes calm as the oceanic vessel approaches, while the wind drops to a breeze. With their passing, the weather and ocean return to their original pattern. No rough passage here! This level of cooperation is literally awesome, a demonstration of what can be achieved by honouring and acknowledging the great devas of water and wind!

The World River now switches my view to what I can only describe as a huge community city. The one I am watching is located in a desert, but I learn that others exist in forests, on the very high, permanent snow-fields, on lower mountains, one or two *on* the oceans, a few *in* the oceans, and several in other natural places. They appear as huge—and I mean *huge*—translucent domes that contain many thousands of smaller dome homes.

Each community city consists of a single huge, flat-based

translucent dome. The top of the dome is translucent, allowing light to enter. I do not know how it is done, but this natural light is even strengthened, or enhanced, in dull and cloudy weather. For about twenty metres in height the sides of the dome are transparent, giving a visual effect of the translucent top seeming to float above the city. The dome reaches up to maybe one hundred metres high. I can only guess at the overall size, but I would say that the dome would hold a city of around two million people. The whole effect is very natural and organic; high-rise buildings and concrete do not exist here.

Looking through a dome into a community city reveals the visual effect of many shades of green, dotted with the many mobile translucent dome homes among all the gardens and vegetation. I should also mention that the dome homes are able to take on colours. How they do this I have no idea. The colours are subtle, a single dome home blending the colour/shades of spring, summer and autumn that are natural in Nature. The effect is very harmonious and relaxing; visually it is quietly beautiful. They can be permanent colour, or ever changing, or any combination!

Under the huge domes that contain the city, there are hundreds of thousands of fruiting trees, fruiting shrubs, and vegetable gardens of designs beyond description. They abound. All this living, ever-available food is for the people to help themselves. Under the city dome, it is a literally a green oasis. All transport roads appear to be like golfing freeways, but they are not grass. They seem to be composed of a form of green/grey, lichen-type growth. Whatever it is, it is both durable and vibrant, and continually replacing itself. Their methods of transport range from hover-seats, to hover-everything you can image! Plus a large amount of easy, flowing, joyful, vibrant, willing walking! As with the homes of the nomadic groups, all the homes under the great dome hover. The pressure and impact on the soil is absolutely minimal. Nature rejoices in these community cities. I learn that the homes are not located permanently. When a family begins another journey, the home floats with them. The city is constantly emptying and filling in a flow of human energy; a flow which means the community city is constantly reshaping and recreating its interior design.

Everywhere I look I see the startling white colour of Balance. The reds of Chaos and blacks of Order seem to be non-existent. Balance is both the dynamic and the structure of life in this three-dimensional world! The World River tells me that even these cities can, and do, move their location every now and then, according to the needs of Nature. A few tens of kilometres of coordinated movement, and they settle again into another naturally prepared area and into another natural cycle of Nature. This is a humanity that places the needs of Nature before its own needs, and all prosper and thrive from this high and fine regard.

Focus now more on the Spirits of Nature. See what is possible when the energies of the physical and the spiritual are joyfully harnessed for the benefit of all.

My vision changes on its own accord. I am still observing the community city. A community city; no other words than these can adequately describe it. Our cities thrive and grow on commerce, depending on such for their continuity, but not so in this reality. Here, the cities are vibrant, holistic communities—thriving on thriving people! Each person shares their creativity and passion for life with all people. I see what we call restaurants, but here, undercover, thus not needing roofs, they are built around multi-tiered community gardens of enormous diversity and complexity. These provide endless varieties of living, organic food from a fully cooperative soil. These areas also contain complex, multi-tiered water gardens, with a large range of amazing, edible, aquatic plants. Some of these aquatic plants even fruit underwater! It is all a very beautiful presentation.

Ah, now I see the Nature Spirits. These are a type I have never before seen, swarming like white bumblebees over all these multi-tiered gardens. I watch as they fly in and out of the leaves, branches, flowers and fruits of the gardens. With them, working in a coordinated pattern of movement, I see large numbers of earth-like Nature Spirits. Looking like clods of animated soil, they swarm through the earth as though utterly frantic, such is their inexhaustible energy. In the water gardens small, sylph-like Nature Spirits dance and flow with the constantly moving water in what, to casual sight, appear as flickering lights moving within and over the water. No frantic soil energy here, but a pace and cadence of flow and grace. And somehow, orchestrating all this, are tall, gnome-like Nature Beings who wander with clear purpose and intent throughout the entire, multi-tiered gardens. These Nature Beings are not performing any task other than holding a laser-like intent for all the Nature Spirits involved in the food production. I am aware that each of these Nature Spirits needs, and fits in with, all the others in One, cohesive whole. No energy is obsolete or wasted. Interestingly, there are many hundreds of these restaurants/gardens scattered throughout the whole city community.

Finally, over lighting each restaurant/food garden, are the individual, devic energies which link and connect holistically with the vast and incredible over-lighting deva of the whole beautiful community/city. Wow! What a triumph of divine order—of complete, holistic cooperation.

"Thank you, World River, for showing me all this. What I have seen and experienced here feeds and nourishes a part of me that I now realise was hungry. I am truly grateful."

I, too, have been nourished. I have shared your experiences as you observed and marvelled at this holistic world. Feeling the newness in you has been a newness within me, for we are not separate. Feeling your wonder and awe has awoken in me something that slumbered, so I, too, am grateful. All that I have received will go into new creation, just as all you have received will gradually recreate your life . . . and with you, the lives of many others. Go in Love.

And I am back with the waterfall.

Still as a misty ghost of my metaphysical self, I am again watching the nymphs playing in the waterfall. "Thank you, thank you," I call to them, but they ignore me. I can also see the little, brown, dumpy Nature Beings in the creek playing the bounce game, and I wave, but they, too, ignore me.

I suspect, my lessons with them finished, I am dismissed.

For the first time I become aware of a rainbow within the permanent mist of the waterfall. How did I fail to notice this earlier? Has it just appeared? It is still drizzling, with no sun, but here is a rainbow! It comes to me that all is in order. I leave my hovering, lotus position, moving closer to the rainbow. As I approach, it seems to recede, bending away from me, which should be impossible! Closer I get, and closer, when suddenly the rainbow snaps back toward me, as though strongly elasticised. As the rainbow engulfs me, I disintegrate into zillions of tiny, rainbow-coloured Nature Spirits. I am One, I am All; there is no distinction. We fly/move/zip through the air as One in complete coordination, for the zillions of me are One.

The spray-wet atmosphere of the waterfall creates an environment of breathtaking scale. As a single Rainbow Spirit, the waterfall is an immensity, a whole world of moisture in which to give and receive energy. This is what I am created for, to exchange energy with the micro-droplets of water molecules. At this scale, the micro-droplets are miniature water-worlds in which I can dive endlessly, giving each world my energy and taking energy with me. Like a bee pollinating flowers, I am pollinating water-worlds. As I do so, I am aware that this micro-level is being reflected somewhere in the galaxy on a more cosmic macro-level—all is connected. This is my human-based realisation, even though I am one Rainbow Spirit and all Rainbow Spirits.

As I/we zip as a glowing cloud of rainbow-coloured light in the fine spray of the waterfall, I am unable to separate this waterfall from all waterfalls. Nor am I able to separate this rainbow from all rainbows—all are One. I am One with the waterfalls of the world, and I am aware of the World River spilling over countless smooth and jagged rock faces, as she journeys her endless way around the world. A never-ending journey, for while she travels the land, she also travels the sky, moving as clouds over the face of the Earth. Rising, falling, endlessly flowing, here racing with speed, there a sluggish movement, here a huge outpouring, there a tiny rivulet—and we are One.

I feel such endless patience. For me, it is patience; for the World River, it is life flowing with life. For me, I feel eternity; for the World River, it is as it is. What a difference in perspective when nothing is measured against time. The nomadic people I observed had released their grip on time, while we continue to relentlessly hold onto it. As Rainbow Spirits, there is no individual focus; we are One. Yet there is an awareness of others, of more than being single, more than being alone. I cannot fathom this complex multiplicity because for them it does not exist: it is as it is. We humans live in duality: the soul-Self and the personality-self. All too often each is going its own separate way, never knowing their Oneness until death does us part—again. Then—another try!

I am aware of the perpetuity of the Rainbow Spirits. They do not cease to be when a rainbow disappears, for it does not. All Rainbows are one rainbow, there is no separation, thus they are always sharing their beauty with the world. All waterfalls are One. Space, time and distance have no meaning, no reality in the energetic and holistic world of Nature. I feel replete with the newness of all I am experiencing. I am finding words to describe it, yet my words are but the skeleton of my metaphysical involvement.

Abruptly, I am thrown out of the rainbow, no longer One with the Rainbow Spirits. I am dismissed. Again, I am standing before the waterfall where it all began.

Moving back to my lotus position, I look around. What further marvels await?

A rather furtive, shadow movement to one side of me catches my attention. Flitting along the creek, from one wet boulder to another, is a tiny, bird-like creature. Appearing as a dark shadow, it flits almost to my feet.

"Hello, who are you?"

The energy of the little, green manikin replies. *I am the astral of a common bird of the creeks. We ask for you to follow me, entering another astral realm of Nature.*

Hmm, I'm not sure how this works. Nevertheless, as a smoky essence of my metaphysical self, I dutifully follow the little, shadow bird as it flits on down the creek. I, too, can flit from one boulder to another, as light as a feather. Ahead of me the whole creek bed and surrounding area seem as though they are softly illuminated, far more so than the slight gloom in the drizzling, misty rain in the forest. The shadow bird flies into the illumination, instantly changing its whole appearance. Gone is the tiny flitting shadow; in its place is a vibrant bird of great beauty. Even though only a few degrees larger than the shadow bird, it *appears* much bigger. As I stare, I notice that, although the bird is vibrant with colour, the colours are browns and greys, yet these normally dull colours seem to be filled with such energy that they appear dynamic, almost effervescent.

I, too, move into the area of illumination.

Oh—jeepers—this is something else! It is as though I have plunged into the Disney movie, *Fantasia*. Okay, not exactly, but this astral reality is so Light, so clear, so defined, so vibrant, so incredibly, utterly, stunningly *alive*, that my normal world reality must surely be cast in permanent shadow.

Not shadow, but illusion. Millennia of incarnations of illusion slowly but surely close down the human relationship with life. People no long see that which is, they see what they expect to see.

I could weep for what we are missing, for the world that is lost to us.

"Are you telling me that this is reality? That *this* is the truth of life on Earth?"

Of course it is. This is the greater reality. It is each one's personal reality that has lost the greater glory of life. Humanity closed its eyes — its true vision—*long, long ago, and forgot to open them. Follow your little guide into the greater astral world of Nature, not the lesser world of human reality.*

Even in all my many incredible journeys, I had no idea of the magnitude of what we have turned our backs on—removed from our lives. Every blow of a sword, every impact of a bullet, every rip of the plough, every blast to open a mine, every forest felled, every action we have ever taken to control and exploit, so we have turned ever further away from the Truth of the Earth on which we live. We, collectively, have reduced and ruined our relationship with beauty. I had no idea of the extent.

I follow the vibrant, multi-brown bird in all its true splendour, as it leads me into the illumination, flitting away from the creek and into the illuminated area of the forest.

This area is a representation of a greater Nature. Do not get attached to expectations of what might be in this forest. The forest encompasses all natural life.

I am not at all sure that I understand the meaning of the little green manikin. But I have no doubt that its meaning will become clear. As I follow my bird guide smoothly through the trees, we suddenly emerge onto a large iceberg. Iceberg! Okay, now I get it. This illuminated section of forest is a metaphysical doorway to *any* place in Nature.

Lying flat on its back on the ice is the biggest male polar bear I have ever seen. Fair enough, I have only ever seen them in various zoos, well fed—and large. This polar bear looks twice the size. And the colour of its coat is gloriously, startlingly white. Lying flat on its back, its four feet flopped out around it, this polar bear is the epitome of complete relaxation. I can see his huge chest rising and falling in the slow, even rhythm of sleep

Not quite sure of what I am supposed to be learning, I simply observe the bear. As I watch, I see another male bear lying in exactly the same place. This polar bear is the size of a normal, large bear, and its fur is a dingy blend of yellowish tinges and a dirty white. I understand. This bear is the physical bear as we normally see it; the first bear is the way it appears in a greater reality. The astral bear smells sweet; our normal bear has a faint stink of dead meat.

The bird flutters around me, then flies off the iceberg and over the sea. Over the sea! But, I follow the bird as we move back into the forest. I smile; neat!

Moving between the great, Southern Beech trees, we come now onto a typical scene in the Oz outback. We are in a large paddock, a broken-down fence defining where the paddock ends and the wild, scrubby vegetation begins. Feeding on the overgrazed grass is a mob of red kangaroos. This time I am seeing them as I would normally see them, and they are impressive. A huge male, boss of the mob and very dominant, is surrounded by his females. A few younger males hang around on the fringe of the mob, not quite sure of their place. When to move on?

As I watch, the forest illumination gradually encompasses the mob, the pasture, and the nearest area of wild scrub. Once again, the scene appears to become larger than life. I sigh. The truth is, this *is* life size. We see a reality reduced and diminished by the way we see and relate to ourselves, each other, and Nature. In fact, diminished by the way we experience life. And yet, it does not have to be this way, although, at this moment, I see no quick way out. We slowly created a reduced relationship with life and, as slowly, we need to rebuild it. Now I know how the nomadic people see and relate to their environment.

My personal view shows overgrazed pasture and a scrubby vegetation that is completely lacking in energy. It all looks flat and lack-lustre. The mob of kangaroos is impressive enough, but I have always liked and admired them. The holistic, astral view shows the pasture is indeed overgrazed, but it also reveals the life within the soil, a dynamic waiting to be released. I realise that an organic farmer or gardener has more to use than the mere tools of trade. They can also use conscious imagination to consciously, and knowingly, connect with the energy within the soil, the energy within the pastures and the energy within the whole property, using it creatively. An organic farmer would never overgraze, having more insight into the harm of this very common error. In this double level of reality, I am seeing the farmer's or gardener's potential of lifting the common level to the higher level, if they consciously interface with Nature.

The bird flits away and I follow it back into the verdant green forest.

And so this continues. I visit many scenes of the astral level interfacing with the physical, and always the physical is the lesser. I learn that this is not the way it need be, but there is a snag! Isn't there always? Humanity and Nature are One. The way we relate to Nature is directly involved with the manner in which we relate to ourselves. When we accept and live our *magnificence,* we will find ourselves surrounded by a magnificent Nature. While we act as though life is no more than a humdrum, boring, repetitious daily struggle, we create and live our mundanity. This is the world of illusion which we have created.

Following the little bird through the forest, we emerge into an area which has been clear-felled. I give thanks that this is not within the Southern Beech forest, although it is a tragedy that clear-felling exists elsewhere in Tasmania. It has the energy of a slaughterhouse. In fact, in some ways this is worse than a slaughterhouse. In a livestock slaughterhouse, they are the only victims, apart from the people who work in such places. But here, in this devastation that was once a forest, the victims are many indeed. The soil is laid bare to pounding rains and blazing sun, eroding and destroying its structure as the micro-organic soil life is obliterated. Every arboreal animal is either killed during the tree felling, or will die as it loses its territorial trees, its place in Nature. All the ground-dwelling animals suffer the same fate. This is senseless, wholesale slaughter, driven by humanity's twin despairs of fear and greed — same thing!

Slowly, almost reluctantly, the astral level of a greater reality emerges into my vision. I realise that this is deliberately different from my recent view of the pastures. Of that, I was shown little, thus enabling me to enlarge and increase my insight into the farmland. But here, in this area of devastation, I see a scene that I once saw long ago.

In this greater reality, every tree is growing magnificently. The whole forest is untouched, untainted by human avarice and greed. The under-storey is alive with vegetation and small marsupials, scurrying about their business. Koalas live in the trees, snakes, small tree dragons, and other reptiles abound, along with all the species of gliders that silently glide from tree to tree when sunlight releases its daily hold, and the moon caresses the forest in soft, vague, shadowy outlines. A few larger wallaroos and wallabies bound through the undergrowth, there to spend the daytime in quiet contemplation, or sleeping, with senses alert. The forest is vibrant with energy, alive with life unseen, unheard, all part of the overall energy of the forest.

Two realities occupying the same space. In a physical reality, death and devastation. On a metaphysical level of reality — the astral level — life continues, untouched by man. The reader might ask, 'Which one is real?' Both are real. The physical is real, but it is not the only reality. In a greater reality, man has no place to reap and ruin. Physically, we are banned. I think that the story of

Adam and Eve in the Garden of Eden describes it perfectly. The story represents our fall from grace. Our fall from the greater, holistic reality, into our physical reality of separation. Both exist, both occupy the same space/moment, but we fell from the grace of Truth into the fear that always accompanies illusion. Like all biblical stories, this story, too, lost much in its multiple translations before reaching our modern languages, each scribe adding his pennyworth of how it should be written!

If a pennyworth it be, this is mine!

The scene now moves slowly back to only the physical reality of devastation. The vibrant forest appears to have vanished. A gloom grows and spreads, and the energy sinks lower and lower. Even in my ghostly metaphysical reality, I shiver. I know what is about to be revealed—a lower astral reality. I am not at all keen to see this. Once, in a ruined forest in a foreign land, I saw a glimpse of the lower astral entities that thrive on pain, fear and suffering. Now, it is happening once more as the gloom deepens, with an accompanying chill of nastiness.

Life is always about attaining Balance. For this to happen every energy expression has an equal and opposite expression. In our books and movies it is depicted as the Light and dark forces. In reality, this is quite close to the truth of it. We can never abolish the dark, any more than we can immortalise the Light; all life needs its opposite, countering energy to learn to attain Balance. So now I watch as the lower astral Beings crawl out of the depths of their lower astral realm, giving me an insight into something I am not keen on facing. I see repulsive, slug-like creatures sliding on a trail of stink and ooze; nothing remotely like the beauty of a slug in our reality. These creatures not only devour the reduced energies of life, they excrete the vapours of death and decay. This is not the natural death and decay of physical substances; this is the decay of invisible life energy, something that is of a whole, different order.

I see spider-like creatures that invoke a shudder in me. I know that I am untouchable, but to see creatures like this is challenging. Maybe they are spider-like because spiders invoke a shudder in me. Or, maybe they invoke a shudder in me, and so many others, because there have been the few, but terrible, incarnations when in the last moments of slowly dying in great fear and pain, we have seen and connected with these monsters of the lower astral. Many of us have had nightmares about such terrifying apparitions. We are not entirely strangers to their astral existence. Many long- term alcoholics lose the last threads of their sanity to such lower astral creatures. This is what I mean when I refer to these creatures as feeding on reduced life energy.

I watch as they prowl and roam the ruin that was once a vibrant forest. No benign Nature Beings of a higher astral order are in this lower astral energy. It is difficult for the human mind to comprehend that the higher and lower astral realms occupy the same space/moment, yet on entirely different frequencies. I could fairly state that the higher astral is a higher Light energy, while the lower has a greater *absence* of Light, and a greater *presence* of dark. I see creatures that hop on two legs, rather like a mutation between a manikin and a grasshopper. As they hop and crawl, they emit low piercing wails of such intense despair and gloom that it penetrates everything. Even I cannot shut it out. It evokes feelings of choking, of drowning, of strangulation. Horrible. Another creature, rather like a grotesque, deformed praying mantis emits loud, piercing screams, sounding as though something is being ripped apart. This invokes my long-dormant memories of being torn apart on the rack in the torture chambers of dark and terrible dungeons in bygone ages. I do not like this, but the little bird that brought me here is not to be seen. What next?

The devastated forest vanishes abruptly—to be replaced by small-acreage green fields that appear to be the abundance of Nature. They are not. I am standing in fields of vegetables for the market. The most alarming of the lower astral nasties have gone, but there are now many of the repulsive slug-like creatures moving over the crops, as well as within the soil. These are GM (genetically modified) vegetables. I stare, appalled. I knew that GM is anti-Nature, but not for a moment did I expect this. These unnatural vegetables are such an abomination in the natural world that they attract lower astral energy. In this one field there are tomatoes, sweet corn, squash and zucchini. Nearby there are fields with much larger acreages of rapeseed for oil — canola. The rapeseed has the same gruesome attendants. This abhorrent, slug-like thing is predominant among the lower astral entities. Disturbingly, there are also astral entities in the rapeseed fields which affect the consumers of the finished products of canola oil. These entities look a bit like hideous, freakish, badly distorted rats, only bigger. They make our wild and mangy rats look cute and cuddly.

As I observe all this, I feel slightly sick with the recognition of what this all reveals. Both the many slug-like nasties, and the even more repulsive rat-like horrors, are feeding from the energy of the vegetables and rapeseed — and replacing it with an exchange of their own lower astral energies. If we continue developing and consuming GM foods — and we are, rapidly — we are heading into whole new arenas of sickness and suffering. As I watch this terrible scene, I can energetically see that it will be our mental health that will take the biggest hit. Over ninety percent of canola oil today comes from GM crops. Need I say more?! Just for clarity, rapeseed oil and canola oil are one and the same.

Even though it is energetically impossible, I feel limp! When the small brown bird comes flitting around me, its vibrant energy is outstanding in these low-energy fields of human food.

"Lead on, little brown friend. I have had enough!"

It flies away, with me closely following — back into the forest of Mystery.

Automatically, I am again with the waterfall, sitting once more in the lotus position. I deliberately relax, becoming aware of my metaphysical tension. Very unusual!

Not the nicest of experiences. I have been able to monitor your energy field, so I am aware of all you have experienced. I know of your insights and deductions, and you have done well. It is almost time for you to go, but do you have any requests of me?

"Yes, a couple. What is your real name? And may I see what the few Nature Beings are doing who seem to be conducting an orchestra? One I cannot hear, but I would like to. Oh, and I am not overly attached to knowing your name!"

A dry chuckle. *I am not Patch, I am provocative. As for the rest, be with it.*

So saying, he waves his arms exactly like Patch! and the scene changes.

More clearly than ever, I see about a dozen of the taller Nature Beings that seem to be conductors. They have a canine/human appearance, not quite one or the other, and not quite either. They are dark-striped brown with pointy faces, prick ears, a human-type mouth, just over a metre tall, slim as reeds, and rather striking in appearance. I watch as they move in upright, two-legged dance steps, that take each of them into a movement that appears as a triangle within an inverted triangle. As they do this, they pause, look at me, then all of them dramatically bring their hands down from a raised position, simultaneously.

Music bursts into my reality. Music beyond any music known to man. Maybe not. Is this where some of the great classics came from? I suspect it is. Inside my metaphysical self, I weep. I cannot listen to this galactic ecstasy brought to Earth and remain calm. It feels that every cell in my physical body is raising its vibration, my emotions straining to contain it. I give up. As a non-musician I have no words to describe this. All I know is that if this sound was heard by every human simultaneously, it would instantly change human reality. Those who could ascend to the heights would do so; those who could not would immediately be elsewhere, in a place compatible with their energy. This is the music of transformation, the music of growth for Nature and humanity. This is the cosmic song on Earth; this is the consciousness of heaven in music.

I listen, drifting in and out of awareness.

At some moment in all this, I become aware of the manikin watching me as I hover in the air close to the waterfall.

You are a rare human to be sure. Thank you for your gifts.

"*My* gifts! What have *I* given? All I am aware of is *receiving* so very much."

You give us the gift of openly receiving. Of openly sharing your emotions with us. Of openly sharing your wonder and awe, and of your despair in the GM fields. Such an open sharing from an aware human is rare beyond measure. Gifts go two ways, remember?

I smile. "I don't know who, or what, you are, but thank you. From the deepest depths of my heart I freely give and share my Love with you, and the Spirits of Nature."

Suddenly, abruptly, I am before a wet and physical waterfall in a very physical world.

I sigh in contentment. Then I step . . . *Between* . . . and out into my study.

CHAPTER TWELVE

THE FIRE BUDDHA

Having returned from another trip to Japan, I have a lot to think about, or feel into. After Carolyn and I had finished our weekend seminar and the 5-Day Intensive, we had some time to spare, owing to our flight home being delayed by a day. Despite enjoying being at home, this was okay with us, for we now had time to see more of the temples and shrines of Japan.

We walked through the Arashiyama bamboo forest—a never-to-be-forgotten experience—and gasped at the breathtaking colours of the Japanese maples as they donned their fiery, autumn finery. The ancient gardens, with their trees ablaze in flaming reds, brilliant yellows, and a wet, burnished orange gleaming through the brief, sunlit showers, were utterly spectacular. One of the outstanding temples we visited was at Nagano. It is called the Kozen-ji. Ji means temple in Japanese.

Carolyn and I were with Yasumi, our Japanese organiser and my book translator for our Japanese publisher, Carol, a good friend visiting from the U.S. and Kei, a Japanese friend who had very kindly offered to drive us in his luxurious Lexus to the various temples. During my years visiting Japan, I seem to have developed some odd connections. First, the Shimyoin Temple with the Stargate that metaphysically opens to another reality, then with the Togakushi Mountain Gods and Goddesses—and Shishi, the incomparable! Now, without any conscious intention from me, it seems to have happened again.

As I stared into the slightly gloomy interior of a small temple in the Nagano Kozen-ji complex, a Buddhist monk was kneeling on the floor, reading aloud from a huge book in a low monotonous chant. I think he was a keeper of the temple. At the very back of the temple, a large picture was hanging among accompanying Buddhist relics. I glanced at it. My first impression was of a dim figure engulfed in fire. It did nothing for me, so I tried to look elsewhere, but I could not easily do so. The picture did not exactly ensnare me, but it seemed to hold my attention despite my wanting to look away.

I stared at it as the minutes passed by. Not many minutes, but a whole lot more than I had intended. Dragging my gaze away, I asked Yasumi what the large picture depicted. She told me that it was considered a national treasure; it was a picture of the Fire Buddha.

Inadvertently, I glanced again at the picture, and again felt a strange compulsion that I had to meld, or merge with the Fire Buddha, and that it/he awaited my metaphysical visit. This was not something that held any appeal for me—a *Fire* Buddha? I mean, fire as in flaming hot! Plus, the vague impression I got from the picture was not exactly benign. He looked ferociously demonic. By the time I could drag my eyes away, the rest of the group had moved on. That's that, I thought. Except it was not!

As I walked along with the others I could not get the picture out of the mind. It seemed stuck in my consciousness, as though it *intended* to accompany me. Okay, I thought, this is weird, even for me. Why do I have a fascination with a bizarre picture of the Fire Buddha when I'm not even a Buddhist? What *is* a Fire Buddha? I admire the traditional Buddha as a spiritual Being, but *this* . . .? Nevertheless, when we eventually neared the exit I noticed a small shop selling the usual various reproductions of temple items. I was about to dismiss it all when my eyes were drawn to a horribly expensive scroll of the Fire Buddha. I should have run away! Instead, I walked over and stared at it, noticing the details I had missed, for we were not allowed to approach the picture in the temple. The face was even more demonic than I realised. I learned that the people call the Fire Buddha, Fudo Myo-O. He/it was once popular over all Japan, which suggests that things have changed. A smile would help, I thought! The Fire Buddha is considered a Guardian with clear intention. He protects people from evil, burning away their earthly desires. This *would* make him popular! In his right hand is a sword which symbolises intelligence; surely—violence! In his left hand is a rope with which to bind the evil mind. Hmm, mind is mind, neither good nor evil—but, people like drama. The rock on which he sits represents the peaceful mind, free of all doubt. His nickname is Ofudo-san. The Japanese like nicknames for their deities.

The compulsion had not finished with me. I watched myself buy the horribly expensive scroll, not vaguely understanding why I was doing so. Not like me at all! It later proved that the cardboard cylinder, in which the scroll was inserted, exactly fitted in my suitcase, corner to corner.

Since we arrived home, I have studied it a few times, and I find it to be both unattractive and repelling. Obviously I have a journey awaiting that I am not sure I want to take. I have to face the fact that we seem to share a metaphysical connection—albeit a reluctant one on my part. The 'why' and 'how' is a complete mystery. But . . . that about sums up my current life!

The 'thinking about and feeling into' I earlier mentioned has led me absolutely nowhere, so it all comes down to a metaphysical journey which I eagerly await, yet equally eagerly would like to forever postpone.

"Pan, my enigmatic mentor, do you have any advice to give me regarding all this?"

Yes . . . it is time to once again look and learn.

"I guessed that, but I'm not really sure that I want to."

Trust me on this . . . you need to be very sure.

"Thanks a lot. That comment is even more off-putting!"

Take another day or so to inner-prepare. Then, we will journey.
"Okay . . . this seems like a good idea."

*　　*　　*

Three days have quickly passed and the time has arrived. I still have reservations about this journey, yet they are not fear-based. I am well used to the unknown, but this seems like a brew of highly-concentrated mega-unknown! As for being inner-prepared, the very thought is a joke. Even as a boy at school, all my preparations were invariably about me completely ignoring whatever examination subject I should have been preparing for.

It works for me!

Relaxed in my study, I connect with Pan. "Okay, I'm ready."

I feel an inner-chuckle. *Are you very sure about this?*

"Of course I am. What's likely to be a problem? I'm metaphysical when we journey, and no matter what might happen . . . hey, I'm *immortal.* I could not be more shocked than when I met Shishi, nor feel more sick than when approaching the Earth's core . . . and I'm still good to go!"

Pan laughs. *Your irreverent approach is certainly better than anxiety. We will go.*

I knew he was satisfied with me, despite my attitude. He knows my energy better than I do.

I step . . . *Between* . . . and out—with no focus at all—straight into a blazing inferno of fire.

"Oh! What in the hell . . . yikes! Is this . . . hell?"

Do you feel heat? Are you burning up?

Hmm, that's a good question! "No, I cannot feel any heat at all. But I'm looking at flames that must be thousands of kilometres high . . . and it is obvious that the heat factor must be far, far beyond absolutely astronomical . . . yet I cannot feel it. Oh gosh . . . this must be impossible."

I seem to be somewhere in space, looking into a raging inferno. I have a sense of the height of the flames, because while I am within them, I am also beyond them. Most odd! It gradually occurs to me that, for the first time, I have a number of reference points within this conflagration. Hmm, this is new. I am here, but also there—and there—and there. Very new!

"Okay, Pan. Look and learn is in place . . . but how can I be in several locations all at the same time? Is there more than one of me . . . or what?"

How could you not be in more than one location? Since when was there only one of you?

Okay. This is going to be *very* interesting! "Pan, my beloved friend . . . I have no idea what you are talking about. What do you mean . . . more than one of me? Don't you think this lesson could have been held in my garden, instead of the . . . the . . . sun! Oh . . . the *SUN!*"

How many lifetimes have you lived? Was every lifetime separate? Or were they all happening simultaneously in a greater reality? Are you not Michael in a personal reality frame, with other body/personality names in simultaneous lifetimes? And Mixael. Which personality 'you' is you? Is not 'here' and 'there' different for every different 'you' in every frame of reality?

My head is spinning. "Okay, okay . . . you have made your point. I concede. I understand what you are saying, I think. But why now, why here . . . in the sun? I take it this *is* the sun?"

Because I like to take you by surprise. And your lack of preparation makes it easy.

"Consider me surprised, shocked and shaken. But, I can do this. You need not answer any of my questions. I can do this. After all, this is only the sun. Just leave it to me."

Such is my intention, oh mighty one!

I feel Pan smilingly withdraw. Ye Gods—I think this must be examination time! Okay, I am here because of my connection with the Fire Buddha. Focus—consciously be Mixael. An inner light switches on. Of course, he is the required connection, not Michael. Mixael is the aspect of me for whom this journey is meaningful. Okay, now this begins to make a lot more sense.

With my focus firmly within Mixael, a whole new clarity emerges. I am now glad of the many reference points; the need was instantly created—and met. No-one is an isolated unit, or person. We isolate ourselves in a body in each so-called lifetime, but we do this only to create a biological and linear reference point for the lessons of each incarnation. In truth, we are each a collective, or, we are each collectively every incarnation we have ever experienced. In my case, I not only have the reference points of Michael's incarnations, but also Mixael's fifth-dimensional references.

Reaching out/within, I consciously connect with the several reference points that I am aware of at this incredible location in the sun. At one reference point, I am out far beyond the majestic sun, observing the utter immensity of the flaming sun-scape beneath me. I know that the heat is here, yet I am aware that I am not within the dimension that expresses sun energy as heat. I realise that, as with our Earth, the sun has many dimensions, and not all of them are a raging inferno of heat. Each and every dimension is pure seething energy. Within the colossal flames, I see heat-balls floating over the sun's surface, as though they are living entities, seemingly changing direction with clear intent. I also see some vast gas-balls lifting into the atmosphere above the sun, some of which are about our moon size, with others bigger than our planet, Earth. I watch in total awe, witnessing an immense cosmic dance above the enormity of the sun. I observe the sun as a profusion of energies, many magnitudes beyond the *vaguest* of human comprehension. I release all my ideas, concepts and beliefs about the sun. I humbly accept that I know less than nothing about it. I let go of whatever education I received regarding the sun, and all the information I held about it. I allow the pure newness of the experience to move through me and make no attempt to understand—*it is as it is*. For me, it is unknowable. I actually rejoice in my openness and, oddly, my *un*knowingness.

The sun is pure Mystery—and I rejoice in life's mysteries.

At another reference point I am deeply within the utterly immeasurable, sheer immensity of the flaming surface of the sun. It *has* no surface, as such, but I am compelled to use inadequate words to describe something beyond my language ability. I see heat-balls of many sizes floating along in the heat haze—it *is* hazy for me. I experience/see all this energetically, rather than with eye vision, and quite probably some of the haze is self-created from the overload of my metaphysical senses. I have the perception of Beings within the heat-balls—for want of a better description— and my senses reel from the impact of such a reality: Beings living in the sun! I have the impression that the Beings are somehow of fire and flame, and yet there is a definition that seems to follow a vague human shape, even though it is a shape that is constantly wavering and changing, growing and receding. As I observe, I see that many of the heat-balls seem to have a clear destination, even stopping and restarting on a few occasions. When they stop, the incandescence from them is so powerful that the rapid increase in the haze erases my view of what is happening. Or, maybe this haze is designed to protect me from stimulus overload.

From yet another reference point, I seem to be *within* the sun. It is different from my other simultaneous experiences, although this difference is easier to experience than describe. I seem to be in a vast chamber of shimmering heat—yet I feel a very unexpected coolness. Maybe this is only comparative to my other reference points of experience, but I feel a welcome and refreshing coolness. Beings of Light are flickering from one place to another within this chamber. When I say a vast chamber, a medium-sized town could be placed in it, with maybe ten thousand people. This is just to give you a scale of reference. I also get a feeling that size is comparative to our experience of life, for this chamber also has an unknown aspect to its dimensions. It does not conform to our three-dimensional reality. I could be within a seven-dimensional chamber, or more—whatever! Forget exact descriptions. The Beings in here *flicker* from one place to another in a micro-moment. I have yet to see any suggestion of a familiar movement, like walking, or even a swimming action.

All these reference points are somehow converging within me, but I am comfortable with this. I, also, am converging into one whole me, although I am aware that I was never separate. Only my points of reference were separate, designed to present a bigger picture. It is a rather strange dichotomy to be separate *and* whole. I see, now, that the reference points have been slowly feeding me with experiences which, as I digest them, are able to become integrated within my greater holistic experience. A type of filtering to assist my assimilation. All my reference points have now amalgamated, with *and* within me, in this huge chamber.

I mentioned the Beings of Light within this chamber. Up until this moment, Beings of Light have always been Light-Beings. Be patient with me on this! As my type of energetic-seeing seems to be becoming more fine-tuned for this experience, the Light-Beings take on a whole different aspect. I realise, in this moment, that most of the Light-Beings I have seen to date appeared to me in a comfortable and familiar three-dimensional way—even though they were not necessarily three-dimensional. Now however, the game has changed. These Beings appear to be continually melting and reforming as I 'look' at them. The process defies description. It is only *because* I have let go of comparisons with anything and everything I have previously experienced, that I can even be here looking at and perceiving this. Seeing these Beings undulating and oscillating in this impossible manner inclines me toward feeling a bit dizzy. And yet, I am deeply moved by an alien, and slightly terrible, transcendent beauty of a quality previously unknown to me.

That these Beings are beautiful is beyond all doubt. Sure, it is a beauty that is indescribable, yet beauty expresses its own unique consciousness, and right now the consciousness of this awe-inspiring beauty is imprinting itself within the soul I am. This takes a timeless time.

I am glad of my inner-steadfastness, gained from my many previous experiences, for what is now gradually unfolding. In the manner of an old-fashioned picture slide, fading from the screen of a projector as it is slowly replaced by another, so the scene in the chamber is gently fading into an utterly impossible outdoor scene. I am standing on a hill. All around me is green grass and very dark-green shrubs. I can see no trees, but impossibly, a brisk stream is running up the hill to plunge as a small waterfall over the sheer rocks and down the other side. I smile in bemusement. Folding my legs into a lotus position, I sit and relax about a metre above the grass, watching the impossible being possible. I am not sure why this makes me smile so much, but my metaphysical heart-space is bubbling with joy.

Once again, timeless-time passes by. I am seeing signs of wildlife here, but it seems to have no relationship with any life-forms I am familiar with. The grass and shrubs seem very Earth-like, yet the hesitant, moving shapes and shadows of strangeness and colour are as alien as the grass is normal. I smile more. Let go of Earth comparisons. *It is as it is.* If it is possible, the joy in my heart is growing and intensifying. I sigh in utter contentment. There is nothing to understand and nothing that needs knowing—*it is as it is.* A question emerges: is this really the sun? Is this reality possible at all? I sigh. *It is as it is.*

Excellent. I am impressed. Not for aeons have I had an Earth visitor here. Be very welcome.

Standing before me is a beautiful man. He did not approach, he appeared. I smile at him, almost lost in a serenity of silent wonder, of immense gratitude.

He nods, knowingly. *Excellent. Surprise is no longer within my reality, but if it was, then surprise would be most appropriate right now. You see, but you do not see. And you are comfortable with this. You hear, but you do not hear, and you are relaxed. You are many, and you are one, and this does not concern you. You are on the Earth, and, within the sun. Yet you smile. Thank you.*

"Why do you thank me? I have done nothing."

The man laughs. *Oh indeed, you have done much. I note that you have a companion who is here, yet not here at all.* He laughs aloud. *How very appropriate in the circumstances.*

"Do you mean Pan? He is not *my* companion, I am *his.* He is my beloved mentor."

Yes, I know of this. But you are alone on the sun. Your mentor withdrew some while ago. Did you not know of this? Did you assume that you were under his protection?

"No. I felt him withdraw. I need no protection. I am a metaphysical human; my mortal body is safe at home. No matter what may happen . . . I choose Love. This is enough."

I stare at the beautiful man before me. He is tall, powerfully built, yet with an aura of grace and elegance that is far beyond earthly. He seems physical to me, but I am very sure he is not. Energetically, he is probably one of the most powerful Beings I have ever encountered.

Do I not overwhelm you? Do you not feel a desire to throw yourself at my feet in worship?

I smile respectfully. "You must read me very easily. Yes, I do feel somewhat overwhelmed, but not enough to throw myself at your feet. I worship at the feet of Divine Love, so in that way I am already worshipping you . . . whoever you are."

And you know not who I am?

I stare at him as comprehension slowly dawns. "Oh! My gosh . . . you're the Fire Buddha."

He smiles at me. Just that simple action feels as though he has projected a mega-flow of Love right through me. I am awash in Love. Such an energy Being is beyond thought.

This is one name I have been given. I have many names amongst humans. Each time I walk among you I am given a different name. Names . . . and mostly meaningless worship.

"Why is such worship meaningless?"

Do the hens that crouch at your feet worship you? Are you a Being with whom they can share a single concept? Do the goldfish, with their mouths agape revere you?

For me, these are valid comments. My hens often crouch in submission at my feet while my goldfish also stare up at me with mouths agape. "Hmm . . . are you saying that where there is Love, no worship is necessary, and where there is no Love, then no worship is possible?"

Very astute.

"Please, tell me why I had such a strong connection with the Fire Buddha picture?" My humour intervenes. "And I have to say that your portrait is fiendishly inappropriate. You need to commission a new painter. It is horrible. It appears to represent everything that you are not. You, surely . . . are Love."

Forget the picture and an artist's worshipful, if distorted impression. Consider the Buddhist monks who take turns in guarding the picture: Is this an act of Love, of selfless devotion, or is it a meaningless act of obedient servitude?

"I would not attempt to answer such a question. Personally, I suspect all of that is mixed within the servants of the temple, but I think they are completely honouring in their intent towards you. After all, you are one of their revered Gods."

Can I be Loved and revered if there is no Love for Self?

"There can be no Love for Self if it is not part of their religion. Surely the very definition of a religion is to love a God, or a deity, that is outside Self. Paradoxically, this cannot be because there is *nothing outside* Self. All the religions that I know anything about— and that is not much—teach of external Gods, rather than the God-Self within."

And what is your religion?

"I am not religious. I am a humble man focused as much as possible—and I often feel to be sadly lacking—in the Love and Light of humanity. To me, God is Love, Light, Life."

Yet, when I felt your energy before the picture, I felt the energy of one of the most religious men I have encountered in a long time. How do you explain this?

"I think you are playing with me in all this conversation. I know that you have no questions regarding me, or anything else known to man. You can see through me, and into me, as though I am completely transparent. So I have no answer, for none is necessary. But I do have a question. You felt my energy when I stood before the picture. This suggests that you have an aspect, or trace, of your energy with the picture, and I connected with this. Am I correct? I can only assume that the monks also feel this. I certainly hope so."

The Fire Buddha laughs. *You are a wise one. Human life should offer little challenge to you.*

"On the contrary, human life is continually challenging me." I gesture around me. "I have no clue how this can exist within the sun, but the energy here is pure Lightness compared with the very much heavier energy of Lightness currently on Earth. Happily, the inner-Light we each have/are, if we acknowledge it, makes it possible to live in our present times, but it is comparatively few who acknowledge, and give credence to, the Light within."

The Fire Buddha smiles at me. *Come, I have enjoyed our conversation. You came into this place in increments, gradually closing down your intellect while opening to intelligence. During our time together you have been assimilating the sun energy, so you can now safely move through the various dimensions of experience that I offer you. Do you feel ready?*

"As ready as I will ever be . . . and very willing."

I have invited a much-loved companion of yours to join us.

As his word-energy moves into me, I see hurtling toward me what momentarily appears as a miniature red sun. Then I am basking in the radiant Love of the huge and beautiful Shishi.

Am called. I come. To you. I Love. Joy you. Joy me.

I am engulfed within the huge God-Being whom I so Love. One-and-a-half times bigger than an elephant, Shishi is a garish, flamingly scarlet-red fur-ball, with the terrifying features of a lion/dog/boar all in one. Shishi is so scarily ugly that he is utterly beautiful—and certainly unique.

For some reason, having Shishi with me here is so breathtakingly perfect, I almost weep.

Expanding my Light-body to a size matching his, I hug him enthusiastically.

Is good. You need. I come. I Love.

I see the Fire Buddha watching us with a fond smile. "How could you know my need before I even knew it myself?"

As you surmised, you are transparent to me. This journey is surpassingly strange and challenging, even for you.

"Oh . . . you are so right. Thank you very much."

Having Shishi with me is rather like a boy having his big brother by his side. I do not feel *reduced* by his magnitude, but *empowered*. The Love of Shishi is an energy beyond our current human Love. It is a power that enters my heart, both allowing for, and creating, newness.

I watch as the Fire Buddha and Shishi respectfully and affectionately greet each other. It becomes obvious that they are on reasonably familiar terms. Of course, they both have a mutual Japanese connection, but I intuit that it goes back far, far beyond this.

It becomes obvious that Shishi also easily reads me. Even with my new skill of focused telepathy, I must still be an open book!

Beloved Buddha. Big brother. Open book. Me, you. I Love.
I smile from a full and open heart. I am content.

The Fire Buddha has a penetrating gaze as he now looks at me.
In your reality on Earth you are in a period of change. The hereabouts of your 2012 is the timing of old cycles coming to an end, and of new cycles beginning. This, however, involves far more than Earth alone, for you are but one wayward planet in a solar system. All is affected. Even your solar system is but one among countless solar systems in this galaxy. All is affected, for all life is holistic. *This is a word to which humans give lip-service, but very few comprehend the profound implications of a holistic universe.*

The holistic concept/reality is known to you. What may not be known is that the energy of the sun will change on Earth over the period ahead. Some people will experience the sun rays as they have been for the last few millennia, while others will feel a subtle difference in the sun's energy. This, of course, will depend on the consciousness of the people. Combined with water, the sun is life to your planet, yet there are people who die from sun-related sicknesses. For many, this will continue. For others, the sun will be a new and transforming energy. For these people, sun-sickness will be impossible.

"Surely this will create a new type of separation. The vulnerable and the invulnerable, the new and the old, or something along those lines."

Or, it will create a new level of awareness as this new reality becomes obvious. Is this not also possible? The people of newness will be the teachers of those who, from excessive fear, strayed from their spiritual journey. There are no evil people on Earth, no matter what their misdeeds; there are only people who have lost their spiritual relationship with Love.

"Yes, I agree. Where there is self-hate, even murder, there is no absence of Love, only an absence of a *conscious connection* with Love. Hmm, an interesting scenario. It will either create world wars beyond any we have seen, or Love and Peace will prevail, if there are enough available teachers. But . . . how do you teach people to Love?"

Is this not your current life's work?

"I teach what unconditional Love *is*, rather than teach people *to* Love. I teach people how it is possible to Love self, and how to Love life and living, and I teach them a direction to take to allow Love to unfold within them, but how do you teach people to actually Love?"

You play with words. In reality you are teaching people to Love. This is why you are here. You are aware of the new energies in so many of your younger children. Great numbers of mature and Loving souls are being drawn to incarnate in your Earth reality to assist in lifting the energy of the masses. When the old gives birth to the new, the old is more open to learning from the new. Is this not so?

I smile. "Yes, the old-consciousness parents who give birth to new-consciousness children are usually very open to inner growth. This could eventually transform humanity."

Nevertheless, the trailblazers will go ahead into new and greater realities. This is how it has always been. But those who linger cannot be abandoned or neglected. They can only be nurtured by their own species to find their maximum potential.

"Are we the only humans capable of nourishing us? I mean, if for millennia the trailblazers have gone ahead, somewhere in our solar system, or in the galaxy, they must have their own huge, very advanced civilisations by now. Are we not their sisters and brothers? Could they not offer us help at this time of human crisis? I know they are there, I have met some of them."

The Fire Buddha chuckles. *This is so. Even as you speculate, it is happening. You are not alone as a species, but one of a vast human family that was thriving before your Earth was born.*

"Yes, so I have learnt. . . but I'm still surprised."

Why so?

"Well . . . I have journeyed into a fifth-dimensional reality, and I have learned that there is far, far more to the big picture than I ever thought possible. But when I metaphysically journey, my relationship with linear time is totally disrupted. So I have little awareness of the 'where' or 'when'. But beyond this, I have read enough of everyday physics and space science to accept that there was a time our galaxy began, of our universe beginning, of the Big Bang . . . that sort of thing. When you state that we were a thriving species before our Earth planet was born, in our solar system, in its corner of our Milky Way Galaxy . . . then I have to release all the guesstimates of science and accept that linear time does not apply on the greater cosmic scales of creation. Does this make sense?"

Another chuckle. *An excellent summary. Yes, throw away the estimation of years. Time and its measure are a human invention. For long ages the seasons of the sun were the only measure, for they told of times of plenty and times of hardship. In your everyday life, the measurement of time has proved to be a very useful tool, but as a reference point to universal creation it offers little, other than to limit the vast scale of intelligent imagination. However, time, as you know it, is also due for a change, for when it is strongly adhered to it creates a false representation of reality.*

"One can only wonder!"

The chuckle becomes a laugh. *Yes, quite possibly. Now it is time to show you what I mean by the new sun and the old. Be aware you need not* understand. *Simply* assimilate, *and in due course, inner-knowing will unfold its truth into your consciousness. This is the way of* soul-knowing.

During this timeless exchange, Shishi has been bounding around us, obviously full of energy. Now, he lunges toward me — and I am engulfed in his long, flaming red-coloured fur. I feel myself spinning within his embrace, losing all sense of reality, when abruptly, I am standing by his side in a changed — environment? I can no longer see the Fire Buddha.

The previous strange Nature, with its shadowy shapes reminiscent of distorted creatures, is gone. With Shishi, I am standing before a sun — or so it seems. I thought that I was *in* the sun, yet here is a sun *before* me. I have no clue how this is possible. The sun appears far distant, as though I am on Earth, except I am not looking up, squinting uncomfortably. I am comfortably looking directly ahead.

You see. I see. Is good. Is clear. Is sun.

I smile fondly at Shishi. His words are always brief, rarely more than two at a time, but his energy speaks for him very powerfully. He has little need of words. As he silently speaks into my consciousness, I become aware of more than my own perceptional ability. Shishi's telepathy is very advanced, offering insight with the words. I am standing before a new sun, or maybe a new sun-energy. Then again, this is not actually a *new* sun; rather it is one that has never before been available to our awareness. I get the insight that, over the years, there will be people who will see *two* suns from Earth, while others will deny any such reality. Let me clarify this; not two *different*, separate suns, but literally, two-suns-in-one. Probably those who experience two suns will be very discreet about it! As should be expected, this sun is *also* hot by countless magnitudes, yet it is a very *different* heat. This is where I do not have sufficient education to explain. There is heat that burns, scorches, and can destroy, and there also is heat that does *not* burn, scorch, or destroy, yet it can be mega-powerful. *This* is such a heat.

As I gaze at this sun, I feel an invitation to connect with it. Despite mild trepidation, I am willing to do so. Although I have no idea what the results will be, I trust.

You ready. I take. I Love. Is good.

I invariably smile at the conciseness of Shishi's words. Why do I need to use so many words to convey my information? Clearly he is a far more advanced communicator than I.

"I'm ready, Shishi. Do your thing."

In a single, twisting bound, I am engulfed by Shishi. Spinning like a top for what seems the briefest moment, we are suddenly in a different place.

We are standing in what I can only describe as a portal. Again, I have several reference points, all feeding me information simultaneously, while I attempt to assimilate and, hopefully, make sense of it all. Now I know what the Fire Buddha meant when he said, *be aware you do not need to understand it.* There are two levels to understanding: our intellect and our intelligence. The intellect attempts to understand information by using prior knowledge, while intelligence is able to embrace information with current wisdom. Wisdom is the distillation of experience and intelligence. This is the path that I now take.

From one reference point, I see a vast, flaming archway, maybe a thousand kilometres high and across. This is purely my perspective. When I say flaming, it is not just *fire* that is flaming, but a brilliant, leaping flame/*Light* that is utterly unique. I have seen many forms or expressions of Light, but I have never seen anything like this. The flames of Light could be a hundred kilometres in height, somehow leaping into the air and dancing in an ordered chaos of continuous movement. Oh, my gosh! Of course! This is a dance of the *Chaos* and *Order* of Light, with the torsion held in complete Balance. So totally all-consuming is the white of Balance that to me, the red of Chaos and the black of Order are practically nullified. The flames of Light are pure, dancing, ethereal Balance. Wow! I had no idea that something like this is possible.

Another reference point brings me in much closer. I am within the portal, yet because my metaphysical senses are *very* non-physical, I do not see from my eyes, as such, but from a level of perceptual awareness. I am tiny within the vast portal, yet I am also one *with* the portal. I cannot explain this, only to say that while I am here, separation is impossible. I can leave this place and be separate from it physically, yet I will never again be *meta*physically separated. I realise that as we continue into this time of energetic planetary change, those people of a raised consciousness on Earth will also be metaphysically connected with this new energy of the sun, whether they are aware of it or not. And paradoxically, when we are connected metaphysically, then we are also connected physically. There are no borders, boundaries, or limits to a holistic Truth!

I have described the portal as vast, which it *is*, yet it is also a portal of almost countless layers of living Light. I am within the portal, but only now am I aware that the portal is also within me. If you look at a very tall, high-rise building, you will observe that the very summit of the building is also one with the base. Between the summit and base there are multiple stories, usually represented by the rows of windows. In this way, the very tall high-rise is one holistic building. Using this as a metaphor, so I experience the portal in a similar way, although nothing like a high-rise! The portal is living, seething *life*. It is Nature unleashed, yet completely Balanced. Equally, if you look into the clear eyes of a person staring at that high-rise, you would see the whole building reflected in their eyes. A visual indication that the observer and the observed are One. Take this metaphor to a far deeper metaphysical level, and you may grasp what I am experiencing.

How do I explain this portal, or even describe it? I am within the Nature of Earth, and yet this is only because I create it this way by being here. If I were a silicon-based alien standing here, I would see/experience a silicon-based Nature that is familiar to me. I am saying that reality is exactly the way we make it through our perceptions and experience. And it is this way in our everyday life. We create all that we are involved in, exactly as is happening in this sun portal. When I am living within my physical body, I, unfortunately, take on the blueprint of my past—we all do—along with all the limitations that we have created within this blueprint. A blueprint, I might add, that is no longer appropriate. A blueprint that needs to be consciously abandoned, or released. And this is the offering of every physical death we experience—the death of the blueprint. Sadly, our emotional attachments are close to, but not quite, indestructible. *Emotionally letting go* is the new game on offer! This requires an alert consciousness, but it can be done.

What I experience in this vast sun portal is a seamless and eternal mixture of a three-dimensional Nature. I see creatures that have long been extinct to us. As I experience this, I am aware that all life is energy. This I knew, but that knowing now takes on a new intensity, a new depth, an entirely new dimension of perspective. Whereas I intellectually know that all life is deathless, and therefore can never become extinct, this *knowing* takes on a whole new meaning. As a human person, I live with linear time. Linear time has its place, but it is not the reality we *believe* it to be. Despite this, to a great extent, time runs our lives, the departure and arrival time of planes, trains, and automobiles! The physical time of pregnancy, of so-called birth and so-called death, of seeds growing, of flowers blooming, of seasons passing—on and on as we are involved in linear time. We are imbibed *by* it, marinated *in* it, and our worldwide human beliefs and conscious memories are finally demolished by the passing centuries of it.

All this is a program. It is all real—but this is only a tiny aspect of reality—and we are all consumed by it. Here, now, in this sun portal, linear time has no reality. I see/experience all Nature as energy, timeless and ageless, beyond birth, death or extinction. I watch as Nature changes form in an endless procession/progression of energy experiencing the greatest range of physical form possible. It seems never-ending. From gases, to minerals, to plants, to the whole range of animals, not so much in an orderly cycle of evolution, but more from expressions of Order and Chaos finding Balance in a dance of energy far beyond a human ability to understand. This indicates to me that all our theories of evolution of the species may well be true, but only true within our tiny linear framework. And Nature is so far above and beyond that framework that it is beyond our wildest projections of possibility. To use time as a metaphor, our linear framework of physical Nature represents perhaps one second—maybe even less!—in a thousand years of a greater metaphysical Nature.

In it, surrounded by it, literally engulfed by a Nature that is beyond all time, I am lost in pure wonder. I wonder how I *know* all that I know. I wonder where my *knowing* comes from, and even as I wonder these things—I *know*. I cannot be here and *not know*. This is impossible.

You know. I know. Time not. No time. All time.

I laugh. Shishi's words seem almost unintelligible in their utter simplicity, yet energetically they say so much more, making deep and profound sense. Linear time is our own three-dimensional construct. I know that time is rather different in a fifth-dimensional reality, although I would get lost in attempting to explain that difference. In this sun portal all time and dimensions somehow cease. It is beyond both, yet it is filled with creatures that defy all reason or logic. I am watching a lion-like animal that seems to be made of a red/green gas. Yet it is rubbing a seemingly solid body on a tree trunk, while the tree, quivering slightly from the animal's enthusiasm, is clearly absorbing gas from its body.

Forget sense. Human sense. Accept now. Here now.

"I am going to call you Succinct Shishi!" I say, smiling. Again, his words are a perfect summary of how to be with this: let go of my physical Earth-sense experiences. I am in the portal of the sun. Be here now! Simply accept . . . *it is as it is.* Oh gosh, how much deeper can these few simple words take me? Somehow I know that it will be far deeper yet. These are words I live by, words I honour for their profound simplicity, their profound depths— *limitless* depths.

In front of me I watch an animal of some completely unknown herbivore species slowly melt, transforming into a single-stemmed blue plant with a huge, soft-hued, violet/purple flower. The flower turns toward me, then advances, not walking or crawling, but *advancing*! As the flower comes closer, I have a brief moment of a whole new level of wonder, for within the flower I see a city—and I am walking into it. Happily, Shishi is by my side!

This is no human city. I am not even sure if it is a city, but I have no other word with which to describe it. I see buildings which seem to be in continuous movement. It is as though all the buildings are made of sheer silk—they are not!—and that a breeze is blowing across them—it is not! But this gives you an impression of what I am seeing. The buildings are in constant movement, yet there is no regular rhythm or rhyme to the movements. They are as random as a fickle breeze moving through a forest. These buildings are coloured, but the colours also refuse to be stable. Colours change from metallic golds to bronzes, and on to silvers, in a mercurial, flowing way that is utterly beautiful. I walk over to one such building—if this is what they are—and as I approach, it comes toward me. Despite my many metaphysical experiences, I am not used to being approached by a building. I stop my advance, and the building stops. I take a small step and the building makes a tiny advance.

"Whoa . . . this is different, Shishi!"

For once, Shishi has nothing to offer. Maybe this is new even for a Heart God! I make my commitment, and moving toward the building, it swiftly proceeds toward me. We meet—and merge. !!!!!!! I am a Being of Exultant Energy. I am not a building. I am not a human Being. I am completely lost in *Beingness.* I am aware of the sun as a tiny speck of heat in a very small solar system, in a fairly small galaxy. I am aware of countless galaxies in a moderate-sized universe, and I am aware of countless universes in countless multiverses. I am awareness of All that Is. I am nothingness in anywhere, in any-when, in nowhere. Mind is snuffed, a discarded candle. Intellect collapses into ashes. Consciousness expands into and throughout the tiny speck of sun. Through the sun portal I/we/nothingness flows into *All that Is*. Beauty, Glorious Beauty . . . everywhere.

I/we/nothingness is overwhelming. All is LIGHT . . . fading . . . Light . . . fading . . .

I become aware of my metaphysical body being held in the arms of Shishi. I have a sense that in a timeless realm, I have spent a long period of timelessness, elsewhere.

Too much. Too big. Too all. So perfect.

I consciously merge with my metaphysical body . . . I am Mixael. I am Michael. I am . . . more.

I smile at Shishi. So perfect.

Gently he puts me to the—*ground?* No, not ground. Under my feet is cloud, but it is not cloud, it is energy. All life is the movement of conscious energy. All intelligence is energy. All energy is yours, is mine, is you, is me, is us. *We* are energy. All energy is *One* energy. Separation is a terrible belief, it is a pain, it is fear, it is a sickness, it is a violation of you, of me, of us, of all. We are One with all life. All life is energy. Nothing else. Everything we see as physical form is a game that conscious energy is playing throughout many dimensional realities. We need to learn from our games. Too many are painful.

The Fire Buddha comes striding toward us. He stops, and I watch him transform into flames, into a lion-like creature, into Shishi, into me—and back as the Fire Buddha.

He smiles at me intently. *Do you get it?*

I nod. "Yes, I do. Everything we see through our physical eyes, where one thing appears to be separate from another, is an illusion, a falsity. Nothing exists in separation. All is connected."

In a new age of humanity, every dimensional level will have a

269

higher, more vibrant energy. The old expressions will rapidly break down. Those who cling to the old will destroy themselves. They will spend further cycles with the old. Those who see Self in all life will move into new expressions of humanity. All is energy. All energy is eternal creation.

"I will never look at the sun again without a sense of wonder."

Allow your horribly expensive picture of a horrible Fire Buddha to be your connection with an eternity of elsewhere. A deep chuckle. *Nothing is as it seems.*

I am embraced by Shishi, engulfed in Love.

I go. You go. I Love. You Love. We Love.

Shishi makes a remarkable exit. He does not zoom away, or fade away. He expands until it would seem that Shishi and the sun are One. Of course! And I am alone in the portal of the sun.

I am in no hurry to return. Folding my legs into my favoured metaphysical position, I sit in the sun portal . . . awaiting what may happen . . . or be . . . or will . . . or . . .

. . . Awareness returns.

I am somehow changed. This is not a change that will be apparent to some people, but it is apparent to me. I have connected with a knowing so vast that it is uncontainable. I realise that our intellect is dedicated to changing present-knowing into past-knowledge. In so doing, it is reduced. This is no longer the way forward. We have to find the ability to embrace universal knowing. As this awareness flows within me, I realise that our right-brain hemisphere is comfortable with unlimited universal knowing, simply embracing it within our holistic self. Our left-brain hemisphere needs to prove and consolidate *mystical* knowing into *practical* knowledge, for this is the only way it can process and accommodate such information.

I have embraced the energy of universal knowing at some deeper level. As I have stated so often, all information is energy, all energy is information. Our human body is seen to be substance, while in reality it is ninety-nine percent energy/information. Max, my body elemental, *is* this information/energy. So long as I simply embrace and Love my energy-self, so the Max elemental will thrive, meaning that I, too, will physically, emotionally and mentally thrive.

If I tell people that I am the sun, they will think I am a fruit-loop! And if I were to make such a statement, I probably *would be*. But—*I am the sun!*

From my place in the portal of the sun, we are One. I cannot repudiate this, nor do I wish to. I am the Fire Buddha, the Fire Buddha is me. I am you, you are me. In this glorious blazing energy of Love, of Newness and Nowness and Foreverness, I see/experience life very differently from when in my human physical body. At this moment I am not sure if I *am* human only. I am not sure if any person is *exclusively* human. No, let me be honest with my knowing. We are *not* exclusively human at all. We cannot be, for we are One with all life. We are One with the multiverse.

I am aware of the sun connection we each have. *I am the sun.* Every person is energetically connected to the sun. We could not be here on Earth without this connection. The sun is actually life to us, not death, yet many people get a melanoma that is medically declared to be sun-induced. We are making the sun an enemy. We are creating fear-campaigns based in protecting ourselves from the sun. In this moment in the sun portal, I see the separation we are creating from our life source. There have been periods in our history when it was believed that water was bad for our health, some even believing water carried the plague. We minimised drinking water and very rarely bathed in it. We look back at this period as though we were crazy! But we are now repeating this insanity with the *sun*. It is not our relationship with the sun that is causing us health problems, it is our disastrous relationship with ourselves. The sun amplifies our relationship with ourselves. I do not mean the relationship that we show to the world, the masks and images of deceit. I mean the deep, old-program feelings we have about ourselves. The majority of people do not have a conscious, Love-based positive relationship with self; they have a subconscious, sub-emotional, fear-based and negative relationship. This is not bad or wrong, but it does not work for our benefit.

Everything we externalise is based in illusion. Based in our self-relationship, all maladies come from within; we create them.

I see/experience the sun as energy. I see humanity as energy. Energy has countless different expressions. Obviously we need to be careful how we relate to various energies in the manner of gases and other chemicals, but in the final analysis, all energy is One. It all comes down to the principles of Truth for human life, and the Great principle is Absolute Love for Self. Here, in the sun portal, I *feel* that Love very powerfully, even while knowing it is minuscule compared with the limitless Love that is available.

I smile in contentment, soaking in the pure knowing that is surging into and through my consciousness. I cannot find words to share it all, for it is a knowing beyond intellect. Only now do I become aware of another reference point to the sun. Whether it has just appeared, or has just reached my attention, I do not know, but I surrender to it as I enter it.

I am on Earth. It appears not to be the Earth that I metaphysically stepped away from, for this Earth has a more golden, glowing daylight than we are used to. Looking up, I can see the sun without any need to squint. The sun appears as a luminous golden ball, radiating an energy that I feel to be benign and supportive of all life. I am standing close to a forest, so I move over to it. I am unable to clearly identify this forest. In our reality we have many types of forests, ranging from the evergreen and deciduous forests in the north, to the hot and humid equatorial jungles and on to the great Southern Beech forests much further south. This forest contains all of these—and much more. Equatorial trees grow alongside cold climate trees! Trees of my time period and trees from long-past Earth periods, all are growing in an ordered profusion of chaos. I smile. Once again another example of the torsion between Chaos and Order finding Balance, in complete denial of the separation—both climatic and linear—that we experience in our current frame of reality.

Within the forest I see huge herbivores from a Jurassic period grazing alongside small deer from our own period. I sense that this place is without the carnivores, not because carnivores are bad or wrong, but because in this frame of reality, the herbivores regulate their *own* life cycles, not requiring carnivores to ensure that over-population and subsequent disease does not occur, as in *our* Nature. I can feel the difference in the energy.

Do you know where you are?

Pan! I smile in delight. "Not really. I have known for quite a while that life is vast, but the Fire Buddha has given me a whole new insight and appreciation of *VAST*. Life is measureless and endless, far, far beyond human comprehension. I assume that this is another frame of reality."

Would you believe that this is your own frame of reality?

"I believe it if you say so . . . but I don't vaguely understand how it's possible."

Would it help if I said it is another page in the Earth's Book of Life?

"But in our same frame of reality? How is this possible?"

Mixael, what is the difference between your current life and your potential life?

"Hmm, this needs thinking about! Maybe my potential is something I am forever reaching toward. Something of that ilk."

Or maybe your potential is the other side of the current life you are living. Maybe your potential is being lived simultaneously by the potential you.

"Oh my gosh! More Oneness. If I separate myself from my potential, my awareness and perception separates me from it. It places my potential into a future I will never reach. Even though my potential and I remain as One. Does this mean that as I struggle to reach my potential, I am forever creating a space between my current and future potential? Gosh, Pan, this is difficult to comprehend."

Let it sit with you.

I gaze back into the forest. "Are you showing that this forest, this Nature, is the potential of the Nature that is happening in my familiar frame of reality? Is this the flip-side? If so, what keeps them apart? Is it people, humanity?"

Every thought and action of every human is forever creating your experience of your world, of life and Nature, of your climates, of all your realities.

"I need to let this percolate, along with my other experiences in the sun's portal."

Yes. I will withdraw. Be with this. Simply, be with it. Do not question; be with it.

Sitting in the lotus position a few metres above the ground, I contemplate the forest.

I allow thoughts and feelings to percolate in my consciousness, rather than fix on something I want to know and then chase it. I am my potential. I am living my potential. I am being my potential. My potential grows as I live it. I grow as I live it. My potential grows as I grow. My potential is not something that I am reaching for, it is the moment of expression in my life. There is no flip-side unless I create the concept of separation between me and my potential. Then I create apartness. Apartness is illusion. Wholeness is reality. Ergo, my potential and I are One!

As I contemplate the forest, it all seems to recede from me. I am within the sun portal, but I am looking at the sun portal as though I am outside of it. I let go of any attempt to understand. I just observe the sun portal before me, from within the sun portal.

A timeless passing of no-time.

Gradually, as I deepen my *letting go* of wanting anything, of wanting to learn, of wanting an experience, of wanting to know, of the very human habit of *wanting,* I accept that all want is based in illusion. I accept that all want is the inability to fully embrace that *it is as it is.*

In my letting go of want, a whole new awareness arises from within.

I am the sun within the sun portal I am . . . within the great *central* sun portal of the galaxy.

I know that this is the way it has always been. The sun of our tiny solar system is One with the great central sun of the Milky Way Galaxy. I have learned that the galaxy has a central sun. It is an immensity that on the scale of size makes our sun tiny by comparison. As I sit in my lotus position, taking care to observe, to be, to connect and not intellectually chase, I realise that this is not just about the size of either sun, it is about the magnitude of *energy.* The galactic central sun is One with the whole galaxy. The central sun of the galaxy is in constant communication with our solar sun, with many other suns, sharing information which is as far beyond my comprehension as these words are beyond the comprehension of an ant. I do not even attempt it. *I am the sun* is enough, even though I have no idea what this means, suggests or indicates.

From my observation within the solar sun portal within the great galactic sun portal, I am aware that the galactic sun is in communication with every star, planet, meteor, asteroid, in fact all the countless heavenly bodies that make up what we call the Milky Way Galaxy—and beyond. As I observe this, I see the same communication taking place with every open heart within the universe. I become aware of human-type Beings who are closed within their own sun/heart/portals and other human-type Beings that are fully open in their sun/heart/portals. Some species of these Beings are all closed, no matter how advanced their technology, while other species of these Beings are all open. I neither marvel nor wonder at this. *It is as it is.* Observing our human species, I see sun/heart/portals that are fully open, with some opening, while others are closed, or are closing.

I sit observing—at One with the solar sun, at One with the galactic sun.

I become aware that our solar sun is the heart of our solar system, while the great galactic sun is the heart of the galactic system. Accepting this, I become aware of a vast universal sun that energetically contains the galactic sun and our solar sun. I am now One with our solar sun, the galactic sun and the *universal* sun. I know that other suns are involved, but I am aware of only the three. I am surprised that I am calm! I am at peace within a cosmic energy of such vastness that I am as nothing . . . and yet I am One with this vastness. I do not quail or cringe. This energy is me, I am this energy. As is every human—for this is our heritage. This is where we were born as Beings of pure energy. We are energy wearing the clothing of flesh. We are energy lost in the world of material illusion. Yet—we are One with our heritage, no matter how lost we appear to be in illusion. It is our destiny, in the fullness of eternity, to find our way Home. And when we arrive Home we will contain the magnitude of our brief, infinite moment of physical form. But by our reckoning in linear time, there remains a lot of water to flow under the metaphorical bridge!

Solar sun, galactic sun, universal sun—endless suns—I am receiving energy/information which is currently unintelligible to me, incomprehensible, yet I am content. I am now aware that each human has a sun/heart/portal within both our mortal physical body, and our immortal metaphysical Being. As I connect with these mighty sun energies I realise that they are communicating not with my brain, or even my heart, but with the DNA of my physical body, and the torus/vortex DNA equivalent within my metaphysical Being. Energy is information, and this information is as universal as I am, as we all are. We are the cosmos in just one stream of consciousness we call human. Our metaphysical DNA torus/vortex portal enables us to communicate with, and receive communication from, the solar sun, the galactic sun and the universal sun. There are many other suns in many other systems, in many other galaxies, in many other universes, but each has a principal, or prime, sun. However, we can only communicate/connect with the principal suns when we reach the state of consciousness that fully embraces holistic life, knowing separation as the projection of illusion.

There is no ending to this I am experiencing, for there is no beginning . . .

About Michael J. Roads

The deep wisdom contained in Michael's spiritual Enlightenment and his inner-experience of unconditional Love is the basis for his 5-Day Intensives, seminars and books, currently in thirteen languages. Michael's public speaking tours have included invitations to Australia, New Zealand, Norfolk Island, South Africa, The Netherlands, Italy, Switzerland, Austria, Belgium, Germany, France, UK, Denmark, Sweden, Norway, West Indies, U.S.A., Canada and Japan.

An extraordinarily gifted communicator, Michael imparts and conveys unconditional Love heart-to-heart, far beyond the reach of words, creating the space to awaken from a dream . . . to ignite the Love that exists within each person.

Michael's 5-Day Intensives are based in Unconditional Love and emotional completeness.

For information on Michael's international events, tour schedule, books, CDs, free audio downloads and much more, please visit:

www.michaelroads.com

RoadsLight pty ltd
PO Box 778
Nambour, QLD 4560
Australia

info@michaelroads.com

CPSIA information can be obtained at www.ICGtesting.com
Printed in the USA
BVOW02s0249231215

430858BV00003B/302/P